ROMAN VERSE SATIRE

Lucilius to Juvenal

A Selection with
an Introduction, Text, Translations, and Notes

by
William J. Dominik
and
William T. Wehrle

Bolchazy-Carducci Publishers, Inc.
Wauconda, Illinois

General Editor
Laurie K. Haight

Cover Design
Charlene M. Hernandez

Latin Text
The Latin text of Lucilius (with some minor changes) is reprinted by permission of the publishers and the Loeb Classical Library from *Remains of Old Latin*, vol. 3: *Lucilius, The Twelve Tables* (Cambridge, Massachusetts: Harvard University Press, 1938), E. H. Warmington, ed. and trans. The Latin text of Horace (with numerous minor changes) is from *Q. Horati Flacci Opera*, second edition, Oxford Classical Texts (Oxford: Clarendon Press, 1901), E. C. Wickham and H. W. Garrod, eds., by permission of Oxford University Press. The Latin text of Persius (with numerous minor changes) and Juvenal (with some major and minor changes) is from *A. Persi Flacci et D. Iuni Iuuenalis Saturae*, second edition, Oxford Classical Texts (Oxford: Clarendon Press, 1992), W. V. Clausen, ed., by permission of Oxford University Press. The minor changes to the Latin text are mainly in orthography, punctuation, and capitalization, while the major changes consist of alternative readings.

Cover Graphic
The cover depicting street musicians is taken from a Roman copy of an original mosaic of the third century B.C.E. in the Museo Nazionale at Naples.

Bolchazy-Carducci Publishers, Inc.
1000 Brown Street, #101, Wauconda, Illinois 60084 USA
http://www.bolchazy.com

ISBN: 0-86516-442-8

Printed in the United States of America
by Bang Printing
1999

Library of Congress Cataloging-in-Publication Data

Roman verse satire : Lucilius to Juvenal : a selection with an introduction, text, translations, and notes / by William J. Dominik and William T. Wehrle.
    p. cm.
Parallel text in English and Latin; introd. and notes in English.
Includes bibliographical references and index.
ISBN 0-86516-442-8 (pbk. : alk paper)
    1. Verse satire, Latin—Translations into English. 2. Latin poetry—Translations into English. 3. Verse satire, Latin. 4. Rome—Poetry. I. Dominik, William J. II. Wehrle, William Thomas.

PA6164.R638 1999
871'.070801—dc21
                                                99-051347
                                                 CIP

For Robert Smutny
and
In Memory of Robert Hanlon

ACKNOWLEDGMENTS

William T. Wehrle and I express special thanks to Susanna Morton Braund (Royal Holloway College, London) for her helpful suggestions on matters of translation and comments on the form and content of this anthology; to Peter Tennant (Natal, Pietermaritzburg) and Malcolm Willcock (University College, London) for reading an earlier version and spotting a number of errors and infelicities of expression in the translation; to the anonymous referee for Bolchazy-Carducci, who made many helpful comments, especially concerning the selection of satires and the Introduction; and to Anne Gosling (Natal, Durban) and Christoff Zietsman (Stellenbosch) for their comments on the format and presentation of the text as well as on the translation.

I also acknowledge the assistance of Terrence Lockyer (Natal, Durban), who edited an earlier draft of this anthology; Justine Wolfenden (Leeds), who checked the text and assisted in compiling the Index; Anne Briggs and Angela Knock (Natal, Durban), who proofread the final version; and Susan Haskins (Natal, Durban), who suggested the Roman mosaic depicting street musicians on the cover.

These acknowledgments would not be complete without expressing appreciation to the students who have helped to give shape to this anthology over many years, namely my undergraduate classical civilization and Latin students, who over the years have encountered various sections of this anthology in their classes; William T. Wehrle's senior high school Latin students, who endured an earlier draft of the manuscript in their classes; and Adam Clulow (Natal, Durban), who as a graduate student of mine in Roman satire and epigram brought his special insight and perspective to bear upon the translations and notes.

I wish also to express my appreciation to Bolchazy-Carducci, especially Laurie Haight for guiding me through the submission, contract, editing and production stages; Charlene Hernandez for her technical assistance and design support during the preparation of the final manuscript for publication; and Ladislaus Bolchazy, who has done so much for Classics over the years by publishing pedagogical and other texts that help to bring life to the discipline in the university and secondary classrooms.

The University of Natal, Durban (South Africa) and The British Council (UK) awarded me research grants that assisted in the preparation and publication of this anthology. I express my thanks to these organizations for their financial support.

The Commonwealth Scholarship Commission in the United Kingdom awarded me a Commonwealth Fellowship for the 1997–1998 academic year, which enabled me to complete a final draft of this anthology while serving as a Visiting Professor of Classics at the University of Leeds. I am especially indebted to my colleagues in the School of Classics at Leeds for providing a congenial and supportive academic environment during my period of residence.

William J. Dominik

DEDICATION

We have dedicated this anthology to Robert Smutny, Professor Emeritus of Classics at the University of Pacific, and to the memory of Robert Hanlon, Master Teacher of Latin and English at Lincoln High School, Stockton, California (USA). Robert Smutny taught us Latin and Greek at the University of the Pacific, where we were awarded BA degrees in Classics. William T. Wehrle succeeded Robert Hanlon as Latin teacher at Lincoln High School, where William J. Dominik was taught by Mr. Hanlon in year 12. It is largely through the inspired and dedicated teaching of Professor Smutny and Mr. Hanlon that we were motivated to pursue teaching careers in Classics.

William J. Dominik
William T. Wehrle

CONTENTS

FOREWORD

This anthology of Roman verse satire is designed to give *representative* selections from Lucilius, Horace, Persius, and Juvenal with exegeses appropriate for the undergraduate and senior secondary market; it therefore should appeal to teachers looking for a text with selections from each of the verse satirists. This volume, however, is not intended to replace editions of individual satirists containing larger selections of satires or even comprehensive volumes such as those published by Penguin Books.

In deciding which of these satires and fragments to include in this anthology, we were faced with some difficult decisions. Achieving both balance in regard to the selections and including teachers' and students' favorite passages is akin to sailing between Scylla and Charybdis. It is impossible to please all readers in this regard. In the end, it becomes a matter of individual preference and judgment as to which satires to include in an anthology designed for student use. The Introduction not only includes brief summaries of the poems included in this anthology but also discusses a few of the famous poems not included in this volume in order to gives students a broader idea regarding the topics and themes of the satirists.

It has been our aim to include a balanced selection of satires and fragments in this anthology. Lucilius is an excellent starting point to explain the basic form and characteristics of satire to students. In selecting the fragments of Lucilius, we attempted to choose passages that linked with the other satires in the volume. Fragments 567–573 on women and 1145–1151 on the urban rat-race, for instance, thematically parallel Juvenal, *Satires* 6 and 3, respectively, while fragment 3–4 with its reference to the snarl of satire is echoed by Persius, *Satire* 1.109–110.

Three of Horace's finest poems are *Satires* 1.9, 2.1, and 2.8, which are included in this volume; however, other well known satires have not been included. *Satire* 1.1 on humanity's discontent and *Satire* 2.6 on city and country life were excluded for different reasons. Since satire is a unique Roman genre of the ancient world, we decided to include the opening satires of Persius and Juvenal, which deal with a literary theme; the decision to exclude Horace, *Satire* 1.1 was made partly on the basis that the programmatic first satires of Persius and Juvenal have been included. On the other hand, Horace, *Satire* 2.6 on city and country life was excluded because Juvenal deals largely with the same theme in *Satire* 3. Among Juvenal's major poems are *Satires* 1, 3, 6, and

10. In the end we decided to include *Satires* 3 on Rome and 6 on women, which meant that *Satire* 10 on the folly of human ambition and prayer was excluded.

Adding additional satires of Horace and Juvenal would have distorted the emphasis in this volume toward these satirists at the expense of Persius. We have therefore attempted to correct the imbalance toward Horace and Juvenal that often occurs in the teaching of satire by giving equal billing to Persius. At the same time, there is a proportional balance in our anthology in terms of the number of lines devoted to these satirists, especially in relation to Juvenal, the main Roman exponent of satire. There are far more lines of Juvenal in this anthology than of either Horace or Persius, which reflects appropriately the much larger corpus of Juvenal.

The inclusion of three satires of Persius may seem to over-represent his importance in the satirical tradition. Owing to the perceived difficulty of his poetry, Persius has almost without exception been under-represented when teaching satire. It is this prejudice that we are attempting partly to counteract by featuring him to the same extent as Horace and Juvenal in terms of the number of satires. Since Persius is difficult to understand and to translate in places, his teachability has been questioned; however, we have endeavored to translate his poetry in a way that we believe makes him accessible to undergraduate and senior secondary students and to provide a commentary consistent with this objective.

Our intention from the beginning was to restrict the anthology to approximately ten satires and 200 pages. Increasing the number of selections with accompanying notes would have expanded the volume to a point whereby it would have become potentially less attractive as a text to be included among a number of pedagogical texts to be used in a classical civilization, world literature, or Latin course. The small but varied selection of Roman verse satire should make it attractive as a set text for a literature-in-translation or culture course but yet contain enough different selections to warrant its inclusion on the booklist of a satire class in the original Latin.

Durban, Natal (South Africa)   W.J.D.
Stockton, California (USA)   W.T.W.
September 1999

PREFACE

This anthology provides a selection of the verse satires of four Roman poets: Lucilius, Horace, Persius, and Juvenal. Its purpose is pedagogical rather than scholarly: it is intended primarily for undergraduate and senior secondary classical civilization students engaged in the study of Roman verse satire in translation (for whom no such anthology previously has been published). The anthology has also been designed to serve as an aid to Latin students at the undergraduate and senior secondary levels in their own translation and understanding of these challenging, sometimes obscure and virtually unintelligible, poets. One of the advantages of this edition for Latin students is that the original text is printed opposite the translation.

All translations of (ancient) texts are approximations. No theory of translation can eliminate altogether the practical problem of how to render an "original" into a decoded "equivalent." The translations that follow, while maintaining as far as possible fidelity to and reflecting the style of the original Latin text, aim at a colloquial and easily understandable rendition. It is our belief that Latin poetry deserves to be (and can be successfully) translated as verse, not prose, since this helps to convey a sense of the text *as* poetry. Accordingly, in our attempt to produce a faithful rendering of the selected fragments and satires, we have endeavored to match the English translation to the Latin text line for line to the greatest extent feasible. We have tried especially to avoid the following two faults at the risk of being thought too literal in places: over-colloquialism, which violates the language, form, and syntax of the original, in some cases actually altering meaning significantly; and glossed-over obscenity, itself a legitimate poetic device, a purposeful and meaningful component whose function is better acknowledged than denied.

It has sometimes been said that the best commentary is a translation. Indeed, our aim in this anthology is to convey our interpretation of the Latin text by our translation and to a somewhat lesser extent by our explanatory and interpretative notes. Consistent with our basic objective of elucidating *what* the satires say rather than *how* they say it, the emphasis in the commentary is on factual explanation and some aspects of literary interpretation rather than on detailed textual and philological issues. In addition, it is our belief that our fairly literal, line-for-line translations have obviated the need for much basic grammatical explanation that can be found in other editions devoted primarily to this purpose, some of which are cited in the lists of texts and commentaries in the Introduction. At the same time, our decision to tread a literal path and generally to avoid "equivalents" for Greek and Roman names and allusions means that we have had to include more notes to explain these references.

The general social context of the verse satires is outlined briefly in the Introduction and in the commentary accompanying the individual satires. Additional information on the social context is available in some of the critical studies and scholarly commentaries cited in the Introduction, for instance, *Satire and Society in Ancient Rome* edited by S. H. Braund (Exeter 1989). In addition, the Introduction gives a general background of Roman satire and the context of the verse satires translated and annotated in this anthology. It briefly treats Roman writers who, despite being outside the scope of this anthology, deserve to be mentioned in any discussion of the Roman satirical tradition.

The Introduction also provides suggestions for further reading consisting of critical works on Roman satire in general as well as more focused books and chapters on individual satirists from which the general reader as well as Latin student can benefit. There are select lists of major editions and translations of each of the Roman verse satirists; further bibliography may be found by consulting the various commentaries and translations listed, most of which contain extensive bibliographies. The lists contain mainly publications in English and interpretative articles from journals have been excluded (with a single exception) because of the limitation of space.

The Notes are necessarily selective and are keyed to the English translation. They include the identification of personalities and locations, the explanation of the context of the individual satires and of literary, historical, mythological and philosophical allusions, and discussion of the untranslatable overtones of certain words and phrases. In the interests of user-friendliness and economy, we have tried to avoid being ponderous and neither to over-explain nor to under-explain in the Notes. We have asterisked and provided explanations of those items that we have deemed most essential for a basic understanding of the translation and of the context of the individual satires, particularly those for which a specific knowledge of classical antiquity is required, since the annotation of all names, words, and expressions in the English translation would have made the commentary uneconomical; where specific myths are referred to in the translation, the best known versions are generally given. When the keyed notes refer to whole lines, asterisks appear at the end of the specified lines in the English translation; specific words and phrases may also be asterisked in these lines for specific comment.

When textual matters are discussed in the Notes, the relevant lines of the Latin text (instead of the English translation) are asterisked. Cross-references have been kept to a minimum, so in some cases persons, places, and terms discussed earlier in the commentary are not cross-referenced when they appear again. The Index lists biographical, mythical, geographical and other names that appear in the Introduction, English translations, and Notes; Latinate forms of Greek names are used.

A NOTE ON THE LATIN TEXT

Our translations are based for the most part on the following Latin texts (with numerous changes in orthography, capitalization, and punctuation), although we have adopted the revisions of various commentators in a few places where their readings seem preferable: for Lucilius the text of E. H. Warmington (ed.), *Remains of Old Latin* 3 (rev. London/Cambridge, Mass. 1967); for Horace the text of E. C. Wickham and H. W. Garrod (eds.), *Q. Horati Flacci Opera*[2] (Oxford 1901); and for Persius and Juvenal the revised edition of W. V. Clausen, *A. Persi Flacci et D. Iuni Iuuenalis Saturae*[2] (Oxford 1992). Consonantal "v" and "j" have been printed as "u" and "i" throughout, while "U" appears as "V".

The major divergences from the aforementioned standard texts are listed below.

Horace, *Satire* 2.8.37: *maledicunt* for *male dicunt*

Persius, *Satire* 4.9: *puto* for *puta*

Juvenal, *Satire* 1.157: *deducis* for *deducit*

Juvenal, *Satire* 6.64: *gannit* for *longum*

Juvenal, *Satire* 6.65: *longum* for *gannit*

Juvenal, *Satire* 6.135: *summumque* for *minimumque*

Juvenal, *Satire* 6. O 9: *Psyllus* for *psyllus; Euhoplo* for *eupholio*

Juvenal, *Satire* 6.558–559: omitted

Juvenal, *Satire* 6.614A–614C: omitted

INTRODUCTION

The Roman Satirical Tradition

Roman satire is a peculiar literary genre; its establishment appears to be a particularly Roman accomplishment. *Satura quidem tota nostra est* ("Satire is altogether ours"), wrote Quintilian, a first century C.E. commentator on rhetorical and literary matters.[1] Satire treats an extraordinarily wide range of issues, a fact reflected by the name "satire" itself, which is derived from the Latin word *satur*, meaning "full" (of variety). Lucilius and Horace call their satires *Sermones* ("Conversations"), which suggests the broad scope and immense variety of the genre. In his programmatic satire, Juvenal calls his writing *farrago* ('stuffing,' 1.86), a mish-mash of grain fed to cattle. At the heart of satire, then, is variety and abundance, but at its most basic level the extensive mixture of topics and elements is accompanied by a certain naturalness, even coarseness, reflecting the most basic concerns and aspects of Roman society. Satire's concern is with daily life—what is happening in the public and private places of Rome and her inhabitants.

As a mirror of Roman society, satire was as powerful and direct in its portrayal as was the Old Comedy of Aristophanes' Athens.[2] Yet while ancient Attic comedy was designed especially to focus on the topical issues of its period, for instance, politics, religion, and socio-economic conflict, the scope of Roman satire involved a far broader view. Thus the thematic plurality encompassed by this genre makes it especially accessible and informative to the modern student of the ancient Roman world. In fact, a reader of the Roman satirists requires relatively little socio-historical background in order to appreciate their criticisms, which are remarkably universal in application, transcending as they do both time and space.

The deepest roots of Roman satire have been traced to primitive Italian dramatic presentations. These were localized skits performed with some degree of religious significance, that is, to gain the favor of the gods during times of

---

[1] See Quintilian, *Institutio Oratoria* 10.1.93. What is meant by 'altogether ours' is, in essence, 'non-Greek'; the formal bases of the genres of epic, lyric, tragedy, and comedy were all established for the Romans by Greek precedent.

[2] Greek Old Comedy is in fact cited by Roman satirists as an ideological and spiritual model: see, for example, Horace, *Satire* 1.4.1–8, where mention is made of three Greek comedians: Cratinus, Eupolis, and Aristophanes.

plague or other collective misfortune. The actors in these skits were accompanied by music, and singing and dancing formed an important part of the action. The festive and humorous (although socially relevant and even unsettling) tone of these early performances was transferred to two subsequent Roman literary genres especially—comedy and satire.

The first Roman author to compose what can be termed "verse satire" was probably Quintus Ennius, who was born in 239 B.C.E.; he is known today primarily for his partially extant historical epic poem *Annales*. Although Ennius' work is now extremely fragmentary, some reconstruction of his satirical *oeuvre* has been achieved. We know that he composed in a variety of meters and on a variety of themes. Thematically mention may be made of the following Ennian treatments: stories involving animals (fables); debates between abstract characters (for example, Life and Death); the complaint of a social parasite (this perhaps a self-mocking monologue); and personal commentary (Ennius' own views stated outright). To what degree Ennius used satire as a means of personal attack (invective) is uncertain. What *is* apparent from the fragments, however, is that even in its very early stages satire was characterized by thematic variety. As a poet, Ennius was well aware of his words' potential immortality, as is seen from what tradition holds to be his self-composed epitaph:

> nemo me lacrimis decoret nec funera fletu
> > faxit. cur? uolito uiuos per ora uirum.
> > > (*Epigrams*, fragment 2)[3]
> Let none honor me with tears or prepare my funeral
> > with weeping. Why? Alive I fly from the lips of men.

Despite the Ennian precedent, the traditional "founder" of Roman verse satire is Gaius Lucilius,[4] who flourished during the second half of the second century B.C.E. Marcus Terentius Varro (116–27 B.C.E.), although he followed Lucilius chronologically, did not follow "the father of satire" ideologically. Instead he composed relatively tame satires based on the precedent set by Menippus of Gadara, a third-century B.C.E. Syrian who wrote in Greek. The Menippean format consisted of a mixture of verse and prose. It was used also by Lucius Annaeus Seneca (*circa* 4 B.C.E.–65 C.E.) in his *Apocolocyntosis*, which seems to mean "Pumpkinification." This work satirizes in an unsympathetic manner the post-mortem fate of the emperor Claudius, who reigned 41–54 C.E. The *Satyricon* of Petronius Arbiter (died *circa* 66 C.E.) is likewise an admixture

---

[3] From the edition (with minor changes) of O. Skutsch, *The Annals of Q. Ennius* (Oxford 1985).

[4] See below, pp. 5–6.

of prose and verse although, since it is a narrative novel, prose far outweighs verse. The work may be described as a "picaresque novel," since it relates the exploits of three main characters—Encolpius, Ascyltus, and Giton—as they travel through southern Italy. The best known section of the *Satyricon* is the *Cena Trimalchionis* ("Dinner of Trimalchio"). While the account of this very extravagant and extremely unusual dinner-party hosted by Trimalchio is highly entertaining, it nonetheless also prompts interesting questions about the Neronian socio-political ambience, as does the *Satyricon* in general.

A native Spaniard, Marcus Valerius Martialis (40–103 C.E.), while working outside the strict field of verse satire, nevertheless merits mention in any discussion of the Roman satirical tradition. Martial published his first poems after the establishment of the Flavian Amphitheater (the Colosseum) at Rome in 80 C.E. The collection was entitled *De Spectaculis* ("On the Games") and the short poems addressed the various aspects of the public spectacles (for example, animal fights). There followed the progressive and steady publication of volumes of *Epigrams*, of which fourteen books are extant. Like the satirists (most notably Persius and Juvenal), Martial, although keeping his poems short and concise, attacked the irrelevance of the literary production of his contemporaries. He (again like the satirists) depicted a society in which there was apparently no shortage of material to illustrate corruption and absurdity at all levels from slave to emperor. Martial directs verbal fusillades at his targets with unrelenting force—fusillades intensified by the bullets of obscenity, personal invective, double entendre and caustic wit. By adopting the stance of outraged observer of societal perversity, Martial realizes the effective technique of apparently answering offense with offense, audacity with audacity, outrage with outrage. The poet's work need not, however, serve to reflect his manner of life, and Martial himself stressed this in one of his better known poems:

> contigeris nostros, Caesar, si forte libellos,
>   terrarum dominum pone supercilium.
> consueuere iocos uestri quoque ferre triumphi,
>   materiam dictis nec pudet esse ducem.
> qua Thymelen spectas derisoremque Latinum,
>   illa fronte precor carmina nostra legas.
> innocuos censura potest permittere lusus:
>   lasciua est nobis pagina, uita proba.
>
> (*Epigrams* 1.4)[5]

---

[5] From the edition (with minor changes) of D. R. Shackleton Bailey, *Martialis Epigrammata* (Stuttgart 1990).

If by chance, Caesar,[6] you should touch upon my little books,
   set aside the censoriousness that is world's lord.
Your triumphs also were accustomed to bear jokes;
   nor does it shame a leader to be material for words of jest.

5   With the outlook you display when you watch Thymele and the joker
         Latinus,[7]
   with that outlook, I pray, may you read my poems.
A censor can allow harmless amusements:
   my page is licentious, my life upright.

We do know of a couple of other Roman writers who wrote satirical poems. Marcus Pacuvius (*circa* 220–130 B.C.E.), a nephew and pupil of Ennius, composed satires, while Turnus, a contemporary of Juvenal, was a popular satirist during the reign of Domitian (81–96 C.E.); unfortunately only a couple of lines written by the latter survive. We can only guess at the other losses incurred by posterity from this most Roman of genres.

General Surveys

Anderson, W. S., *Essays on Roman Satire* (Princeton 1982).
Braund, S. H., *Roman Verse Satire* (Oxford 1992).
———— (ed.), *Satire and Society in Ancient Rome* (Exeter 1989).
Braund, S. M., *The Roman Satirists and Their Masks* (London 1996).
Classen, C., "Satire—The Elusive Genre," *Symbolae Osloenses* 63 (1988) 95–121.
Coffey, M., *Roman Satire*[2] (Bristol 1989).
Gowers, E. G., "Satire," in S. Hornblower and A. Spawforth (eds.), *The Oxford Classical Dictionary*[3] (Oxford 1996) 1358–1359.
Knoche, U. (trans. E. S. Ramage), *Roman Satire* (Bloomington 1975).
Ramage, E. S., D. L. Sigsbee, and S. L. Fredericks, *Roman Satirists and Their Satire: The Fine Art of Criticism in Ancient Rome* (Park Ridge 1974).
Relihan, J. C., *Ancient Menippean Satire* (Baltimore 1993).
Rudd, N., *Themes in Roman Satire* (London 1986).
Sullivan, J. P. (ed.), *Critical Essays on Roman Literature* 2: *Satire* (London 1963).
Van Rooy, C. A., *Studies in Classical Satire and Related Literary Theory* (Leiden 1965).
Witke, C., *Latin Satire: The Structure of Persuasion* (Leiden 1970).

---

[6] 'Caesar' here is in reference to the emperor Domitian (who reigned 81–96 C.E.), under whom Martial was writing.

[7] Thymele was either a stage-actress or a character portrayed on stage; Latinus was a comic actor. Both figures were active under Domitian and are mentioned in Juvenal, *Satire* 1.36.

Lucilius

Lucilius (*circa* 180–102/1 B.C.E.), "the father of satire," was born at Suessa Aurunca in the southwestern Italian region of Campania. Entirely fragmentary, his writings display the salient qualities of personal invective, autobiography and (importantly for his followers) coarse humor. Lucilius set the tone of satire as one of glib conversation, referring to his verse as "sport" (*ludus*) and "talk" (*sermo*). With Lucilius too came the adoption of dactylic hexameter as the conventional meter for satire. This meter had been established by the Greeks as the standard one for epic poetry as far back as Homer (eighth century B.C.E.) and Hesiod (*circa* 700 B.C.E.); it seems somewhat paradoxical, on the surface at any rate, that the meter of "lofty" (Greek) epic should be adopted by Lucilius for the composition of a "base" sort of poetry like satire. In fact, however, one of the important characteristics of Roman satire in general, as is demonstrated by the selections in this anthology, is attack on other literary genres, especially epic—thus parody by metrical imitation. Not all subsequent Roman satirical writers, however, adhered to the use of the dactylic hexameter.

The Lucilian fragments presented in this anthology have been selected with a view toward illustration of the diversity of his subject-matter. Although many of the fragments are very short (only one or two lines), their tone and design are quite informative, especially when viewed in conjunction with certain (longer) passages in the works of the subsequent satirists, who in many instances pointedly call attention to their own status as self-proclaimed followers of the Lucilian model.

Texts and Translations

There are three readily available catalogues of Lucilius' fragments, as listed below. The translation in this anthology is based on the text (with some minor changes) of Warmington (rev. 1967).

Krenkel, W. (ed. and trans.), *C. Lucilius. Satiren: lateinisch und deutsch* (Leiden 1970). Critical text.
Marx, F. (ed.), *C. Lucilii Carminum Reliquiae* (repr. Amsterdam 1963). Critical text.
Warmington, E. H. (ed. and trans.), *Remains of Old Latin* 3 (rev. London 1967). Text and translation.

Critical Studies

Fiske, G. C., *Lucilius and Horace: A Study in the Classical Theory of Imitation* (repr. Westport 1970).

Gratwick, A. S., "The Satires of Ennius and Lucilius," in E. J. Kenney and W. V.
    Clausen (eds.), *The Cambridge History of Classical Literature* 2 (Cambridge
    1983) 156–171.

Horace

Lucilius' successor in the new-fashioned genre of main-line verse (that is,
dactylic hexameter) satire, Quintus Horatius Flaccus (65–8 B.C.E.), capitalized
on a perceived opportunity for further revision and invention. His two books of
eighteen *Satires* (or, as he prefers to call them, *Sermones*, "Conversations") can
be dated to the period *circa* 38–30 B.C.E.,[8] a period during which Octavian and
Mark Antony were engaged in a struggle for political dominion. The *Satires*
deal with a wide variety of themes, including personal biography, travel, women,
social class and economics, philosophy, gastronomy, and literary criticism. The
flavor of the *Satires* is anecdotal, lightly humorous, and personal, even ostensibly
autobiographical. The representative selection given in the pages of this anthology
(*Satires* 1.9, 2.1, and 2.8) illustrates well the unique stance of Horace as satirist.
Lucilian personal invective is relatively absent and the poetic voice is constrained,
which in part reflects the political and social uncertainty of the 30s B.C.E. and
the more restrictive environment of the Augustan era.

Satire 1.9, which we have subtitled "The Pest," is a narrative account,
assisted by intermittent dialogue, of the accidental meeting between Horace
himself and an obnoxious pest.[9] This person ("known," says Horace, "to me
only by name," *notus mihi nomine tantum*, *Satire* 1.9.3) seems to be seeking
recognition as a man of letters. The outcome of the encounter, however, is not
an introduction to any of Rome's circle of current literary figures or patrons,
such as Maecenas, the patron of Horace and Vergil, but rather a court-summons
for the pest, which Horace as narrator is all too happy to facilitate.

Satire 2.1 is in form a dialogue between Horace and one Gaius Trebatius
Testa. Trebatius, evidently a renowned lawyer from the time of Cicero (106–43
B.C.E.), is given the role of counselor to Horace, who defends his right to pro-
duce satire rather than, for instance, historical epic. In this respect, the satire is
somewhat programmatic, although the emphasis is not on the (projected) content

---

[8] Horace's other surviving works and their approximate dates of publication are as follows:
Epodes (*circa* 30 B.C.E.); *Odes* (books 1–3 *circa* 23 B.C.E.; book 4 *circa* 13 B.C.E.); *Epistles* (book
1 *circa* 20 B.C.E.; book 2 *circa* 15 B.C.E.); and *Carmen Saeculare* (17 B.C.E.).

[9] This satire is commonly subtitled 'The Bore.' The satirisation of a 'bore' was evidently
undertaken by Lucilius (book 6) and Horace's adaptation of that theme is closely connected to
the Lucilian model.

of Horace's other satires but rather on the legitimacy of satire itself as a genre. Lucilius is cited by Horace as his literary/spiritual model and there is some emphasis on the fact that Horace must write, whatever the nature of his life. The role of Trebatius is that of objector. He warns Horace that satire may offend, which may cause him to lose friends and perhaps even be taken to court on charges of slander. In the end, however, even Trebatius has to admit that humor will prevail.

Satire 2.8 has as its theme a dinner party, a subject commonly treated by Roman satirists across the authorial spectrum. In this case the host of the dinner is a somewhat paradoxical figure—at once both extravagant and offensive. The narrator is one Fundanius, apparently a comic writer (also mentioned by Horace at *Satire* 1.10.42), and the formal model of the piece was once again probably a work of Lucilius. The host of the dinner-party, Nasidienus, is wealthy yet highly pretentious. The dishes are ludicrously exotic and their presentation is accompanied by much ostentation. Present as guests are Maecenas (compare Horace, *Satire* 1.9) as well as a pair of parasitic buffoons. The dinner itself is marred by the catastrophic collapse of the dining-room's overhanging awnings; before the meal is completed Fundanius and the other guests depart in disgust. A close parallel to Horace's Nasidienus is Petronius' Trimalchio.[10]

While *Satires* 1.9, 2.1, and 2.8 are well known and give us a glimpse into some of Horace's concerns as a satirist, many of his other *Satires* such as 1.1 and 2.6 employ themes with a particular relevance to our own age. *Satire* 1.1 is notable for its treatment of humanity's habitual discontent with its assigned lot. The central theme is man's greed, which emerges as the main impediment to a happy life. *Satire* 2.6, which contains the famous story of the town and country mouse, contrasts the simple pleasures of country life with the pressures of urban existence. It was much admired by poets of the eighteenth century, including Alexander Pope (1688–1744) and Jonathan Swift (1667–1745), who imitated it.

Texts, Translations, and Commentaries

Editions and translations of the *Satires* (*Sermones*) are numerous; only a selection of those most widely available is listed below. The present translations are based (with numerous minor changes) on the edition by Wickham and Garrod (1901).

Bovie, S. P. (trans.), *The Satires and Epistles of Horace: A Modern English Verse Translation* (Chicago 1959). Verse translation with notes.

---

[10] See above, p. 3.

Brown, P. M. (ed. and trans.), *Horace: Satires I* (repr. Warminster 1995). Text, translation, and commentary on the translation.

Carne-Ross, D. S. and K. Haynes (eds.), *Horace in English* (Harmondsworth 1996). Selection of English translations by various hands.

Fairclough, H. R. (ed. and trans.), *Horace: Satires, Epistles, Ars Poetica* (rev. London 1929). Text and translation.

Fuchs, J., *Horace's Satires and Epistles* (New York 1977). Verse translation.

Muecke, F. (ed. and trans.), *Horace: Satires II* (Warminster 1993). Text, translation, and commentary on the translation.

Palmer, A. (ed.), *The Satires of Horace* (repr. London 1971). Text and commentary.

Rudd, N. (trans.), *Horace: Satires and Epistles. Persius: Satires* (rev. Harmondsworth 1987). Verse translation with notes.

Rushton Fairclough, H. (ed. and trans.), *Horace: Satires, Epistles and Ars Poetica* (repr. London 1966). Text and translation.

Shackleton Bailey, D. R. (ed.), *Q. Horatii Flacci Opera* (Stuttgart 1985). Critical text.

Wickham, E. C. (ed.), *Quinti Horati Flacci Opera Omnia. The Works of Horace 2: The Satires, Epistles and De Arte Poetica* (Oxford 1891). Text and commentary.

Wickham, E. C. and H. W. Garrod (eds.), *Q. Horati Flacci Opera*[2] (Oxford 1901). Critical text.

Critical Studies

Armstrong, D., *Horace* (New Haven 1989).

Costa, C. D. N. (ed.), *Horace* (London 1973).

Fraenkel, E., *Horace* (Oxford 1957).

Freudenburg, K., *The Walking Muse: Horace on the Theory of Satire* (Princeton 1993).

Oliensis, E., *Horace and the Rhetoric of Authority* (Cambridge 1998).

Porter, D. H., "Horace," in T. J. Luce (ed.), *Ancient Writers: Greece and Rome 2* (New York 1982) 703–731.

Reckford, K. J., *Horace* (New York 1969).

Rudd, N., "Horace," in E. J. Kenney and W. V. Clausen (eds.), *The Cambridge History of Classical Literature 2* (Cambridge 1983) 370–404.

———, *The Satires of Horace: A Study* (Cambridge 1966).

West, D. A., *Reading Horace* (Edinburgh 1967).

Persius

Aulus Persius Flaccus has had a significant and permanent impact not only on subsequent Roman literature but also on the readers, writers, and thinkers of early and recent modernity. Lucilius and Horace are his main influences, but his *Satires* are entirely original and distinctive. Persius lived not quite twenty-eight years (34–62 C.E.), dying of a stomach condition, as we are told by the ancient "Life" (*Vita*). His *oeuvre* is relatively slight (his six *Satires* and introductory prologue total only 664 lines), especially in comparison with Lucilius and Horace, but this seems consistent with his poetic objective of composing a "little book" (*libelle*, *Satire* 1.120). According to the ancient biography, Persius had links with the Stoic opposition to Nero, and in his opening, programmatic satire he attacks the poetry being written by Neronian *dilettanti*—presumably this includes Nero and his circle. But the *Satires* themselves are avowedly more concerned with poetry and ethics than with politics. Literary bad taste and moral debasement are Persius' main themes—what he calls the "biting truth" (*mordaci uero*, *Satire* 1.107).

As a literary figure, however, Persius has unfortunately been poorly received by some modern critics. With Persius the invective of Lucilius and the genial mocking tone of Horace becomes what his interlocutor in the first satire asserts "tastes of bitten nails" (*demorsos sapit unguis*, *Satire* 1.106). His manner, unusual choice of diction, the density of his language, employment of complex imagery and metaphor, and general unorthodoxy of expression have all contributed to modern readers' misassessment of his poetry. Persius' Latinity is itself difficult, the meaning of many passages ambiguous, even elusive. Yet those who choose to ignore (or worse, to disparage) Persius' *Satires* are led to do so simply by their unwillingness or inability to see them for what they are: unconventional (both for their time and our own), purposefully experimental, aggressively extravagant, and even iconoclastic from a literary standpoint, as the poetic value-assumptions of Persius' contemporaries are questioned and even deliberately dissolved.

As preface to Persius' *Satires* stands a fourteen-verse prologue, the main concern of which is the dichotomy of false poets, who are likened to mimetic birds, and the satirist, who denies similar "poetic" inspiration altogether. The language of the prologue is forceful, experimental, and virulently original, as tends to be Persius' language in general. The metrical scheme of the original Latin verse is choliambic, otherwise known as "limping iambic," itself remarkable in that it shows Persius' singular repartee in ridicule by imitation; Persius attacks "lame" poets and poesy in "lame" or "limping" metrics.[11] The thrust of the prologue involves primarily two important ideas: the self-dissociation of Persius as satirist from contemporary Neronian *literati* and the monumental irrelevancy and disgustingly mercenary nature of contemporary literary production.

Satire 1 is Persius' program piece and a truly remarkable piece of literary criticism. It opens with a line probably taken from Lucilius: *O curas hominum!*

---

[11] Persius does not actually call contemporary literary figures 'lame'; his maligning of them is more wide ranging, citing especially their effeminacy, hypocrisy, and lack of self-knowledge.

o quantum est in rebus inane! ("Oh the cares of human beings! Oh how much emptiness there is in things!"), the immediate effect of which is to confirm a generic, if not ideological, bond between the two authors. The Persian program is highly critical of Roman literary taste. The creators of literature, their products and, in fact, their audience are all similar in their perversion, hypocrisy, and critical inability. Yet the satirist, because of an innate and overwhelming drive, must write; he will write, therefore, in the only area still uncontaminated by contemporary poets—satire. Persius' justification for writing satire is combined with an incisive, multi-faceted attack on literary pretension and is assisted (as are the justifications of Horace and Juvenal) by the device of dialogue. The satirist sets up an opposing voice, whose basic message is "you really shouldn't offend people by satirizing them," only to dismantle this voice's arguments and further his own.

    Satire 3 is a highly original experiment involving a complex interaction between different "voices" assumed by Persius and his interlocutor. Persius seems to shift between two voices—that of the narrator and that of the lazy student, while a third voice, a "censorious companion," is also distinguishable. There is nonetheless a unifying theme: mental and physical sloth, philosophical and moral retardation, and an unwillingness to confront one's shortcomings on the one hand versus the call to Stoic philosophy's healthy influence on the other. The core of the argument is aimed at those who do not allow philosophy to help them regulate their lives. Physical parallels moral: while bodily symptoms index moral defects, good health is attained by living according to the precepts of Stoicism.

    Satire 4 is modeled on the Greek Socratic/Platonic dialogic tradition. The two main characters in this piece, both Greek, are "Socrates," who is assigned the role of fault-finding critic, and "Alcibiades," who embodies various moral/ethical shortcomings. In this piece the "Socrates" figure is actually designed by Persius to resemble in viewpoint and language the prototypical "Roman" satirist. "Alcibiades" as symbol represents one of satire's universal objects of attack: the hypocritical, incompetent, and intellectually underdeveloped young dilettante.

Texts, Translations, and Commentaries

The standard text for Persius is that of Clausen (rev. 1992), which is the one used in this anthology (with numerous minor changes). There are also several editions, including the recent ones of Lee and Barr (1987) and of Jenkinson (1980), which combine the Latin text with an English translation and explanatory notes.

Clausen, W. V. (ed.), *A. Persi Flacci Saturarum Liber, Accedit Vita* (Oxford 1956). Critical text with textual introduction.

—— (ed.), *A. Persi Flacci et D. Iuni Iuuenalis Saturae*[2] (Oxford 1992). Critical text.

Conington, J. and H. Nettleship (ed. and trans.), *The Satires of A. Persius Flaccus*[3] (repr. Hildesheim 1967). Text, translation, and commentary.

Cowherd, C. (ed.), *Persius: Saturae* (Bryn Mawr 1986). Text and notes.

Gifford, W., J. Warrington, and S. H. Braund (trans.), *Juvenal: Satires with the Satires of Persius* (London 1992). Early nineteenth-century verse translation with notes.

Harvey, R. A., *A Commentary on Persius* (Leiden 1981). Commentary.

Jahn, O. (ed.), *Auli Persii Flacci Saturarum Liber* (repr. Stuttgart 1967).

Jenkinson, J. R. (ed. and trans.), *Persius: The Satires* (Warminster 1980). Text, translation, and commentary on the translation.

Lee, G. (ed. and trans.) and W. Barr, *The Satires of Persius* (Liverpool 1987). Text, translation, and commentary.

Merwin, W. W. (trans.; introd. and notes W. S. Anderson), *The Satires of Persius* (Indiana 1961). Translation with notes.

Ramsay, G. G. (ed. and trans.), *Juvenal and Persius* (rev. London 1940). Text and translation.

Rudd, N. (trans.), *Horace: Satires and Epistles. Persius: Satires* (rev. Harmondsworth 1987). Verse translation with notes.

Tate, J. (trans.), *The Satires of A. Persius Flaccus* (Oxford 1930). Translation.

Critical Studies

Anderson, W. S., "Persius and Juvenal," in T. J. Luce (ed.), *Ancient Writers: Greece and Rome* 2 (New York 1982) 855–876.

Bramble, J. C., *Persius and the Programmatic Satire: A Study in Form and Imagery* (Cambridge 1974).

Dessen, C. S., *Iunctura Callidus Acri: A Study of Persius' Satires* (Urbana 1968).

Hooley, D. M., *The Knotted Thong: Structures of Mimesis in Persius* (Ann Arbor 1997).

Rudd, N., "Persius," in E. J. Kenney and W. V. Clausen (eds.), *The Cambridge History of Classical Literature* 2 (Cambridge 1983) 503–510.

Wehrle, W. T., *The Satiric Voice: Program, Form, and Meaning in Persius and Juvenal* (Hildesheim 1992).

Juvenal

Relatively few biographical details are known about Decimus Iunius Iuvenalis. The date of his birth is speculative, resting probably somewhere between 55 and 67 C.E. For the date of his death, evidence from the *Satires* themselves points to sometime after 127 C.E. At any rate Juvenal was not, it appears, extremely popular or even well-known in literary circles during his lifetime. He may have been quite poor at some point in his life, even dependent on the more wealthy for his sustenance. He may also have undertaken military service and even gained significant office. These conjectures (and again, this is all they are), however, have their foundations not in irrefutable historical evidence but rather in imaginative inferences drawn from certain passages of the *Satires*.

The Juvenalian *oeuvre* consists of sixteen *Satires* on an extremely wide range of themes, the last satire of which was apparently never finished. The compositional style of Juvenal can perhaps most accurately be described as "paragraphic." Although rhetorical questions are posed, these questions in many cases lead not to logically drawn out expositions but rather to other spheres of digressive discourse. This stylistic aspect has led many modern critics to examine the *Satires* for evidence of identifiable, if not predictable, structure. Lack of "logical" structure, however, is itself a poetic technique—a technique that adds spontaneity and liveliness.

As poetry Juvenal's *Satires* lead the reader through an intricate yet constantly entertaining nexus of images and characters. In contrast to the comparatively restrained satire of Horace, Juvenal stretches Lucilian invective to the limit by adopting a stance of moral outrage (especially in *Satires* 1–6) to describe what he perceives as the depravity of contemporary Rome. What emerges through his eyes is a picture of a society in which the established traditions and codes buttressing the Roman élite have disintegrated. Corruption and absurdity abound at all levels from slave to emperor. The aristocratic classes are portrayed as paradigms of moral and political corruption. This includes the emperor Domitian, who is depicted as a sexual hypocrite and tyrant.

Satire 1 serves to define Juvenal's satirical stance—his relative position in spheres primarily social and literary. It can appropriately be termed a "programmatic" satire since on the surface, if not in actuality, it sets forth a kind of prospectus for the remaining satires. The declaration that professes to be programmatic index, however, somewhat misleads: *quidquid agunt homines, uotum, timor, ira, uoluptas, / gaudia, discursus, nostri farrago libelli est* ("Whatever people do—prayer, fear, anger, pleasure, rejoicing, running about—is the stuffing of my little book," 1.86–87). As will be seen, the "stuffing" of the *Satires* is of limited scope, presented by voice(s) of limited, although artistically designed, perspective.

The fancied dramatic setting of *Satire* 1 involves the picture of the satirist standing at a Roman cross-roads with writing tools in hand. Various manifestations of contemporary Roman vice, corruption, perversity, and absurdity pass into the sphere of his literary vision and these are enumerated for us one by one. The predominant tone of the piece is one of savage indignation. Especially important from a programmatic perspective is Juvenal's attack on his contemporary *literati*. Stock (for example, mythological) themes are disparaged as socially irrelevant as well as burdensome to those forced to sit at formal recitations of such literary treatments. In form the poem mirrors its contents: the structure suggests random composition, a sort of "formless form." Complementary to the adamantly indignant tone (*difficile est saturam non scribere*, "it is difficult *not* to write satire," 1.30) is a train of thought that jumps rail without warning, as though itself propelled by the indomitable engine of societal corruption.

Satire 3, an elaborate sketch of urban "disease," is voiced by a character called Umbricius, who is quitting Rome to relocate to Cumae, a resort town south of Rome. The indignant narrative tone of this satire echoes that of *Satire* 1. While the *persona* of Umbricius may not have been designed to elicit unmixed sympathy from the reader, some of his criticisms of city-life, for instance, the ever-present threat of fire and ruin and the prevalence of violent crime, are by no means alien to the readers and writers of modern times. Prominent in Umbricius' monologue is a sustained expression of xenophobia, especially toward Greeks and Greek culture; for instance, he calls Rome a "Greek city." Overstated is a fancied distinction between "true Roman," the paragon of which is Umbricius himself, and invasive non-Roman. In short, Umbricius posits no advantage of city-life but espouses instead country-life and a return to simple values and an unaffected life-style. This satire was imitated by Samuel Johnson (1709–1784) in his poem entitled *London*, while Nicolas Boileau-Despréaux (1636–1711) turned its subject Rome into Paris in two separate satires.

Satire 6, in superficial form an admonition against marriage addressed to a certain Postumus, has been widely celebrated as one of ancient literature's greatest pieces of raw misogyny. The satire disturbs with its relentless portrayal of women as depraved freaks of nature; this pointedly anti-feminine tone in combination with singular (for Juvenal) and emphatic obscenity is what makes this satire especially curious. The poem is long, the narrative voice unrelenting. Practically no stone is left unturned in the woman-hater's quite single-minded search for hideous and disagreeable feminine traits and practices.

Although *Satires* 1, 3, and 6 give the reader an idea of Juvenal's disgust with contemporary society and its standards, the other *Satires* complete his treatment of this theme. A poem not included in this anthology is *Satire* 10 on the folly of human ambition and prayer, which Samuel Johnson adapted in composing *The Vanity of Human Wishes*. In this poem Juvenal successively exposes the dangers of wealth, power, eloquence, military success, long life, and beauty. The poem contains one of the most famous quotations handed down to us from antiquity—*mens sana in corpore sano*, "a healthy mind in a sound body"— which is the one thing for which humankind should pray.

Texts, Translations, and Commentaries

For the text of the *Satires* there are the recent editions of Clausen (1992), Courtney (1984), Martyn (1987), and Willis (1997). The translation given here is based on Clausen's text (with some major and minor changes).

Braund, S. M. (ed.), *Juvenal: Satires Book I* (Cambridge 1996).

Clausen, W. V. (ed.), *A. Persi Flacci et D. Iuni Iuuenalis Saturae²* (Oxford 1992). Critical text.

Courtney, E. (ed.), *A Commentary on the Satires of Juvenal* (London 1980). The standard scholarly commentary.

——— (ed.), *Juvenal. The Satires: A Text with Brief Critical Notes* (Rome 1984). Critical text.

Duff, J. D. and M. D. Coffey (ed.), *D. Iunii Iuvenalis Saturae XIV: Fourteen Satires of Juvenal* (Cambridge 1970). Partly expurgated text with commentary.

Ferguson, J. (ed.), *Juvenal: The Satires* (New York 1979). Text with commentary.

Gifford, W., J. Warrington, and S. H. Braund (trans.), *Juvenal: Satires with the Satires of Persius* (London 1992). Early nineteenth-century verse translation with notes.

Green, P. (trans.), *Juvenal: The Sixteen Satires* (rev. Harmondsworth 1998). Verse translation with notes.

Martyn, J. R. C. (ed.), *D. Iuni Iuvenalis Saturae* (Amsterdam 1987). Critical text.

Ramsay, G. G. (ed. and trans.), *Juvenal and Persius* (rev. London 1940). Text and translation.

Rudd, N. (trans.) and W. Barr, *Juvenal: The Satires* (Oxford 1992). Verse translation with notes.

Willis, J. A. (ed.), *Iuvenalis Saturae* (Stuttgart 1997). Critical text.

Critical Studies

Anderson, W. S., "Persius and Juvenal," in T. J. Luce (ed.), *Ancient Writers: Greece and Rome* 2 (New York 1982) 855–876.

Bramble, J. C., "Martial and Juvenal," in E. J. Kenney and W. V. Clausen (eds.), *The Cambridge History of Classical Literature* 2 (Cambridge 1983) 597–623.

Braund, S. H., *Beyond Anger: A Study of Juvenal's Third Book of Satires* (Cambridge 1988).

Colton, R. E., *Juvenal's Use of Martial's Epigrams: A Study of Literary Influence* (Amsterdam 1991).

Ferguson, J., *A Prosopography to the Poems of Juvenal* (Brussels 1987).

Friedländer, L. (trans. J. R. C. Martyn), *Essays on Juvenal* (Amsterdam 1969).

Highet, G., *Juvenal the Satirist: A Study* (London 1954).

Jenkyns, R., *Three Classical Poets: Sappho, Catullus and Juvenal* (London 1982) 151–221.

Winkler, M. M., *The Persona in Three Satires of Juvenal* (Hildesheim 1983).

LUCILIUS, FRAGMENTS

2

o curas hominum! o quantum est in rebus inane!

3–4

                                                     <r littera . . .>
inritata canes quam homo quam planius dicit.

36–37

"quae facies, qui uultus uiro?"
"uultus item ut facies, mors, icterus morbus, uenenum."

70

"uiuite lurcones, comedones, uiuite uentris!"

87–93

"Graecum te, Albuci, quam Romanum atque Sabinum
municipem Ponti, Tritani, centurionum,
praeclarorum hominum ac primorum signiferumque,
maluisti dici. Graece ergo praetor Athenis,   90
id quod maluisti te, cum ad me accedis, saluto:
'chaere' inquam 'Tite.' lictores, turma omnis chorusque:
'chaere Tite.' hinc hostis mi Albucius, hinc inimicus!"

LUCILIUS, FRAGMENTS

2

Oh the cares of human beings! Oh how much emptiness there is in
    things!*

3–4

The letter *r*,*
which an angry dog says more plainly than a human being.*

36–37

"What's the appearance, what's the face of the man like?"*
"His appearance is just like his face: death, jaundice-disease, poison."*

70

"Live, gluttons, devourers; live, you bellies!"*

87–93

"You have preferred to be called a Greek, Albucius,* rather than Roman
    and Sabine,*
citizen of Pontius, of Tritanus, of centurions,*
of illustrious and foremost men, of standard bearers.*
90   As praetor* in Athens, therefore, in Greek*
(that which you've preferred) I greet you when you approach me:*
'Chaere,'* I say, 'Titus.' The lictors,* the entire throng and chorus: *
'Chaere, Titus.' Hence is Albucius a foe to me, hence an enemy!"*

567–573

"num censes calliplocamon callisphyron ullam
non licitum esse uterum atque etiam inguina tangere mammis,
conpernem aut uaram fuisse Amphitryonis acoetin
Alcmenam atque alias, Helenam ipsam denique—nolo　　　　　570
dicere; tute uide atque disyllabon elige quoduis—
κούρην eupatereiam aliquam rem insignem habuisse,
uerrucam naeuum punctum dentem eminulum unum?"

713–714

hunc laborem sumas laudem qui tibi ac fructum ferat.
percrepa pugnam Popili, facta Corneli cane.

1145–1151

nunc uero a mani ad noctem festo atque profesto　　　　　1145
totus item pariterque die populusque patresque
iactare indu foro se omnes, decedere nusquam;
uni se atque eidem studio omnes dedere et arti—
uerba dare ut caute possint, pugnare dolose,
blanditia certare, bonum simulare uirum se,　　　　　1150
insidias facere ut si hostes sint omnibus omnes.

567–573

"Surely you don't think that any woman with beautiful locks and
     beautiful ankles*
could not touch her belly and even her groin with her breasts,*
and that Amphitryon's wife Alcmena* could not have been knock-
     kneed or bow-legged,*

570   and that others, even Helen* herself, could not have been—I don't want*
to say it; see to it yourself and choose any bisyllabic word you like*—
that a 'maiden' born of a noble father could not have had some
     distinguishing mark,*
a wart, a mole, a pit in the skin, one tooth projecting a bit?"*

713–714

You should undertake this task, which might bring to you praise and
     profit.*
Sound loudly about the fight of Popillius;* sing the deeds of Cornelius.*

1145–1151

1145   But, as it is, from morning until night, on holiday and workday,*
the whole people and the senators too all alike*
bustle about in the forum and on no occasion leave it.*
To one and the same pursuit and artifice all devote themselves:*
to be able to cheat with cunning, to fight cleverly,*

1150   to struggle charmingly, to pretend to be a good man,*
to lay a trap, as if everyone were everyone's enemies.*

1196–1208

uirtus, Albine, est pretium persoluere uerum
quis in uersamur quis uiuimus rebus potesse;
uirtus est homini scire id quod quaeque habeat res;
uirtus scire homini rectum utile quid sit honestum,
quae bona quae mala item, quid inutile turpe inhonestum;   1200
uirtus quaerendae finem re scire modumque;
uirtus diuitiis pretium persoluere posse;
uirtus id dare quod re ipsa debetur honori,
hostem esse atque inimicum hominum morumque malorum
contra defensorem hominum morumque bonorum,   1205
hos magni facere, his bene uelle, his uiuere amicum,
commoda praeterea patriai prima putare,
deinde parentum, tertia iam postremaque nostra.

1196–1208

Virtue, Albinus,* is to be able to pay out the true price*
in matters in which we find ourselves involved and in which we live;*
virtue is to know what it is that each thing contains for a person;*
virtue is to know what is right for a person, what is useful, what is
      honorable,*
1200   what things are good and likewise what are bad, what is useless, what
      is disgraceful, what is dishonorable;*
virtue is to know a thing's boundary and proper measure of seeking;*
virtue is to be able to pay out a price from one's supply of wealth;*
virtue is to give that which in a matter itself is owed to honor,*
to be an enemy and non-friend of bad people and bad character*
1205   and on the contrary to be the defender of good people and good character,*
to take great account of these, to wish well for these, to live as a friend
      to these;*
furthermore, to think that the interests of fatherland come first,*
then those of parents, thirdly and lastly those of ourselves.*

HORACE, *SATIRE* 1.9

ibam forte uia Sacra, sicut meus est mos,
nescio quid meditans nugarum, totus in illis.
accurrit quidam notus mihi nomine tantum,
arreptaque manu "quid agis, dulcissime rerum?"
"suauiter, ut nunc est," inquam, "et cupio omnia quae uis."   5
cum adsectaretur, "num quid uis?" occupo. at ille
"noris nos" inquit; "docti sumus." hic ego "pluris
hoc" inquam "mihi eris." misere discedere quaerens,
ire modo ocius, interdum consistere, in aurem
dicere nescio quid puero, cum sudor ad imos   10
manaret talos. "o te, Bolane, cerebri
felicem!" aiebam tacitus, cum quidlibet ille
garriret, uicos, urbem laudaret. ut illi
nil respondebam, "misere cupis" inquit "abire;
iamdudum uideo: sed nil agis; usque tenebo;   15
persequar hinc quo nunc iter est tibi." "nil opus est te
circumagi: quendam uolo uisere non tibi notum:
trans Tiberim longe cubat is, prope Caesaris hortos."
"nil habeo quod agam et non sum piger: usque sequar te."
demitto auriculas, ut iniquae mentis asellus,   20
cum grauius dorso subiit onus. incipit ille:
"si bene me noui non Viscum pluris amicum,
non Varium facies: nam quis me scribere pluris
aut citius possit uersus? quis membra mouere
mollius? inuideat quod et Hermogenes ego canto."   25
interpellandi locus hic erat: "est tibi mater,
cognati, quis te saluo est opus?" "haud mihi quisquam:
omnis composui." "felices! nunc ego resto.

HORACE, *SATIRE* 1.9

(The Pest)

I was going by chance along the Sacred Way,* as is my habit,
thinking over some trifles or other, entirely absorbed in them.
Up runs a certain character known to me only by name;
he grabs my hand and says: "How are you doing, best of friends?"
5   "Just fine, as it now stands," I said, "and I wish you all the best."
When he stuck close, I got in quickly: "You don't want anything, do
      you?"
But he replied, "You know me. I'm clever!" Here I responded, "In this
      then
you'll be of greater esteem to me." Striving miserably to get away,
now I go more quickly; periodically I stop to say
10   something or other into my slave's ear; all the while sweat
is running to the bottom of my heels. "Oh Bolanus,* of lucky temperament
are you!" I kept saying silently, while he kept ranting about
anything at all as he praised the streets and the city. As I made
no reply to him, "Wretchedly you desire," he said, "to escape;
15   I've seen it for some time now. But you accomplish nothing; I'll hang
      on all the way,
I'll follow wherever your journey takes you." "There's no need for you
to go out of your way; I want to visit someone you don't know.
Far across the Tiber* he's sick in bed, near the Gardens of Caesar."*
"I have nothing to do and I'm not lazy. I'll follow you all the way!"
20   I drop my ears like a depressed donkey
when he has taken on a load too heavy for his back. He starts in:
"If I know myself well, you won't regard Viscus* more a friend,
or Varius.* For who can write more
verses than I, or more quickly? Who can move his limbs
25   more gracefully? What I sing even Hermogenes* might envy."
Here was opportunity for interruption: "Do you have a mother,
relatives, anyone to whom your well-being matters?" "I've no one at
      all:
I've put them all to rest." "Fortunate are they! Now I remain.

confice; namque instat fatum mihi triste, Sabella
quod puero cecinit diuina mota anus urna: 30
'hunc neque dira uenena nec hosticus auferet ensis,
nec laterum dolor aut tussis, nec tarda podagra;
garrulus hunc quando consumet cumque: loquaces,
si sapiat, uitet, simul atque adoleuerit aetas.'"
uentum erat ad Vestae, quarta iam parte diei   35
praeterita, et casu tunc respondere uadato
debebat; quod ni fecisset, perdere litem.
"si me amas" inquit "paulum hic ades." "interea si
aut ualeo stare aut noui ciuilia iura;
et propero quo scis." "dubius sum quid faciam" inquit,   40
"tene relinquam an rem." "me, sodes." "non faciam" ille,
et praecedere coepit. ego, ut contendere durum est
cum uictore, sequor. "Maecenas quomodo tecum?"
hinc repetit: "paucorum hominum et mentis bene sanae;
nemo dexterius fortuna est usus. haberes   45
magnum adiutorem, posset qui ferre secundas,
hunc hominem uelles si tradere: dispeream ni
summosses omnis." "non isto uiuimus illic
quo tu rere modo; domus hac nec purior ulla est
nec magis his aliena malis; nil mi officit" inquam   50
"ditior hic aut est quia doctior; est locus uni
cuique suus." "magnum narras, uix credibile." "atqui
sic habet." "accendis, quare cupiam magis illi
proximus esse." "uelis tantummodo, quae tua uirtus,
expugnabis; et est qui uinci possit, eoque   55
difficilis aditus primos habet." "haud mihi deero:
muneribus seruos corrumpam; non, hodie si
exclusus fuero, desistam; tempora quaeram;
occurram in triuiis; deducam. nil sine magno
uita labore dedit mortalibus." haec dum agit, ecce   60
Fuscus Aristius occurrit, mihi carus et illum
qui pulchre nosset. consistimus. "unde uenis?" et

Finish me off! For that grim fate threatens me which a Sabine

30   hag, her divine jar shaken,* sang to me as a boy:
'Neither dire poisons nor hostile sword shall kill this man,
not internal pain nor cough nor slow gout;
sometime, some blabbermouth or other shall consume him. Talkers,
if he is wise, he will avoid as soon as old age catches up with him.'"

35   We had arrived at Vesta's temple,* now with a quarter of the day
gone, and then (by chance) he had to respond to a legal foe;
if he didn't do this, he would lose the case.
"If you love me," he said, "support me here a bit." "May I die if
I either have the power to stand up for you or know about civil law;

40   and I'm hurrying to you know where." "I'm hesitant as to what to do,"
he said,
"whether to abandon you or the legal matter." "Me, please!" "I won't,"
said he,
and he began to walk on. I, as it's tough to contend
with a conqueror, follow. "How does Maecenas* relate to you?"
Thence he starts up again: "He's a man of few associates and of perfectly
sound mind;

45   no one has used his fortune more opportunely. You would have
a great helper, one who could play second fiddle to you,
if you were willing to introduce me to him. May I die if
you wouldn't displace everybody!" "We don't live there in quite the
way you think; no house is purer than that one

50   nor more foreign to those evils. It bothers me not at all," I said,
"that someone is richer or more learned; for one and each is a place
his own." "A great thing you tell—hardly believable!" "Nevertheless,
it is so." "You inflame me even more in my desire to be
next to him!" "Just wish it. Your virtue is such that

55   you'll win him over; and he's the type who *can* be won over, and that's
why he makes first approaches difficult." "No way will I fail:
I'll bribe his slaves with gifts; I won't, if today
I'm shut out, desist. I'll seek the proper time;
I'll meet him at the cross-roads; I'll escort him. Nothing, without great

60   labor, has life granted to mortals." While he's on about these things,
behold!
Fuscus Aristius* runs up, one dear to me and who
knew *him* well. We stop short. "Where are you coming from?" and

"quo tendis?" rogat et respondet. uellere coepi,
et prensare manu lentissima bracchia, nutans,
distorquens oculos, ut me eriperet. male salsus   65
ridens dissimulare: meum iecur urere bilis.
"certe nescio quid secreto uelle loqui te
aiebas mecum." "memini bene, sed meliore
tempore dicam: hodie tricesima sabbata: uin tu
curtis Iudaeis oppedere?" "nulla mihi" inquam   70
"religio est." "at mi: sum paulo infirmior, unus
multorum: ignosces: alias loquar." huncine solem
tam nigrum surrexe mihi! fugit improbus ac me
sub cultro linquit. casu uenit obuius illi
aduersarius et "quo tu turpissime?" magna   75
inclamat uoce, et "licet antestari?" ego uero
oppono auriculam. rapit in ius: clamor utrimque:
undique concursus. sic me seruauit Apollo.

"Where are you headed?" he asks in reply to my greeting. I began to
     tug at him
and to squeeze his reluctant arms with my hand, nodding,
65   rolling my eyes, so that he might rescue me. As a bad joke,
smiling, he pretended he didn't follow: my liver burned with bile.*
"Certainly you were saying that you wanted to speak about something
     or
other with me in private." "I remember well, but at a better
time I'll tell you. Today's the thirtieth Sabbath.* Or do you want
70   to insult the circumcised Jews?"* "Religion is," I said,
"nothing to me." "But it is to me; I'm a little weaker, one
of many. Forgive me; I'll talk another time." What a
black cloud came over me! The rogue fled and left
me under the knife.* By chance there came to meet him
75   his court-opponent, and "Where are you off to, you filth?" in a loud
voice he yells, and "Can you serve as witness?" Indeed, I
put forth my ear.* He drags him to court; there's shouting on both
     sides,
running about everywhere. Thus Apollo saved me.*

HORACE, *SATIRE* 2.1

Horatius: "sunt quibus in satira uidear nimis acer et ultra
legem tendere opus; sine neruis altera quidquid
composui pars esse putat, similisque meorum
mille die uersus deduci posse. Trebati,
quid faciam praescribe." *Trebatius:* "quiescas." *Horatius:*
      "ne faciam, inquis,   5
omnino uersus?" *Trebatius:* "aio." *Horatius:* "peream male
      si non
optimum erat: uerum nequeo dormire." *Trebatius:* "ter uncti
transnanto Tiberim somno quibus est opus alto,
irriguumque mero sub noctem corpus habento.
aut si tantus amor scribendi te rapit, aude   10
Caesaris inuicti res dicere, multa laborum
praemia laturus." *Horatius:* "cupidum, pater optime, uires
deficiunt: neque enim quiuis horrentia pilis
agmina nec fracta pereuntis cuspide Gallos
aut labentis equo describat uulnera Parthi."   15
Trebatius: "attamen et iustum poteras et scribere fortem,
Scipiadam ut sapiens Lucilius." *Horatius:* "haud mihi deero
cum res ipsa feret: nisi dextro tempore, Flacci
uerba per attentam non ibunt Caesaris aurem,
cui male si palpere recalcitrat undique tutus."   20
Trebatius: "quanto rectius hoc quam tristi laedere uersu
Pantolabum scurram Nomentanumque nepotem,
cum sibi quisque timet, quamquam est intactus, et odit!"
Horatius: "quid faciam? saltat Milonius, ut semel icto
accessit feruor capiti numerusque lucernis;   25

HORACE, *SATIRE* 2.1

(In Defense of Satire)

Horace: "There are those to whom I seem, in satire, excessively harsh
    and
to stretch my work beyond the law.* The other faction thinks that
    whatever
I have composed is nerveless, and that verses similar to mine
can be drawn up a thousand a day. Trebatius,*

5   lay down what I should do." *Trebatius:* "You should rest." *Horace:* "I
        shouldn't compose, you say,
any verses at all?" *Trebatius:* "So I say." *Horace:* "May I die miserably
    were that not
the best option; but I can't sleep." *Trebatius:* "Three times, after being
    oiled,*
let those who need deep sleep swim across the Tiber;*
at night let them keep their bodies soaked in undiluted wine.

10   Or if so great a love of writing grabs you, dare
to tell of unconquered Caesar's exploits;* many rewards for your efforts
you will obtain." *Horace:* "Although I desire it, good father,* my
    strength*
does not suffice; nor does it come to just anyone to describe*
battle-lines bristling with lances* or Gauls* dying with broken spear-
    point,*

15   or the wounds of a Parthian* as he slips from his horse."*
Trebatius: "But yet you could have written of him as just and brave,
just as wise Lucilius* did of Scipio."* *Horace:* "I'll not fail myself
when the occasion presents itself. Unless the time is right, Flaccus'
words* will not penetrate the attentive ear of Caesar,*

20   who, if you flatter poorly, might kick back, safe on all sides."
Trebatius: "How much more right is this than to wound with grim verse
Pantolabus* the buffoon or Nomentanus* the prodigal,
when each fears for himself, although he's untouched, and hates!"
Horace: "What am I supposed to do? Milonius* dances as soon as

25   passion has reached his hammered head and the lamps seem numerous;

29

Castor gaudet equis, ouo prognatus eodem
pugnis; quot capitum uiuunt, totidem studiorum
milia: me pedibus delectat claudere uerba
Lucili ritu nostrum melioris utroque.
ille uelut fidis arcana sodalibus olim   30
credebat libris, neque si male cesserat usquam
decurrens alio, neque si bene; quo fit ut omnis
uotiua pateat ueluti descripta tabella
uita senis. sequor hunc, Lucanus an Apulus anceps:
nam Venusinus arat finem sub utrumque colonus,   35
missus ad hoc, pulsis, uetus est ut fama, Sabellis,
quo ne per uacuum Romano incurreret hostis,
siue quod Apula gens seu quod Lucania bellum
incuteret uiolenta. sed hic stilus haud petet ultro
quemquam animantem et me ueluti custodiet ensis   40
uagina tectus; quem cur destringere coner
tutus ab infestis latronibus? o pater et rex
Iuppiter, ut pereat positum robigine telum,
nec quisquam noceat cupido mihi pacis! at ille
qui me commorit ('melius non tangere,' clamo),   45
flebit et insignis tota cantabitur urbe.
Ceruius iratus leges minitatur et urnam,
Canidia Albuci quibus est inimica uenenum,
grande malum Turius, si quid se iudice certes.
ut quo quisque ualet suspectos terreat, utque   50
imperet hoc natura potens, sic collige mecum:
dente lupus, cornu taurus petit: unde nisi intus
monstratum? Scaeuae uiuacem crede nepoti
matrem: nil faciet sceleris pia dextera: mirum,
ut neque calce lupus quemquam neque dente petit bos: 55
sed mala tollet anum uitiato melle cicuta.

Castor* rejoices in horses, he born from the same egg*
in fist-fights. As many characters as live, so are there just as many
        thousand pursuits.
It delights me to wrap words in meter-feet
in the manner of Lucilius* (one better than us both).
30   He once, as though to faithful comrades, entrusted his secrets
to books, seeking refuge elsewhere neither if it went badly
for him in any way, nor if it went well. So it happens that
open to view, as though inscribed on a votive tablet,
is the old man's whole life. I follow *this* man, of dual nature as I am
        Lucanian or Apulian,*
35   for a Venusian colonist plows what underlies the border of both,*
sent as he was to this place, the Samnites* expelled, as the old story
        goes,*
lest an enemy might charge into empty space past any Roman,*
whether the Apulian race or violent Lucania strike up any*
war.* But this stylus* shall in no way willingly seek out
40   any living creature, and it shall protect me like a sword*
covered by its sheath. Why should I try to draw it
when I'm safe from hostile bandits? Oh Father and King
Jupiter, may the discarded weapon perish with rust,
and may no one harm me, desirous as I am of peace! But he
45   who shakes me up ('Better not touch me!' I shout.)
shall weep. And he'll be sung of, infamous throughout the whole city.
The angry Cervius* threatens with laws and voting urn;
whosoever is Canidia's enemy* she threatens with Albucius' poison;*
Turius* will impose a massive evil* on you if you litigate with him as
        judge.
50   How everybody terrorizes those he suspects with whatever strength he
        has, and how
powerful Nature orders this, reason with me in the following way:
the wolf attacks with teeth, the bull with horns; from what source other
        than instinct
is this taught? Entrust to money-wasting Scaeva* a
long-lived mother. He'll do no crime with his 'pious' right hand:
        wonderful!
55   Just as the wolf neither attacks anyone with its heel nor the ox with its
        teeth.
But evil hemlock in spiked honey will do the old hag in.

ne longum faciam: seu me tranquilla senectus
exspectat seu Mors atris circumuolat alis,
diues, inops, Romae seu Fors ita iusserit exsul,
quisquis erit uitae scribam color." *Trebatius:* "o puer, ut sis   60
uitalis metuo, et maiorum ne quis amicus
frigore te feriat." *Horatius:* "quid, cum est Lucilius ausus
primus in hunc operis componere carmina morem,
detrahere et pellem, nitidus qua quisque per ora
cederet, introrsum turpis, num Laelius aut qui   65
duxit ab oppressa meritum Carthagine nomen
ingenio offensi aut laeso doluere Metello
famosisque Lupo cooperto uersibus? atqui
primores populi arripuit populumque tributim,
scilicet uni aequus uirtuti atque eius amicis.   70
quin ubi se a uulgo et scaena in secreta remorant
uirtus Scipiadae et mitis sapientia Laeli,
nugari cum illo et discincti ludere donec
decoqueretur holus soliti. quidquid sum ego, quamuis
infra Lucili censum ingeniumque, tamen me   75
cum magnis uixisse inuita fatebitur usque
inuidia, et fragili quaerens illidere dentem
offendet solido; nisi quid tu, docte Trebati,
dissentis." *Trebatius:* "equidem nihil hinc diffindere possum;
sed tamen ut monitus caueas, ne forte negoti   80
incutiat tibi quid sanctarum inscitia legum:
'si mala condiderit in quem quis carmina, ius est
iudiciumque.'" *Horatius:* "esto, si quis mala; sed bona si quis
iudice condiderit laudatus Caesare? si quis
opprobriis dignum latrauerit, integer ipse?"   85
Trebatius: "soluentur risu tabulae, tu missus abibis."

Not to ramble on—whether a tranquil old age
awaits me or whether Death encircles me on dark wings,
be I rich, broke, at Rome, or whether Chance decrees it, an exile—
60   whatever the color of my life,* *I shall write.*" Trebatius: "Boy, I fear
you may not be long-lived, and that some 'great friend' of yours
may strike you with a chill."* *Horace:* "What! When Lucilius first
         dared
to compose his work's poems in this manner,*
and to peel off the skin in which each paraded gleaming
65   in public, polluted as he was internally, was Laelius* or he who
took his well-earned name from defeated Carthage*
offended at his genius? Or did they grieve when Metellus* was hurt
and Lupus* was overwhelmed by slanderous verses? Indeed,
he seized upon the foremost of the populace, and the populace a whole
         tribe at a time,*
70   being fair, of course, to Virtue alone and to her friends.
Why even when virtuous Scipio and wise and gentle Laelius
removed themselves from the mob and the public stage to privacy,
they were accustomed to trifle with him* and to joke relaxed while
their vegetables boiled.* Whatever *I* am, although
75   beneath the rank and genius of Lucilius, nevertheless Envy,
unwilling, shall always confess that I lived with the great,
and seeking to strike her tooth on something breakable
she will hit on something solid. That is unless you, learned Trebatius,
have some objection." *Trebatius:* "Indeed I can shatter nothing in your
         argument;
80   but nevertheless consider yourself warned and watch out, lest by chance
some litigation fall upon you out of your ignorance of the sacred laws:*
'If anyone composes bad poems against anyone else, there is right to
         action*
and legal judgment.'"* *Horace:* "So be it, if anyone composes bad
         poems; but what if one composes good poems
and merits praise with Caesar as judge? What if one
85   barks at somebody worthy of castigation, he himself being unbiased?"
Trebatius: "The proceedings will be dissolved with a laugh! You'll
         leave acquitted."

HORACE, *SATIRE* 2.8

Horatius: "ut Nasidieni iuuit te cena beati?
nam mihi quaerenti conuiuam dictus here illic
de medio potare die." *Fundanius:* "sic ut mihi numquam
in uita fuerit melius." *Horatius:* "da, si graue non est,
quae prima iratum uentrem placauerit esca."   5
Fundanius: "in primis Lucanus aper; leni fuit Austro
captus, ut aiebat cenae pater; acria circum
rapula, lactucae, radices, qualia lassum
peruellunt stomachum, siser, allec, faecula Coa.
his ubi sublatis puer alte cinctus acernam   10
gausape purpureo mensam pertersit, et alter
sublegit quodcumque iaceret inutile quodque
posset cenantis offendere; ut Attica uirgo
cum sacris Cereris procedit fuscus Hydaspes
Caecuba uina ferens, Alcon Chium maris expers.   15
hic erus: 'Albanum, Maecenas, siue Falernum
te magis appositis delectat, habemus utrumque.'"
Horatius: "diuitias miseras! sed quis cenantibus una,
Fundani, pulchre fuerit tibi, nosse laboro."
Fundanius: "summus ego et prope me Viscus Thurinus
      et infra,   20
si memini, Varius; cum Seruilio Balatrone
Vibidius, quos Maecenas adduxerat umbras.
Nomentanus erat super ipsum, Porcius infra
ridiculus totas simul absorbere placentas;
Nomentanus ad hoc, qui si quid forte lateret   25
indice monstraret digito: nam cetera turba,
nos, inquam, cenamus auis, conchylia, piscis,
longe dissimilem noto celantia sucum;

HORACE, *SATIRE* 2.8

(A Pretentious Dinner)

Horace: "How did rich Nasidienus' dinner* go with you?
For as I myself wanted you as dinner-guest yesterday, you were said
to be drinking over there since mid-day." *Fundanius:* "It was better
    than I've ever
experienced in my life." *Horace:* "Tell me, if it's no burden,
what was the first morsel to please an angry belly?"
Fundanius: "First off, a Lucanian* boar; under gentle south-wind it
    was
caught, as the feast's father said. Surrounding it were sharp
little turnips, lettuces, radishes—the sorts of things to stimulate a worn-
    out
stomach—tubers, fish-pickles, the lees of Coan wine.*
When these were removed, a slave-boy dressed in a short tunic wiped
    clean
the maple table with a purple cloth of wool,* and another
gathered away whatever was lying useless and whatever
could offend the diners. Like an Attic maiden,
with her sacred objects of Ceres,* there came forth black Hydaspes*
with Caecuban wine* and Alcon* with Chian devoid of sea-water.*
Here the feastmaster said: 'Maecenas,* whether Alban* or Falernian*
delights you more than what has been served, we have both.'"
Horace: "Ah, wealth's miseries! But I'm dying to know with whom
you were dining, Fundanius,* since it was so nice for you."
Fundanius: "I was at the top, and next to me was Viscus the Thurian,*
    and below,*
if I remember, was Varius.* Then was Vibidius,* along with Servilius*
Balatro,* parasites whom Maecenas had brought along.*
Nomentanus* was above the host himself, Porcius* below,*
hilarious as he slurped down whole cakes all at once.
Nomentanus' job was this: if anything by chance was hidden,
he was to point it out with his finger. For the remaining mob,
(we, I'm talking about) dine on birds, shell-fish, fish:
things concealing a flavor far from what we know,

ut uel continuo patuit, cum passeris atque
ingustata mihi porrexerat ilia rhombi.   30
post hoc me docuit melimela rubere minorem
ad lunam delecta. quid hoc intersit ab ipso
audieris melius. tum Vibidius Balatroni:
'nos nisi damnose bibimus moriemur inulti,'
et calices poscit maiores. uertere pallor   35
tum parochi faciem nil sic metuentis ut acris
potores, uel quod maledicunt liberius uel
feruida quod subtile exsurdant uina palatum.
inuertunt Allifanis uinaria tota
Vibidius Balatroque, secutis omnibus; imi   40
conuiuae lecti nihilum nocuere lagoenis.
adfertur squillas inter murena natantis
in patina porrecta. sub hoc erus: 'haec grauida' inquit
'capta est, deterior post partum carne futura.
his mixtum ius est: oleo quod prima Venafri   45
pressit cella; garo de sucis piscis Hiberi;
uino quinquenni, uerum citra mare nato,
dum coquitur (cocto Chium sic conuenit, ut non
hoc magis ullum aliud); pipere albo, non sine aceto
quod Methymnaeam uitio mutauerit uuam.   50
erucas uiridis, inulas ego primus amaras
monstraui incoquere, illutos Curtillus echinos,
ut melius muria quod testa marina remittat.'
interea suspensa grauis aulaea ruinas
in patinam fecere, trahentia pulueris atri   55
quantum non Aquilo Campanis excitat agris.
nos maius ueriti, postquam nihil esse pericli
sensimus, erigimur. Rufus posito capite, ut si
filius immaturus obisset, flere. quis esset
finis ni sapiens sic Nomentanus amicum   60
tolleret 'heu, Fortuna, quis est crudelior in nos
te deus? ut semper gaudes illudere rebus
humanis!' Varius mappa compescere risum
uix poterat. Balatro suspendens omnia naso,
'haec est condicio uiuendi' aiebat, 'eoque   65
responsura tuo numquam est par fama labori.

as was clear immediately when he had offered a flounder's
30   guts to me (things I'd never tasted) and those of a turbot.
After this he taught me that honey-apples blush
when picked during the lesser moon. What difference this makes
you'd do better to hear from him. Then Vibidius says to Balatro:
'Unless we drink him to ruin, we'll die unavenged!'
35   and he asks for bigger wine-cups. Pallor changed
the face of our provider then, as he feared nothing so much as heavy
drinkers, either because they bad-mouth rather freely or
because burning wines make the delicate palate dull.
Vibidius and Balatro empty whole storage jars of wine
40   into Allifanian cups,* with everyone following suit. Only
the guests of the couch's low end did no harm to the vessels.
Brought forth among teeming crawfish is an eel
stretched out on a platter. On this the feastmaster: 'When pregnant,'
he said, 'this was caught. Its meat would be worse after it's given birth.
45   The sauce is a mixture of these: olive oil of the first Venafran
pressing;* roe-juice of Spanish fish;
five-year-old wine (but produced this side of the sea*)
added while it's being boiled (once boiled, Chian does the job—no
other's better); white pepper, not without vinegar
50   that has changed by acidity the Methymnean grape.*
I was first to point out that green colewart and bitter elecampane
should be stewed. Curtillus* adds unwashed sea-urchins,
as the sea-shell gives off a better juice than brine.'
Meanwhile the overhanging canopies crashed hard
55   on the platter, dragging along as much black dust
as even the North Wind can't stir up in Campanian* fields!
We feared something greater, yet after we perceived that there was
no danger, we cheered up. Rufus,* bowing his head as if
his son had died prematurely, wept. This would have been
60   the end, had the wise Nomentanus not raised his friend's spirits
thus: 'Ah, Fortune! What god is more cruel to us than
you? How you always rejoice in playing tricks
on human affairs!' Varius could scarcely check his laughter
with his napkin. Balatro, looking down his nose at everything,
65   kept saying 'This is the nature of living, and for that reason
fame's response will never be on a par with your toil.

tene, ut ego accipiar laute, torquerier omni
sollicitudine districtum, ne panis adustus,
ne male conditum ius apponatur, ut omnes
praecincti recte pueri comptique ministrent!   70
adde hos praeterea casus, aulaea ruant si,
ut modo; si patinam pede lapsus frangat agaso.
sed conuiuatoris uti ducis ingenium res
aduersae nudare solent, celare secundae.'
Nasidienus ad haec 'tibi di quaecumque preceris   75
commoda dent! ita uir bonus es conuiuaque comis':
et soleas poscit. tum in lecto quoque uideres
stridere secreta diuisos aure susurros."
Horatius: "nullos his mallem ludos spectasse; sed illa
redde age quae deinceps risisti." *Fundanius:* "Vibidius dum   80
quaerit de pueris num sit quoque fracta lagoena,
quod sibi poscenti non dantur pocula, dumque
ridetur fictis rerum, Balatrone secundo,
Nasidiene, redis mutatae frontis, ut arte
emendaturus fortunam: deinde secuti   85
mazonomo pueri magno discerpta ferentes
membra gruis sparsi sale multo, non sine farre,
pinguibus et ficis pastum iecur anseris albae,
et leporum auulsos, ut multo suauius, armos,
quam si cum lumbis quis edit; tum pectore adusto   90
uidimus et merulas poni et sine clune palumbes,
suauis res, si non causas narraret earum et
naturas dominus; quem nos sic fugimus ulti,
ut nihil omnino gustaremus, uelut illis
Canidia adflasset peior serpentibus Afris."   95

That *you*, so that *I* be received lavishly, should be tortured
and busied by every anxiety: lest the bread be burnt,
lest a badly spiced sauce be served, that all
70   the slave-boys serve rightly dressed and adorned!
Add too these catastrophes: if the canopies collapse,
as they just did, if a lackey's foot slips and he breaks a dish!
But adverse conditions usually reveal a host's genius,
just as they do a general's. Favorable ones conceal it.'
75   To all this Nasidienus responds: 'May the gods grant you whatever
pleasures you pray for! You're so good a man and an amiable guest.'
And he asked for his slippers. Then on every couch you'd have seen
separate whispers hissing secretly into ears."
Horace: "I'd have preferred no play to these happenings. But come on
80   and tell me what you laughed at next." *Fundanius:* "While Vibidius
asks the serving-boys whether the wine-jugs were also broken,
since the cups aren't given to him as he asks; and while
we laugh at the pretended jests acted out by Balatro,
you, Nasidienus, return with changed expression, as though
85   about to redeem your misfortune by art. Then there follow
serving-boys carrying on a huge serving-dish the torn-off
limbs of a stork sprinkled with a lot of salt and some meal,
and the liver of a white goose fed on fat figs,
and rabbits' shoulders, separated so as to be much more delicious
90   than if one ate them with the loins. Then we saw served both
blackbirds with burnt breasts and rumpless pigeons—
fine delicacies, had not the feastmaster told of their origins
and nature.* We fled from him thus avenged,
as we tasted nothing at all, as though
95   Canidia,* worse than African serpents, had breathed on the food."

PERSIUS, PROLOGUE

nec fonte labra prolui caballino*
nec in bicipiti somniasse Parnaso*
memini, ut repente sic poeta prodirem.*
Heliconidasque pallidamque Pirenen*
illis remitto quorum imagines lambunt*   5
hederae sequaces; ipse semipaganus*
ad sacra uatum carmen adfero nostrum.*
quis expediuit psittaco suum "chaere"*
picamque docuit nostra uerba conari?*
magister artis ingenique largitor*   10
uenter, negatas artifex sequi uoces.*
quod si dolosi spes refulserit nummi,*
coruos poetas et poetridas picas*
cantare credas Pegaseium nectar?*

PERSIUS, PROLOGUE

I neither washed my lips in horse-fount*
nor dreaming on two-headed Parnassus*
do I remember, that I should suddenly come forth thus—a poet.*
The daughters of Mount Helicon* and pallid Pirene*
5   I leave to them whose busts are licked*
by adherent ivy;* myself, a half-constituent,*
I bear our song to bards' rites.
Who achieved for the parrot his "chaere!"*
and taught the magpie to try our words?
10   Master of Arts and briber of genius:
Belly, artist at following voices denied.
But if hope of tricky cash should radiate,
would you believe that crow-poets and
magpie-poetesses sing Pegasian nectar?*

PERSIUS, *SATIRE* 1

Persius: "o curas hominum! o quantum est in rebus inane!"
Aduersarius: "quis leget haec?" *Persius:* "min tu istud ais?
     nemo hercule." *Aduersarius:* "nemo?"
Persius: "uel duo uel nemo." *Aduersarius:* "turpe et
     miserabile." *Persius:* "quare?
ne mihi Polydamas et Troiades Labeonem
praetulerint? nugae. non, si quid turbida Roma   5
eleuet, accedas examenue inprobum in illa
castiges trutina nec te quaesiueris extra.
nam Romae quis non—a, si fas dicere—sed fas
tum cum ad canitiem et nostrum istud uiuere triste
aspexi ac nucibus facimus quaecumque relictis,   10
cum sapimus patruos. tunc tunc—ignoscite (nolo,
quid faciam?) sed sum petulanti splene—cachinno.
    "scribimus inclusi, numeros ille, hic pede liber,
grande aliquid quod pulmo animae praelargus anhelet.
scilicet haec populo pexusque togaque recenti   15
et natalicia tandem cum sardonyche albus
sede leges celsa, liquido cum plasmate guttur
mobile conlueris, patranti fractus ocello.
tunc neque more probo uideas nec uoce serena
ingentis trepidare Titos, cum carmina lumbum   20
intrant et tremulo scalpuntur ubi intima uersu.
tun, uetule, auriculis alienis colligis escas,
articulis quibus et dicas cute perditus 'ohe'?"
Aduersarius: "quo didicisse, nisi hoc fermentum et quae
     semel intus
innata est rupto iecore exierit caprificus?"   25
Persius: "en pallor seniumque! o mores, usque adeone

PERSIUS, *SATIRE* 1

(Program Piece)

Persius: "Oh the cares of human beings! Oh how much emptiness there
is in things!"*
Adversary: "Who shall read these things?" *Persius:* "You ask me that?
By Hercules, nobody." *Adversary:* "Nobody?"
Persius: "Either two or none." *Adversary:* "Disgraceful as well as sad."
Persius: "Why?
Lest Polydamas* and the Trojan ladies* prefer Labeo*
5 to me? Nonsense. You should not, if disordered Rome disparages
anything,
concede or reprove the inferior tongue in *that*
pair of scales; nor should you seek opinion outside yourself.
For at Rome who doesn't . . . ah, if it were proper to speak . . . but
proper it is
then, when gray hair and that grim living of ours
10 I see, and whatever we do with play-nuts left behind,
when we're wise as uncles. Then, *then* (excuse me—I don't want to—
what can I do?), as I'm of rascally disposition, I laugh.
"Enclosed we write—that one verses, this one free of meter,*
something massive that takes a lung of huge blustering to bellow out.
15 These things, of course, to the populace, combed and in fresh toga,
and then whitewashed, with your sardonyx birthday-ring,*
you will read on lofty seat, once with fluid gargle-juice you've
rinsed your pliable gullet, effeminate with eye's orgasmic sparkle.
Then neither in chaste manner nor with calm voice you might see
20 massive Tituses* tremble, when into the loin the poems
enter and private parts are massaged by quivering verse.
Are you, old goat, gathering morsels for the ears of others,
you who are dissipated in limbs and skin, and should yourself say
'Enough!'?"
Adversary: "What good to have learned, unless this ferment,* and fig-
tree* which now is inside
25 rooted, should shatter the liver and spring forth?"*
Persius: "Behold pallor and old age's decay! Oh morals! Is your
knowledge

43

scire tuum nihil est nisi te scire hoc sciat alter?"
Aduersarius: "at pulchrum est digito monstrari et dicier
      'hic est.'
ten cirratorum centum dictata fuisse
pro nihilo pendes?" *Persius:* "ecce inter pocula quaerunt   30
Romulidae saturi quid dia poemata narrent.
hic aliquis, cui circum umeros hyacinthina laena est,
rancidulum quiddam balba de nare locutus
Phyllidas, Hypsipylas, uatum et plorabile siquid,
eliquat ac tenero subplantat uerba palato.   35
adsensere uiri: nunc non cinis ille poetae
felix? non leuior cippus nunc imprimit ossa?
laudant conuiuae: nunc non e manibus illis,
nunc non e tumulo fortunataque fauilla
nascentur uiolae?" *Aduersarius:* "rides" ait "et nimis uncis   40
naribus indulges. an erit qui uelle recuset
os populi meruisse et cedro digna locutus
linquere nec scombros metuentia carmina nec tus?"
    Persius: "quisquis es, o modo quem ex aduerso dicere
      feci,
non ego cum scribo, si forte quid aptius exit,   45
quando haec rara auis est, si quid tamen aptius exit,
laudari metuam; neque enim mihi cornea fibra est.
sed recti finemque extremumque esse recuso
'euge' tuum et 'belle.' nam 'belle' hoc excute totum:
quid non intus habet? non hic est Ilias Atti   50
ebria ueratro? non siqua elegidia crudi
dictarunt proceres? non quidquid denique lectis
scribitur in citreis? calidum scis ponere sumen,
scis comitem horridulum trita donare lacerna,

such a nothing, unless another knows that you know it?"

Adversary: "But it's wonderful to be pointed out and said of 'This is
 he!'

That you have stood as the dictation-exercises of a hundred curly headed
 boys*

30 you value at nothing?" *Persius:* "Behold, among their wine-cups
 Romulids* ask,

as they're stuffed, what things the god-inspired poems tell.

Here someone, around whose shoulders there's a hyacinth-colored
 shawl,

after he's mumbled some putrid gibberish from stammering nose,

dribbles out Phyllises, Hypsipyles, and something or other deplorable
 of the 'bards,'

35 and he trips up the words on his tender palate.

The 'men' nod their approval; now isn't that ash of the poet

fortunate? Does not the tombstone press his bones more lightly?

The dinner-guests give praise; now out of those dead spirits,

now out of the grave and from the fortunate glowing ashes

40 won't violets be born?" *Adversary:* "You laugh" (he says) "and excessively
 you

impose your curled-up nostrils. Or will there be anyone who'd refuse
 to want

to have merited the populace's mouth and, having uttered things worthy
 of cedar,

to leave behind poems fearing neither mackerel nor incense?"*

 Persius: "Oh, whoever you are whom I just made speak as adversary,

45 I do not, when I write, if by chance something rather apt comes out,

(seeing that this is a rare bird), if nevertheless something rather apt
 comes out,

fear to be praised; for my bowels are not of horn.

But I object that the end and point of right is

your 'good' and 'gorgeous.' Just shake out that whole 'gorgeous.'

50 What doesn't it have inside? Isn't the *Iliad* of Attius* here

drunk on hellebore? Any paltry elegies the gastric

nobles have composed? Even whatever's written on citrus-wood
 couches?

You know how to serve a warm sow's udder, how to

treat a raw companion to a worn mantle,

et 'uerum' inquis 'amo, uerum mihi dicite de me.'   55
qui pote? uis dicam? nugaris, cum tibi, calue,
pinguis aqualiculus propenso sesquipede extet.
o Iane, a tergo quem nulla ciconia pinsit
nec manus auriculas imitari mobilis albas
nec linguae quantum sitiat canis Apula tantae.   60
uos, o patricius sanguis, quos uiuere fas est
occipiti caeco, posticae occurrite sannae.
    "'quis populi sermo est?' quis enim nisi carmina molli
nunc demum numero fluere, ut per leue seueros
effundat iunctura unguis? scit tendere uersum   65
non secus ac si oculo rubricam derigat uno.
siue opus in mores, in luxum, in prandia regum
dicere, res grandes nostro dat Musa poetae.
ecce modo heroas sensus adferre docemus
nugari solitos Graece, nec ponere lucum   70
artifices nec rus saturum laudare, ubi corbes
et focus et porci et fumosa Palilia feno,
unde Remus sulcoque terens dentalia, Quinti,
cum trepida ante boues dictatorem induit uxor
et tua aratra domum lictor tulit—euge poeta!   75
est nunc Brisaei quem uenosus liber Acci,
sunt quos Pacuuiusque et uerrucosa moretur
Antiopa aerumnis cor luctificabile fulta?
hos pueris monitus patres infundere lippos
cum uideas, quaerisne unde haec sartago loquendi   80
uenerit in linguas, unde istud dedecus in quo
trossulus exultat tibi per subsellia leuis?
nilne pudet capiti non posse pericula cano
pellere quin tepidum hoc optes audire 'decenter'?
'fur es' ait Pedio. Pedius quid? crimina rasis   85
librat in antithetis, doctas posuisse figuras

55   and 'Truth I love,' you say; 'tell me the truth about me.'
      How's it possible? You wish me to speak? You trifle with yourself,
            baldhead,
      your fat pork-belly sticks out in a foot-and-a-half slope.
      Oh Janus, at whom no stork clacks from behind your back
      nor moving hands in imitation of white ass-ears
60   nor tongue stuck out as far as thirsty Apulian dog's!
      You, oh patrician blood-line, for whom it's proper to live
      with a blind back-side to your skull, meet the sneer from the rear!
            "'What's the talk of the populace?' Well what, except that poems
      now at last flow in smooth meter so that the seam
65   allows severe nails to glide smoothly? He knows how to draw out a
            verse
      no differently than if he were with one eye aligning red line.
      Whether the need's to talk of morals, luxury or kings' banquets,
      the Muse gives great themes to our poet.
      Behold! The transmission of heroic sentiments we now teach to
70   those accustomed to trifle in Greek—'artists' who can neither portray a
            grove
      nor praise the bountiful countryside where there are wicker-baskets
      and hearth and swine and Palilia smoky with hay,*
      whence Remus* and you, Quintius,* polishing plow-shares* in groove,
      when anxious wife clothed you dictator before the oxen
75   and lictor brought home your plows—bravo, poet!
      Now there's one whom the veiny book of Brisaean Accius* detains,
      so too some Pacuvius* and his warty
      Antiope*—her sorrowific heart propped on afflictions.
      When you see blear-eyed fathers pouring these admonitions into their
            boys,
80   do you ask whence this stir-fry manner of speaking
      came to our tongues, whence that disgrace in which
      your smooth-skinned Trossulus* exults along the benches?
      Is it no shame whatever that you are unable to remove the perils from a
            gray-head
      and not desire to hear the tepid phrase 'properly done!'
85   'You're a thief!' he says to Pedius. What's Pedius say? The charges
      he balances on shaven oppositions; he's praised for having placed
            learned tropes:

laudatur: 'bellum hoc.' hoc bellum? an, Romule, ceues?
men moueat? quippe, et, cantet si naufragus, assem
protulerim? cantas, cum fracta te in trabe pictum
ex umero portes? uerum nec nocte paratum   90
plorabit qui me uolet incuruasse querella."
     Aduersarius: "sed numeris decor est et iunctura addita
        crudis."
Persius: "cludere sic uersum didicit 'Berecyntius Attis'
et 'qui caeruleum dirimebat Nerea delphin,'
sic 'costam longo subduximus Appennino.'"   95
Aduersarius: "'Arma uirum,' nonne hoc spumosum et
        cortice pingui
ut ramale uetus uegrandi subere coctum?"
Persius: "quidnam igitur tenerum et laxa ceruice legendum?
'torua Mimalloneis inplerunt cornua bombis,
et raptum uitulo caput ablatura superbo   100
Bassaris et lyncem Maenas flexura corymbis
"euhion" ingeminat, reparabilis adsonat echo.'
haec fierent si testiculi uena ulla paterni
uiueret in nobis? summa delumbe saliua
hoc natat in labris et in udo est Maenas et Attis   105
nec pluteum caedit nec demorsos sapit unguis."
     Aduersarius: "sed quid opus teneras mordaci radere uero
auriculas? uide sis ne maiorum tibi forte
limina frigescant: sonat hic de nare canina
littera." *Persius:* "per me equidem sint omnia protinus alba;   110
nil moror. euge omnes, omnes bene, mirae eritis res.
hoc iuuat? 'hic' inquis 'ueto quisquam faxit oletum.'
pinge duos anguis: pueri, sacer est locus, extra
meiite. discedo. secuit Lucilius urbem,
te Lupe, te Muci, et genuinum fregit in illis.   115
omne uafer uitium ridenti Flaccus amico
tangit et admissus circum praecordia ludit,

'This is gorgeous.' This gorgeous? Or, Romulus, do you gyrate?
Should that really move me? And, if a castaway *sings*,
am I to offer him a coin? Do you sing, when you bear on your shoulder
90   yourself painted on a broken board? True disaster, not that prepared
        over-night,
he will lament who wants to influence me with his complaint."
     Adversary: "But style and fit juncture have been added to unfinished
        verses."
Persius: "Thus 'Berecyntius Attis'* has learned to close a verse,
and 'Which dolphin was dividing sky-blue Nereus';
95   thus: 'We withdrew a rib from long Appenine.'"
     Adversary: "'Arms, the man'*—isn't this just foam and swollen* with
        bark
like an old branch stewed with stunted sponge-cork?"
Persius: "Something then tender and to be read with lax neck?:
'Grim horns they filled with Mimallonian* rumbles,
100   Bassarid,* about to carry off the head snatched from proud yearling,
and Maenad,* about to flex the lynx with fruit clusters,
repeat "euhion";* restoring echo replies.'
Would these come about if a single vein of paternal ball
were living in us? Limp on the spit's surface
105   this swims on the lips, and Maenas is permeated and Attis
neither strikes the writing-couch nor tastes of bitten nails."
     Adversary: "But what need is there to scrape with biting truth
delicate ears? Just look out that the thresholds of the great don't by
       chance
turn frozen on you; here there resounds from the nose the dog-
110   letter."* *Persius:* "As far as I'm concerned, let everything straight-away
       be snow-white;
I'm not holding things up. Bravo, everyone! Everyone, well-done!
       You'll be wonderful!
Does this help? 'Here,' you say, 'I forbid that one make excrement.'
Depict a couple of snakes: *Boys, the place is sacred. Piss*
outside. I'm leaving. Lucilius* cut up the city—
115   you, Lupus*, you, Mucius*—and he shattered his molar on them.
Every vice for his laughing friend clever Flaccus*
touches on and, when he's been let in, he jests around the heart-strings,

callidus excusso populum suspendere naso.
me muttire nefas? nec clam? nec cum scrobe?" *Aduersarius:*
    "nusquam?"
Persius: "hic tamen infodiam. uidi, uidi ipse, libelle: 120
auriculas asini quis non habet? hoc ego opertum,
hoc ridere meum, tam nil, nulla tibi uendo
Iliade. audaci quicumque adflate Cratino
iratum Eupolidem praegrandi cum sene palles,
aspice et haec, si forte aliquid decoctius audis.   125
inde uaporata lector mihi ferueat aure,
non hic qui in crepidas Graiorum ludere gestit
sordidus et lusco qui possit dicere 'lusce,'
sese aliquem credens Italo quod honore supinus
fregerit heminas Arreti aedilis iniquas,   130
nec qui abaco numeros et secto in puluere metas
scit risisse uafer, multum gaudere paratus
si cynico barbam petulans nonaria uellat.
his mane edictum, post prandia Callirhoen do."

skilled as he is in suspending the populace from cleared-out nose.

That I mutter is wrong? Not secretly? Not to a ditch?" *Adversary:* "No place?"

120 *Persius:* "Nevertheless I'll bury it here. I saw it; I saw it myself, little book:

who does not have the narrow ears of an ass? This secret,

this joke of mine, such a trifle, I sell to you for no

Iliad. Whoever of you are inspired by fierce Cratinus*

and grow pallid with the study of irate Eupolis,* along with the great old man,*

125 have a look at these things too, if by chance you're a hearer of decoctions.

Thence* let my reader seethe with steam-cleaned ear—

not he who longs to jest about the sandals of Greeks;

not he who, mean as he is, can say to a one-eyed person 'one-eye,'

thinking he's someone because, proud in Italian office,

130 he as aedile* at Arretium* has shattered deficient half-pint flasks;

nor he who, thinking he's clever, knows how to laugh at numbers on the abacus

and geometry-cones carved in the sand, ready to jump with much joy

if a feisty Nones-girl* should tug a Cynic's beard.*

To these I give the play-schedule in the morning, after lunch *Callirhoe.*"*

PERSIUS, *SATIRE* 3

nempe haec adsidue. iam clarum mane fenestras
intrat et angustas extendit lumine rimas.
stertimus, indomitum quod despumare Falernum
sufficiat, quinta dum linea tangitur umbra.
 "en quid agis? siccas insana canicula messes   5
iam dudum coquit et patula pecus omne sub ulmo est"
unus ait comitum. *Persius:* "uerumne? itan? ocius adsit
huc aliquis. nemon?" turgescit uitrea bilis:
findor, ut Arcadiae pecuaria rudere credas.
iam liber et positis bicolor membrana capillis   10
inque manus chartae nodosaque uenit harundo.
tum querimur crassus calamo quod pendeat umor.
nigra sed infusa uanescit sepia lympha,
dilutas querimur geminet quod fistula guttas.
Comes: "o miser inque dies ultra miser, hucine rerum   15
uenimus? a, cur non potius teneroque columbo
et similis regum pueris pappare minutum
poscis et iratus mammae lallare recusas?
'an tali studeam calamo?' cui uerba? quid istas
succinis ambages? tibi luditur. effluis amens,   20
contemnere. sonat uitium percussa, maligne
respondet uiridi non cocta fidelia limo.
udum et molle lutum es, nunc nunc properandus et acri
fingendus sine fine rota. sed rure paterno
est tibi far modicum, purum et sine labe salinum   25

PERSIUS, *SATIRE 3*

(Wasted Youth)

To be sure, these things continuously. Clear morning now penetrates shuttered windows

and extends their narrow cracks with light.*

We snore, sufficiently to settle down untamed Falernian,*

while the sun-dial's fifth line is touched by shadow.*

5   "Well, what are you doing? Unhealthy Sirius* has been baking the dried-out crops

for a long while already, and every herd is under over-spreading elm tree,"

a companion speaks. *Persius:* "Truly? Is it so? Let someone come here right away!

Nobody?" Glassy bile* gradually swells up:

I'm split open with rage, so that you'd believe the flocks of Arcadia* were bellowing.

10   Now a book and bicolor writing-sheet with hairs removed,*

as well as papyrus rolls and knotty reed has come to hand.

Then we complain because the fluid hangs thick on the stylus.

But clear water poured in; the black cuttlefish* vanishes;

we complain because the stick repeatedly produces diluted dribbles.

15   *Companion:* "You wretch, and beyond wretch daily, as far as this in things

have we come? Ah yes: why not preferably, like both a baby dove

and kings' boys, beg to nibble tid-bits and,

enraged, refuse to lullaby nurse-mommy?

'What else? Am I supposed to study with such a reed-pen?' Whom are you kidding?

20   Why do you spout those ambiguities? The game's on you. Mindless you're dissolving away;

you'll be held in contempt: the pot sounds flawed when struck, badly

it responds unfired with its unchanged clay.*

You are wet and soft mud; now, now you have to be sped on and on the swift

wheel endlessly shaped. But on paternal countryside

25   there waits for you moderate wheat-supply, clean salt-cellar without stain

53

(quid metuas?) cultrixque foci secura patella.
hoc satis? an deceat pulmonem rumpere uentis
stemmate quod Tusco ramum millesime ducis
censoremue tuum uel quod trabeate salutas?
ad populum phaleras! ego te intus et in cute noui.   30
non pudet ad morem discincti uiuere Nattae
sed stupet hic uitio et fibris increuit opimum
pingue, caret culpa, nescit quid perdat, et alto
demersus summa rursus non bullit in unda.
    "magne pater diuum, saeuos punire tyrannos   35
haut alia ratione uelis, cum dira libido
mouerit ingenium feruenti tincta ueneno:
uirtutem uideant intabescantque relicta.
anne magis Siculi gemuerunt aera iuuenci
et magis auratis pendens laquearibus ensis   40
purpureas subter ceruices terruit, 'imus,
imus praecipites' quam si sibi dicat et intus
palleat infelix quod proxima nesciat uxor?"
    Persius: "saepe oculos, memini, tangebam paruus oliuo,
grandia si nollem morituri uerba Catonis   45
discere non sano multum laudanda magistro,
quae pater adductis sudans audiret amicis."
Comes: "iure; etenim id summum, quid dexter senio ferret,
scire erat in uoto, damnosa canicula quantum
raderet, angustae collo non fallier orcae,   50
neu quis callidior buxum torquere flagello."
Persius: "haut tibi inexpertum curuos deprendere mores

(what do you have to fear?) and unconcerned platter as hearth's caretaker.
Is this enough? Or is it appropriate to pop your lung with wind-gusts
because you draw the thousandth branch from Etruscan pedigree*
or because you greet your censor dressed in the trabea?*

30 To the common herd with ornaments! I know you inside and on the
surface.
You're not embarrassed to live in the manner of dissolute Natta.*
But he is dumb with vice, and rich fat has grown over his heartstrings.
He's without blame; he knows not what he's losing; and in the deep
drowned, he bubbles not again on wave's surface.

35 "Oh great Father of the gods, may you be willing to punish savage
tyrants
with by no means different system, when dire whim
tainted with boiling poison moves their temperament!
Let them gaze on virtue and wither away when she's been abandoned.
Or did the bronze of Sicilian bullock groan more,*

40 and did the sword dangling from gold-paneled ceiling* more
terrorize the purple-clad neck below, than if one were to say to himself,
'To the bottom,
the very bottom you're falling!' and inwardly
turn pale wretchedly at what the wife lying beside him must not know?"
Persius: "As a child, I remember, often I used to dab my eyes with
olive oil*

45 if I was unwilling to recite the mighty words of Cato* on the verge of
death—
words to be much-praised by the insane teacher,
which my sweating father would listen to having dragged his friends
along."
Companion: "Justly, for the highest goal in our prayer was to know
what the advantageous 'six'* would bring,
how much the ruinous 'one'* would take away,

50 not to be led astray of the neck of narrow jar,*
that no one should be more skilled at spinning the wooden top with its
string."
Persius: "Hardly unknown to you is the practice of seizing on bent
morals

quaeque docet sapiens bracatis inlita Medis
porticus, insomnis quibus et detonsa iuuentus
inuigilat siliquis et grandi pasta polenta."   55
Comes: "et tibi quae Samios diduxit littera ramos
surgentem dextro monstrauit limite callem.
stertis adhuc laxumque caput conpage soluta
oscitat hesternum dissutis undique malis.
est aliquid quo tendis et in quod derigis arcum?   60
an passim sequeris coruos testaque lutoque,
securus quo pes ferat, atque ex tempore uiuis?
        "elleborum frustra, cum iam cutis aegra tumebit,
poscentis uideas; uenienti occurrite morbo,
et quid opus Cratero magnos promittere montis?   65
discite et, o miseri, causas cognoscite rerum:
quid sumus et quidnam uicturi gignimur, ordo
quis datus, aut metae qua mollis flexus et unde,
quis modus argento, quid fas optare, quid asper
utile nummus habet, patriae carisque propinquis   70
quantum elargiri deceat, quem te deus esse
iussit et humana qua parte locatus es in re.
disce nec inuideas quod multa fidelia putet
in locuplete penu, defensis pinguibus Vmbris,
et piper et pernae, Marsi monumenta clientis,   75
maenaque quod prima nondum defecerit orca.
        "hic aliquis de gente hircosa centurionum
dicat: 'quod sapio satis est mihi. non ego curo
esse quod Arcesilas aerumnosique Solones
obstipo capite et figentes lumine terram,   80
murmura cum secum et rabiosa silentia rodunt
atque exporrecto trutinantur uerba labello,
aegroti ueteris meditantes somnia, gigni
de nihilo nihilum, in nihilum nil posse reuerti.
hoc est quod palles? cur quis non prandeat hoc est?'   85

and whatever things the wise portico* teaches (painted over with trouser-
    wearing Medes),*
and the things for which sleepless and shaven youth*
55   stay awake (fed on pea-pods and ample barley grits)."*
Companion: "And to you the letter that has drawn apart Samian
    branches*
has pointed out the hill on the right-hand path.*
You're still snoring, and your loose head (neck-hinge released)
yawns yesterday's yawn, your jaws unstitched all around.
60   Is there something after which you strive and at which you aim your
    bow?
Or do you follow after crows here and there with clay-shards and
    dirt-clods,
careless of where your foot takes you as you live on the spur of the
    moment?
    "That you demand hellebore* in vain when already sick skin begins
    to swell
you must see; meet disease head-on,
65   and what need to promise great mountains to Craterus?*
Learn, and, you wretches, come to know the causes of things:
what we are and what (pray tell) life we're born to live, which
position's been given, or where and whence turn's bend is smooth,
what's silver's limit, what's it right to hope for, what
70   use has embossed coin, to homeland and to dear relations
how much it's appropriate to outlay, whom god has ordered you to be
and in what part of the human situation you're placed.
Learn; and don't look askance because many a storage-jar rots
in full warehouse (fat Umbrians* having been defended),
75   both pepper and hog-legs,* remembrances of a Marsian client,
because first sprat-jug has not yet let you down.
    "Here someone of the goatish race of centurions
might say 'What I know's* enough for me. *I* don't care
to be what Arcesilas* and gloomy Solons* are,
80   with head bowed and fastening their eyes on the earth,
when they gnaw whispers and rabid silences with themselves
and they balance their words on outthrust lip,
meditating over the dreams of an ancient invalid:
that nothing can rise from nothing; nothing can return to nothing.
85   This is why you're pale? This is why one misses his lunch?'

his populus ridet, multumque torosa iuuentus
ingeminat tremulos naso crispante cachinnos.
    "'inspice, nescio quid trepidat mihi pectus et aegris
faucibus exsuperat grauis halitus, inspice sodes'
qui dicit medico, iussus requiescere, postquam   90
tertia conpositas uidit nox currere uenas,
de maiore domo modice sitiente lagoena
lenia loturo sibi Surrentina rogabit.
'heus bone, tu palles.' 'nihil est.' 'uideas tamen istuc,
quidquid id est. surgit tacite tibi lutea pellis.'   95
'at tu deterius palles, ne sis mihi tutor.
iam pridem hunc sepeli; tu restas.' 'perge, tacebo.'
turgidus hic epulis atque albo uentre lauatur,
gutture sulpureas lente exhalante mefites.
sed tremor inter uina subit calidumque trientem   100
excutit e manibus, dentes crepuere retecti,
uncta cadunt laxis tunc pulmentaria labris.
hinc tuba, candelae, tandemque beatulus alto
conpositus lecto crassisque lutatus amomis
in portam rigidas calces extendit. at illum   105
hesterni capite induto subiere Quirites."
    Persius: "tange, miser, uenas et pone in pectore dextram;
nil calet hic. summosque pedes attinge manusque;
non frigent." *Comes:* "uisa est si forte pecunia, siue
candida uicini subrisit molle puella,   110
cor tibi rite salit? positum est algente catino
durum holus et populi cribro decussa farina:
temptemus fauces; tenero latet ulcus in ore
putre quod haut deceat plebeia radere beta.
alges, cum excussit membris timor albus aristas;   115
nunc face supposita feruescit sanguis et ira
scintillant oculi, dicisque facisque quod ipse
non sani esse hominis non sanus iuret Orestes."

At this the populace laughs, and much the muscular youth
doubles the rippling cacchinations with curled nose.
   "'Examine me: I've got strange palpitations in my chest
and a foul breath is rising from my sore throat. Examine me, please,'
90   says a patient to his doctor. The doctor orders rest. But when
on the third night his veins are flowing steadily,*
he's round at a well-off friend's house with a good-sized bottle,
begging some smooth Surrentine* to drink before his bath.
'Hey, my good man, you're pale.' 'It's nothing.' 'Still, you should watch
     it,
95   whatever it is. Your skin's yellow and swelling quietly.'
'You're even more pale yourself. Don't play the guardian with me!
I buried him long ago; only you are left.' 'Carry on. I'll keep quiet.'
Stuffed with fine food and queasy in the stomach, he goes bathing,
with his throat slowly exhaling sulphurous belches.
100   But as he drinks his wine the shakes come over him and knock
the warm cup from his hand; his teeth are laid bare and chatter;
then greasy hors-d'œuvres slide from his slackened lips.
Then follow the trumpet and the candles and finally our dearly departed,
laid out on a high couch and besmeared with strong unguents,
105   with rigid heels pointing toward the door. Yesterday's new Romans,*
donning caps on their heads,* carry him on raised shoulders to burial."
     Persius: "Take my pulse, you wretch, and put your right hand on
      my chest:*
no fever here! Touch the tips of my toes and fingers:*
they're not cold!" *Companion:* "Should you happen to spot some cash,
110   or should your neighbor's pretty girl smile enticingly,
does your heart beat normally then? You're served tough vegetables
on a cold plate with flour sifted through a common sieve.
Let's see your throat: a putrid ulcer lies hidden in your tender mouth,
which certainly no plebeian beet should rub against.
115   You shiver when pale fear has lifted the stubble on your body;
now your blood boils when a fire is lit under you;
your eyes flash with rage; and you say and do things that even
the mad Orestes* himself would swear were signs of madness."

PERSIUS, *SATIRE* 4

Socrates: "rem populi tractas?" (barbatum haec crede
      magistrum
dicere, sorbitio tollit quem dira cicutae)
"quo fretus? dic hoc, magni pupille Pericli.
scilicet ingenium et rerum prudentia uelox
ante pilos uenit, dicenda tacendaue calles.   5
ergo ubi commota feruet plebecula bile,
fert animus calidae fecisse silentia turbae
maiestate manus. quid deinde loquere? 'Quirites,
hoc puto non iustum est, illud male, rectius illud.'
scis etenim iustum gemina suspendere lance   10
ancipitis librae, rectum discernis ubi inter
curua subit uel cum fallit pede regula uaro,
et potis es nigrum uitio praefigere theta.
quin tu igitur summa nequiquam pelle decorus
ante diem blando caudam iactare popello   15
desinis, Anticyras melior sorbere meracas?
quae tibi summa boni est? uncta uixisse patella
semper et adsiduo curata cuticula sole?
expecta, haut aliud respondeat haec anus. i nunc,
'Dinomaches ego sum' suffla, 'sum candidus.' esto,   20
dum ne deterius sapiat pannucia Baucis,
cum bene discincto cantauerit ocima uernae."
    Alcibiades: "ut nemo in sese temptat descendere, nemo,
sed praecedenti spectatur mantica tergo!
quaesieris 'nostin Vettidi praedia?' 'cuius?'   25
'diues arat Curibus quantum non miluus errat.'
'hunc ais, hunc dis iratis genioque sinistro,
qui, quandoque iugum pertusa ad compita figit,
seriolae ueterem metuens deradere limum

PERSIUS, SATIRE 4

(Self-Deception)

Socrates: "Do you handle the interest of the populace?"* (Believe that
    the bearded teacher
whom dire sip of hemlock removed* is saying these things).
"Relying on what? Tell us this, little pupil of great Pericles.*
Of course, natural ability and quick wisdom of the world

5   came to you before whiskers; you're skilled in when to speak and when
    to keep still.
Therefore when petty mob boils with stirred-up bile,
your mind moves you to impose silence on the hot-headed throng
by your hand's majesty. What then will you say? 'Romans:*
this, I think, is not just; that is bad; more right is that other.'

10   For indeed you know how to suspend the just in the double pan
of a wavering balance; you perceive what's right where it
passes between crooked, or when ruler deceives with malaligned base;
and you can fix the black theta* to a vice.
Pretty on the surface of your skin (to no purpose), then, why don't you

15   desist from prematurely wagging your tail for the flattering little mob,
since it's better that you swallow undiluted Anticyras?*
What's your idea of the highest good? To have lived with greased dish
always and with your little hide pampered by constant sun?
Wait! This old hag might respond hardly otherwise. Go now,

20   puff out, 'Son of Dinomache* am I—I am dazzling white!' So be it,
so long as shriveled Baucis* is no less wise
when she hawks basil to well-stripped home-slave."
    Alcibiades: "How nobody tries to descend into himself, nobody,
but the knapsack is watched on the one ahead of him!

25   Should you ask: 'Do you know the estates of Vettidius?'* 'Whose?'
'The rich man who tills at Cures* so much as a hawk can't cover.'
'You speak of *this one*, born under the gods' wrath with mean guardian
    spirit,
the one who, whenever he plants his yoke at perforated cross-road's
    shrine,
afraid to scrape long-standing filth from small wine-jar,

ingemit "hoc bene sit" tunicatum cum sale mordens   30
cepe et farratam pueris plaudentibus ollam
pannosam faecem morientis sorbet aceti?'"
Socrates: "at si unctus cesses et figas in cute solem,
est prope te ignotus cubito qui tangat et acre
despuat: 'hi mores! penemque arcanaque lumbi   35
runcantem populo marcentis pandere uuluas.
tum, cum maxillis balanatum gausape pectas,
inguinibus quare detonsus gurgulio extat?'
quinque palaestritae licet haec plantaria uellant
elixasque nates labefactent forcipe adunca,   40
non tamen ista filix ullo mansuescit aratro."
          Alcibiades: "caedimus inque uicem praebemus crura
                    sagittis.
uiuitur hoc pacto, sic nouimus." *Socrates:* "ilia subter
caecum uulnus habes, sed lato balteus auro
praetegit. ut mauis, da uerba et decipe neruos,   45
si potes." *Alcibiades:* "egregium cum me uicinia dicat,
non credam?" *Socrates:* "uiso si palles, inprobe, nummo,
si facis in penem quidquid tibi uenit, amarum
si puteal multa cautus uibice flagellas,
nequiquam populo bibulas donaueris aures.   50
respue quod non es; tollat sua munera cerdo.
tecum habita: noris quam sit tibi curta supellex."

30   sighs "May this be well!" while munching salted onion with skin
        retained,
and, as his slave-boys applaud their flour-based porridge,
swallows the ragged dregs of dying vinegar!'"
Socrates: "But if you idle greased and fix the sun on your skin,
near you is someone unknown who pushes you with his elbow and
        sharply
35   spits out: 'These morals! Both penis and loin's secret recesses
weeding, you display to the populace a withered cunt!
Then, when on your jaws you comb scented beard-rug,
for what reason does a shaven little worm protrude from your groin?'
Let five wrestling coaches pluck these little plants out,
40   and let them shake violently your buttock-cheeks with hooked forceps;
nevertheless that fern-patch will be tamed by no plow."
    Alcibiades: "We inflict wounds and in turn offer our shins to arrows.
People live with this policy—so we know." *Socrates:* "Under the groin
you have a blind wound, but a belt with broad gold
45   covers it over. As you prefer, lie and deceive your strength,
if you are able." *Alcibiades:* "When the neighborhood says that I am
        admirable,
should I not believe it?" *Socrates:* "If you grow pale, pervert, when
        coin's been seen,
if you do whatever occurs to your penis,
if, careful, you whip up bitter interest rates with multiple weal,
50   to no purpose you will have given to the populace ears fond of drinking.
Spit out that which you aren't; let Cerdo* remove his presents.
Reside with yourself:* you will know how defective your furniture is."

JUVENAL, *SATIRE* 1

semper ego auditor tantum? numquamne reponam
uexatus totiens rauci Theseide Cordi?
inpune ergo mihi recitauerit ille togatas,
hic elegos? inpune diem consumpserit ingens
Telephus aut summi plena iam margine libri   5
scriptus et in tergo necdum finitus Orestes?
nota magis nulli domus est sua quam mihi lucus
Martis et Aeoliis uicinum rupibus antrum
Vulcani; quid agant uenti, quas torqueat umbras
Aeacus, unde alius furtiuae deuehat aurum   10
pelliculae, quantas iaculetur Monychus ornos,
Frontonis platani conuolsaque marmora clamant
semper et adsiduo ruptae lectore columnae.
expectes eadem a summo minimoque poeta.
et nos ergo manum ferulae subduximus, et nos   15
consilium dedimus Sullae, priuatus ut altum
dormiret. stulta est clementia, cum tot ubique
uatibus occurras, periturae parcere chartae.
cur tamen hoc potius libeat decurrere campo,
per quem magnus equos Auruncae flexit alumnus,   20
si uacat ac placidi rationem admittitis, edam.
    cum tener uxorem ducat spado, Meuia Tuscum
figat aprum et nuda teneat uenabula mamma,
patricios omnis opibus cum prouocet unus
quo tondente grauis iuueni mihi barba sonabat,   25
cum pars Niliacae plebis, cum uerna Canopi
Crispinus Tyrias umero reuocante lacernas
uentilet aestiuum digitis sudantibus aurum
nec sufferre queat maioris pondera gemmae,
difficile est saturam non scribere. nam quis iniquae   30
tam patiens urbis, tam ferreus, ut teneat se,
causidici noua cum ueniat lectica Mathonis

JUVENAL, *SATIRE* 1

(Program Piece)

Am I always a *listener* only?* Shall I never strike back,
so often annoyed by the *Theseid* of rasping Cordus?*
With impunity therefore shall that one have recited to me dramas,*
this one his elegiacs? With impunity shall enormous *Telephus** have
    wasted
5   the day, or *Orestes*,* now written to fill margin
and reverse side and still not finished?
Known more to no one is his own house than to me the wood
of Mars* and the Cave of Vulcan* neighboring the Aeolean*
cliffs. What the winds are doing, what shades Aeacus* is torturing,
10   whence another swipes the gold of pilfered petty hide,*
how great are the ash-trunks Monychus* flings:
so always shout Fronto's plane-trees and the broken-down marbles*
and columns, themselves fractured by the incessant reciter.*
You may expect the same things from the greatest and the least "poet."
15   Yet I too have drawn back my hand from the rod; I too
gave advice to Sulla*—that he should sleep deep, a private citizen.
Foolish is the clemency, when you meet everywhere so many "bards,"
to spare paper destined to be wasted.
Why, then, it's a better option to gallop across the plain
20   over which the great son of Aurunca* steered his horses;
I'll tell you all, if you've the time and patiently accept my reasoning.
    When a delicate eunuch takes a wife, and Mevia stabs
an Etruscan boar and grasps spears nude-titted,*
when one now challenges with his wealth all the patricians,
25   one under whose shaving my beard used to grate when I was young,
when part of the Nile-mob, the home-bred Crispinus of Canopus,*
ventilates (as he pulls up on his shoulder Tyrian capes*)
summer-time gold on sweaty fingers
(for he is not able to tolerate the heft of a greater jewel),
30   it is difficult *not* to write satire.* For of an unfair
city who is so tolerant, so steeled, that he can restrain himself when
up rolls the new-fashioned litter of the shyster Matho,

plena ipso, post hunc magni delator amici
et cito rapturus de nobilitate comesa
quod superest, quem Massa timet, quem munere palpat   35
Carus et a trepido Thymele summissa Latino;
cum te summoueant qui testamenta merentur
noctibus, in caelum quos euehit optima summi
nunc uia processus, uetulae uesica beatae?
unciolam Proculeius habet, sed Gillo deuncem,   40
partes quisque suas ad mensuram inguinis heres.
accipiat sane mercedem sanguinis et sic
palleat ut nudis pressit qui calcibus anguem
aut Lugudunensem rhetor dicturus ad aram.
quid referam quanta siccum iecur ardeat ira,   45
cum populum gregibus comitum premit hic spoliator
pupilli prostantis et hic damnatus inani
iudicio? quid enim saluis infamia nummis?
exul ab octaua Marius bibit et fruitur dis
iratis, at tu uictrix, prouincia, ploras.   50
haec ego non credam Venusina digna lucerna?
haec ego non agitem? sed quid magis? Heracleas
aut Diomedeas aut mugitum labyrinthi
et mare percussum puero fabrumque uolantem,
cum leno accipiat moechi bona, si capiendi   55
ius nullum uxori, doctus spectare lacunar,
doctus et ad calicem uigilanti stertere naso;
cum fas esse putet curam sperare cohortis
qui bona donauit praesepibus et caret omni
maiorum censu, dum peruolat axe citato   60
Flaminiam puer Automedon? nam lora tenebat
ipse, lacernatae cum se iactaret amicae.
nonne libet medio ceras inplere capaces
quadriuio, cum iam sexta ceruice feratur
hinc atque inde patens ac nuda paene cathedra   65

filled up with just himself; after him comes the betrayer of a "dear
    friend,"
about to snatch up quickly whatever is left of now chewed-up nobility,
35   one whom Massa* fears, whom Carus* appeases by a "donation,"
and a fearful Latinus* by "Thymele* submitted";
when *they* displace you who earn their "testaments"
by means of night-duties, whom the highest paths carry to heaven
(now the best route): the wet slit of a rich old hag?
40   Proculeius has a mere twelfth portion, but Gillo eleven twelfths;
each heir has his portion in accord with his dick-measure.
Let him, by all means, receive his blood's reward
and let him turn pale* like someone who's stepped with bare feet on a
    snake
or an orator about to speak at Lugudunum's altar.*
45   Need I relate with what anger my dry liver* burns,
when this despoiler of a debauched schoolboy pushes aside the people
with his mob of followers, this one convicted by an empty
verdict? For what's ill-repute as long as money's stashed away?
Marius,* in exile, drinks from the eighth hour* and gloats over
50   angry gods while you, victorious province, lament.*
Am I not to believe these things worthy of the Venusian lamp?*
Shouldn't I pursue these things? Yet what's better? Yarns about Hercules*
or Diomedes* or Labyrinth's "moo"*
and sea smashed by boy and the flying craftsman?*
55   These themes, when pimp-husband accepts the goods of an adulterer
    (if his
wife has no means of gaining an inheritance), trained to stare at the
    ceiling,
trained to snore in his wine-glass with wakeful nose;
when *he* thinks it reasonable to hope for control of a cohort
who has squandered his goods on horse-stalls* and loses the entire
60   fortune of his ancestors, while as boy Automedon* he races along
the Flaminian Way* on speedy wheel? For he grasps the reins
himself while he shows off in front of his flashy-caped girlfriend.
Can't I choose to fill up massive wax-sheets*
in the middle of the cross-roads, when now on six necks
65   an open forger is carried here and there in an almost exposed sedan-
    chair

et multum referens de Maecenate supino
signator falsi, qui se lautum atque beatum
exiguis tabulis et gemma fecerit uda?
occurrit matrona potens, quae molle Calenum
porrectura uiro miscet sitiente rubetam   70
instituitque rudes melior Lucusta propinquas
per famam et populum nigros efferre maritos.
aude aliquid breuibus Gyaris et carcere dignum,
si uis esse aliquid. probitas laudatur et alget;
criminibus debent hortos, praetoria, mensas,   75
argentum uetus et stantem extra pocula caprum.
quem patitur dormire nurus corruptor auarae,
quem sponsae turpes et praetextatus adulter?
si natura negat, facit indignatio uersum
qualemcumque potest, quales ego uel Cluuienus.   80
     ex quo Deucalion nimbis tollentibus aequor
nauigio montem ascendit sortesque poposcit
paulatimque anima caluerunt mollia saxa
et maribus nudas ostendit Pyrrha puellas,
quidquid agunt homines, uotum, timor, ira, uoluptas,   85
gaudia, discursus, nostri farrago libelli est.
et quando uberior uitiorum copia? quando
maior auaritiae patuit sinus? alea quando
hos animos? neque enim loculis comitantibus itur
ad casum tabulae, posita sed luditur arca.   90
proelia quanta illic dispensatore uidebis
armigero! simplexne furor sestertia centum
perdere et horrenti tunicam non reddere seruo?
quis totidem erexit uillas, quis fercula septem
secreto cenauit auus? nunc sportula primo   95
limine parua sedet turbae rapienda togatae.
ille tamen faciem prius inspicit et trepidat ne
suppositus uenias ac falso nomine poscas:
agnitus accipies. iubet a praecone uocari
ipsos Troiugenas, nam uexant limen et ipsi   100
nobiscum. "da praetori, da deinde tribuno."

(reminding one much of sprawled-out Maecenas*),
a forger who made himself refined and well-to-do
by means of a couple of pages and a wet signet ring?
Up runs a powerful "lady," one who mixes toxic toad
70   with smooth Calenian,* about to offer it to her thirsty husband;
better than Lucusta* she instructs her "uneducated" neighbors
to carry death-darkened husbands out through gossip and in public.
Dare something worthy of minute Gyara* and the jailhouse,
if you want *to be something.* Uprightness is praised and freezes;
75   to their crimes they owe their gardens, palaces, tables,
old silver and goat standing in relief on the cups.
Whom does the seducer of a greedy daughter-in-law allow to sleep,
whom sluttish fiancées and child-adulterer?*
Indignation makes my verse (if innate ability fails me),
80   however it be, the type I can compose (or the scribbler Cluvienus).*
     From the time when Deucalion* (storm clouds raising the water-
          level)
climbed up the mountain* in his row-boat and sought an oracle,
and malleable stones* gradually grew warm with life,
and Pyrrha* displayed to males naked girls—from that time,
85   whatever people do (prayer, fear, anger, pleasure,*
rejoicing, running about) is the stuffing of my little book.*
And when has the supply-bag of depravity been more bloated? When
has a greater gulf of Greed* lain open? When have the dice
roused so many spirits? For one doesn't approach with mere wallets
90   the gambling-board, but the game's played with a treasure-chest at hand.
What great battles you'll witness there, with a cashier as arms-bearer!
Is it not pure rabidity to lose a half a million
yet deny a shivering slave a jacket?
Who among our grandfathers built up so many mansion-estates,
95   ate in isolation a seven-course dinner? Nowadays a paltry picnic basket
sits just outside the doorway for the toga'd mob to grab.*
The door-man, however, first checks your face, fearing lest
you come in disguise and ask for your due under a false name;
recognized, you'll get it. He bids the crier to call forth
100   the very Sons of Troy,* for they themselves crowd the doorway
along with us. "Give the praetor his, then the tribune his!"*

sed libertinus prior est. "prior" inquit "ego adsum.
cur timeam dubitemue locum defendere, quamuis
natus ad Euphraten, molles quod in aure fenestrae
arguerint, licet ipse negem? sed quinque tabernae   105
quadringenta parant. quid confert purpura maior
optandum, si Laurenti custodit in agro
conductas Coruinus ouis, ego possideo plus
Pallante et Licinis?" expectent ergo tribuni,
uincant diuitiae, sacro ne cedat honori   110
nuper in hanc urbem pedibus qui uenerat albis,
quandoquidem inter nos sanctissima diuitiarum
maiestas, etsi funesta Pecunia templo
nondum habitat, nullas nummorum ereximus aras,
ut colitur Pax atque Fides, Victoria, Virtus   115
quaeque salutato crepitat Concordia nido.
sed cum summus honor finito conputet anno,
sportula quid referat, quantum rationibus addat,
quid facient comites quibus hinc toga, calceus hinc est
et panis fumusque domi? densissima centum   120
quadrantes lectica petit, sequiturque maritum
languida uel praegnas et circumducitur uxor.
hic petit absenti nota iam callidus arte
ostendens uacuam et clausam pro coniuge sellam.
"Galla mea est" inquit, "citius dimitte. moraris?   125
profer, Galla, caput. noli uexare, quiescet."
    ipse dies pulchro distinguitur ordine rerum:
sportula, deinde forum iurisque peritus Apollo
atque triumphales, inter quas ausus habere
nescio quis titulos Aegyptius atque Arabarches,   130
cuius ad effigiem non tantum meiiere fas est.
uestibulis abeunt ueteres lassique clientes
uotaque deponunt, quamquam longissima cenae
spes homini; caulis miseris atque ignis emendus.

But a freedman is in line first: "Hey, I was here before them!" he says.
"Why should I be afraid or hesitate to defend my place, just because*
I was born by the Euphrates (a fact that the tender holes in my ear*
105   would verify, even if I myself denied it)?* Nevertheless, my five flea-markets
       yield a million.* What does the wider purple stripe*
have to offer, if in Laurentum's field* Corvinus* guards
rented sheep, while I control more than
Pallas* or Licinus?"* Let the tribunes wait, therefore;
110   let riches conquer, lest to the sacred office* yield
he who had recently entered this city with white feet,*
seeing that the majesty of riches is the most holy among us
(even if deadly Money does not yet reside
in a temple; we've set up no altars of cash,
115   as are worshipped Peace and Fidelity, Victory and Virtue
and Concord, who clacks, her nest greeted*).
But when the highest office adds up at year's end
what the hand-out brings in, how much it adds to the accounts,
what will "buddies" do for whom from this, *from this*, come clothes, shoes,
120   bread and firewood? Sedan-chair jam
seeks the hundred coins;* what's more a wife sick or pregnant
follows her husband in doing the rounds.
This one makes the request for an absent wife (skilled in a ruse now known),
pointing at an empty and closed sedan (as though his wife were really there).
125   "Hey, it's my Galla," he says, "Let us off a little quicker. You're dithering?
Galla, stick your head out! Don't bother her—she's resting."
     The day itself is marked by a "fine" arrangement of affairs:
hand-out, then the forum and Apollo the expert lawyer,*
and the row of conquering heroes, among whom some
130   Egyptian Arabarches* or other has dared to have his record
(at whose likeness it's right *not only* to piss).
Haggard, long-time clients from the porches leave
and lay aside their vows, even though the most long-lived hope for a
person is that of a meal; cabbage and coal will have to be bought by the wretches.

optima siluarum interea pelagique uorabit   135
rex horum uacuisque toris tantum ipse iacebit.
nam de tot pulchris et latis orbibus et tam
antiquis una comedunt patrimonia mensa.
nullus iam parasitus erit. sed quis ferat istas
luxuriae sordes? quanta est gula quae sibi totos   140
ponit apros, animal propter conuiuia natum!
poena tamen praesens, cum tu deponis amictus
turgidus et crudum pauonem in balnea portas.
hinc subitae mortes atque intestata senectus.
it noua nec tristis per cunctas fabula cenas;   145
ducitur iratis plaudendum funus amicis.
      nil erit ulterius quod nostris moribus addat
posteritas, eadem facient cupientque minores,
omne in praecipiti uitium stetit. utere uelis,
totos pande sinus. dices hic forsitan "unde   150
ingenium par materiae? unde illa priorum
scribendi quodcumque animo flagrante liberet
simplicitas? 'cuius non audeo dicere nomen?
quid refert dictis ignoscat Mucius an non?'
pone Tigillinum, taeda lucebis in illa   155
qua stantes ardent qui fixo gutture fumant,
et latum media sulcum deducis harena."
qui dedit ergo tribus patruis aconita, uehatur
pensilibus plumis atque illinc despiciat nos?
"cum ueniet contra, digito compesce labellum: 160
accusator erit qui uerbum dixerit 'hic est.'
securus licet Aenean Rutulumque ferocem
committas, nulli grauis est percussus Achilles
aut multum quaesitus Hylas urnamque secutus:

135   Meanwhile the best produce of wood and wave
      the "King" of these men sucks down—he'll sprawl, single occupant of
            empty couch.
      For from so many beautiful, broad, and antique round-tables
      they chew up patrimonies in one sitting.
      Now there won't remain even a single parasite! But who can put up
            with those
140   filthy displays of extravagance? How great is the gut that sets for itself
      whole porkers, a beast born for banquets!
      The penalty's at hand, however, when you're bloated and throw off
            your
      wraps and haul that half-digested peacock into the hot tub!
      Hence come sudden deaths and old age intestate.
145   Report of your death (new but not sad) runs the dinner-table circuit;
      a funeral is held to be applauded by incensed "friends."
            Nothing further will there be for posterity to add to our character;
      those to come will do and lust after the same things—
      each vice stands ready at the spring-board. Spread sail;
150   spread wide the full furls! You might by chance here interject, "Whence
      the talent equal to the subject? Whence that candor of our predecessors
      in writing whatever struck a blazing soul?
      'Whose name do I not dare mention?
      What's it to me whether or not Mucius* forgives my words?'
155   Caricature Tigellinus:* you'll light up in that pyrotechnic,*
      the one in which they burn standing, those who fry with neck nailed
            down,*
      and you'll carve a wide groove along the middle of the sand-lot."*
      Is he, therefore, who served poison to three of his father's brothers to
            be hefted along
      on down comforters and from there look down at us in disgust?
160   "When he happens by, check your lips with your finger:
      whoever says that phrase 'this is he' will be automatically an accuser.
      Safe and sound you're permitted to set at odds Aeneas and the fierce
            Rutulian;*
      Achilles* struck down is dreadful to no one;
      nor is Hylas, much sought after while he chased a jug.*

ense uelut stricto quotiens Lucilius ardens   165
infremuit, rubet auditor cui frigida mens est
criminibus, tacita sudant praecordia culpa.
inde ira et lacrimae. tecum prius ergo uoluta
haec animo ante tubas: galeatum sero duelli
paenitet." experiar quid concedatur in illos   170
quorum Flaminia tegitur cinis atque Latina.

165 Whenever burning Lucilius growled, as though with drawn sword,
     the hearer (whose mind chills with guilt over crimes committed)
     is red with shame; his heart sweats with silent guilt.
     Hence both rage and tears. Ponder over with yourself therefore*
     these things before sounding the battle-trumpets; regret about combat
          comes too late to the helmeted."*
170 I'll make a stab at what offers itself against those—
     those whose ash is hidden by the Flaminian and Latin ways.*

JUVENAL, *SATIRE* 3

quamuis digressu ueteris confusus amici
laudo tamen, uacuis quod sedem figere Cumis
destinet atque unum ciuem donare Sibyllae.
ianua Baiarum est et gratum litus amoeni
secessus. ego uel Prochytam praepono Suburae;   5
nam quid tam miserum, tam solum uidimus, ut non
deterius credas horrere incendia, lapsus
tectorum adsiduos ac mille pericula saeuae
urbis et Augusto recitantes mense poetas?
sed dum tota domus raeda componitur una,   10
substitit ad ueteres arcus madidamque Capenam.
hic, ubi nocturnae Numa constituebat amicae
(nunc sacri fontis nemus et delubra locantur
Iudaeis, quorum cophinus fenumque supellex;
omnis enim populo mercedem pendere iussa est   15
arbor et eiectis mendicat silua Camenis),
in uallem Egeriae descendimus et speluncas
dissimiles ueris. quanto praesentius esset
numen aquis, uiridi si margine cluderet undas
herba nec ingenuum uiolarent marmora tofum.   20
      hic tunc Vmbricius "quando artibus" inquit "honestis
nullus in urbe locus, nulla emolumenta laborum,
res hodie minor est here quam fuit atque eadem cras
deteret exiguis aliquid, proponimus illuc
ire, fatigatas ubi Daedalus exuit alas,   25
dum noua canities, dum prima et recta senectus,
dum superest Lachesi quod torqueat et pedibus me
porto meis nullo dextram subeunte bacillo.
cedamus patria. uiuant Artorius istic
et Catulus, maneant qui nigrum in candida uertunt,   30

JUVENAL, *SATIRE 3*

(Umbricius' City)

Although upset by my long-time friend's departure,
nevertheless I praise the fact that he intends to establish his residence
    in
Cumae* and to give the Sibyl* one fellow-citizen.
There is Baiae's gateway,* a pleasant coast of lovely
5   seclusion. For my part, I place even Prochyta* before the Subura;*
for what have we seen that's so joyless, so off the beaten path, that you
wouldn't think it worse to fear fire-alarms, constant collapse
of roof-tops, a *thousand* dangers of a savage
city and "poets" reciting* in the month of August?
10   But while his entire household is being arranged on a single carriage,
he stops short at the old arches and moist Capena.*
Here, where Numa used to get together with his night-time girl,*
now the grove of the holy spring, as well as the shrines, are rented
to Jews, whose house-hold consists of bushel-basket and straw.
15   For each *tree* has been ordered to donate goods to the populace,*
and the wood begs (the Camenae* having been cast out).
We move downward into the vale of Egeria and the caves
different from their true selves. How much more present divinity would
        be
to the waters if plant-life enclosed the ripples with green border,
20   and marble-stones did not spoil the natural tufa.
      Here then Umbricius* said, "When for honorable skills
there is no place in the city, no return for one's exertions;
today my capital's smaller than it was yesterday and tomorrow
will rub something from the bit remaining; there I propose
25   to go where Daedalus shed exhausted wings*
while gray hair is new to me, while old age is in its first stage and not
        yet stooped,
while there remains *something* for Lachesis to spin* and
I carry myself on my own feet (with no walking-stick under hand).
It's best that I abandon my fatherland. Let Artorius*
30   and Catulus* live in that place; let those stay who turn black to white,

quis facile est aedem conducere, flumina, portus,
siccandam eluuiem, portandum ad busta cadauer,
et praebere caput domina uenale sub hasta.
quondam hi cornicines et municipalis harenae
perpetui comites notaeque per oppida buccae   35
munera nunc edunt et, uerso pollice uulgus
cum iubet, occidunt populariter; inde reuersi
conducunt foricas, et cur non omnia? cum sint
quales ex humili magna ad fastigia rerum
extollit quotiens uoluit Fortuna iocari.   40
quid Romae faciam? mentiri nescio; librum,
si malus est, nequeo laudare et poscere; motus
astrorum ignoro; funus promittere patris
nec uolo nec possum; ranarum uiscera numquam
inspexi; ferre ad nuptam quae mittit adulter,   45
quae mandat, norunt alii; me nemo ministro
fur erit, atque ideo nulli comes exeo tamquam
mancus et extinctae corpus non utile dextrae.
quis nunc diligitur nisi conscius et cui feruens
aestuat occultis animus semperque tacendis?   50
nil tibi se debere putat, nil conferet umquam,
participem qui te secreti fecit honesti.
carus erit Verri qui Verrem tempore quo uult
accusare potest. tanti tibi non sit opaci
omnis harena Tagi quodque in mare uoluitur aurum,   55
ut somno careas ponendaque praemia sumas
tristis et a magno semper timearis amico.
   "quae nunc diuitibus gens acceptissima nostris
et quos praecipue fugiam, properabo fateri,
nec pudor obstabit. non possum ferre, Quirites,   60
Graecam urbem. quamuis quota portio faecis Achaei?

for whom it's a breeze to contract for buildings, rivers, ports,
drying out swamp-land, transporting a cadaver to the pyre,
and to offer venal head under the spear of control.*
These one-time bugle-biters and constant companions of the village
        sand-lot,
35   these bloated cheeks known throughout the hick-towns,
now sponsor public displays and when, with turned thumb,* the crowd
gives the order, they set about killing with popular approval. Having
        returned thence,
they contract for public toilets—and why not everything, since they are
the kind Fortune lifts up out of the dirt to the great heights
40   as often as she wants to joke.
What am *I* to do at Rome? I don't know how to lie; a book,
if it's poor, I can't praise and seek out.
I don't know astrology; I neither want to, nor can,
promise a father's death; frog's guts I've never
45   inspected;* others know how to carry to a bride what an adulterer sends,
what he orders. No one shall be a thief with me as accomplice,
and for that I go about as a companion to nobody—
just like a crippled corpse useless with its right hand.*
Who now is esteemed except he who is in the know and whose agitated
        heart
50   is warm with secrets and items always to be kept quiet?
He thinks he owes you nothing, will bestow nothing upon you ever,
who has made you participant of a honest secret.
He shall be dear to Verres* who at the time he wishes
can accuse Verres. Let not all the sand of the opaque Tagus
55   (and whatever gold it rolls into the sea)* be of so great value to you
that you lack sleep and sadly take up rewards that must be lain aside,
and that you be always feared by a 'great friend.'
    "Of the tribe most well-received by our own wealthy
(and whom I would especially shun) I shall now hasten to tell;
60   nor will shame hold me back. I cannot bear, sons of Quirinus,*
a *Greek Rome*! Although what a small proportion of the sludge are
        Achaeans?*

iam pridem Syrus in Tiberim defluxit Orontes
et linguam et mores et cum tibicine chordas
obliquas nec non gentilia tympana secum
uexit et ad circum iussas prostare puellas.   65
ite, quibus grata est picta lupa barbara mitra.
rusticus ille tuus sumit trechedipna, Quirine,
et ceromatico fert niceteria collo.
hic alta Sicyone, ast hic Amydone relicta,
hic Andro, ille Samo, hic Trallibus aut Alabandis,   70
Esquilias dictumque petunt a uimine collem,
uiscera magnarum domuum dominique futuri.
ingenium uelox, audacia perdita, sermo
promptus et Isaeo torrentior. ede quid illum
esse putes. quemuis hominem secum attulit ad nos: 75
grammaticus, rhetor, geometres, pictor, aliptes,
augur, schoenobates, medicus, magus, omnia nouit
Graeculus esuriens: in caelum iusseris ibit.
in summa non Maurus erat neque Sarmata nec Thrax
qui sumpsit pinnas, mediis sed natus Athenis.   80
horum ego non fugiam conchylia? me prior ille
signabit fultusque toro meliore recumbet,
aduectus Romam quo pruna et cottana uento?
usque adeo nihil est quod nostra infantia caelum
hausit Auentini baca nutrita Sabina?   85
quid quod adulandi gens prudentissima laudat
sermonem indocti, faciem deformis amici,
et longum inualidi collum ceruicibus aequat
Herculis Antaeum procul a tellure tenentis,
miratur uocem angustam, qua deterius nec   90
ille sonat quo mordetur gallina marito?
haec eadem licet et nobis laudare, sed illis

For a long while now the Syrian Orontes has flowed down into the
    Tiber*
and carried with it its language, customs, along with the flute,
slanting harp-strings, plus its ethnic tambourines

65   and hooker-girls ordered to strut at the Circus.
Go ahead, you to whom barbarian* hooker with colorful bonnet is pleasing!
Even that rustic of yours, son of Quirinus, puts on a 'run-to-dine jacket'*
and wears 'Nike-prizes'* on his perfumed* neck.
This one comes from high Sicyon* left behind, but this one from
    Amydon,*

70   this one from Andros,* that one from Samos,* this one from Tralles*
    or Alabanda*—
they seek the Esquiline* and the hill named after a sprig,*
intent on becoming the vital organs and lords of great houses.
Swift intellect, unfathomable audacity, as smooth-
talking and more fluent than Isaeus:* tell what you

75   suppose *him* to be! He brings to us with him whatever person you like:
grammarian, rhetorician, geometrician, painter, wrestling-coach,
seer, tight-rope dancer, physician, magic-man; the hungry little
Greek knows everything. You tell him to fly skyward—he'll go.
In sum, it was neither Moor* nor Sarmatian* nor Thracian*

80   who donned feathers,* but he born in mid-Athens.
Should *I* not shun the purple robes of *these*? Prior to me
shall *he* sign and lie back supported by a better couch—
he who breezed into Rome on the gust that brought prunes and Syrian
    figs?
Is it so much for nothing that my infanthood, nourished

85   by Sabine berry,* gulped down the atmosphere of the Aventine?*
What of the fact that the race (most accomplished at flattery) praises
the chatter of an idiot, the face of a freak-friend,
and equates the long neck of a weakling to the shoulders
of Hercules as he holds Antaeus high off the ground;*

90   what of the fact that he admires a shrill voice worse than
the sound a hen makes as she's bitten by the rooster?
We too may praise these same things, but it is to *them*

creditur. an melior cum Thaida sustinet aut cum
uxorem comoedus agit uel Dorida nullo
cultam palliolo? mulier nempe ipsa uidetur,   95
non persona, loqui: uacua et plana omnia dicas
infra uentriculum et tenui distantia rima.
nec tamen Antiochus nec erit mirabilis illic
aut Stratocles aut cum molli Demetrius Haemo:
natio comoeda est. rides, maiore cachinno   100
concutitur; flet, si lacrimas conspexit amici,
nec dolet; igniculum brumae si tempore poscas,
accipit endromidem; si dixeris 'aestuo,' sudat.
non sumus ergo pares: melior, qui semper et omni
nocte dieque potest aliena sumere uultum   105
a facie, iactare manus laudare paratus,
si bene ructauit, si rectum minxit amicus,
si trulla inuerso crepitum dedit aurea fundo.
praeterea sanctum nihil †aut† ab inguine tutum,
non matrona laris, non filia uirgo, nec ipse   110
sponsus leuis adhuc, non filius ante pudicus.
horum si nihil est, auiam resupinat amici.
[scire uolunt secreta domus atque inde timeri.]*
et quoniam coepit Graecorum mentio, transi
gymnasia atque audi facinus maioris abollae.   115
Stoicus occidit Baream delator amicum
discipulumque senex ripa nutritus in illa
ad quam Gorgonei delapsa est pinna caballi.
non est Romano cuiquam locus hic, ubi regnat
Protogenes aliquis uel Diphilus aut Hermarchus,   120
qui gentis uitio numquam partitur amicum,
solus habet. nam cum facilem stillauit in aurem
exiguum de naturae patriaeque ueneno,
limine summoueor, perierunt tempora longi
seruitii; nusquam minor est iactura clientis.   125
    "quod porro officium, ne nobis blandiar, aut quod
pauperis hic meritum, si curet nocte togatus
currere, cum praetor lictorem inpellat et ire

that credence is given. Is anyone better when he maintains the role of
    Thais*

95   or when, as comic-actor, he plays a wife* or Doris* (adorned
by no mantle)? To be sure, it seems a woman herself,
not a mask, is speaking. You'd say that all is empty and flat
below the paunch, and separated by a slender cleft.
Nevertheless, neither Antiochus* shall provoke amazement *there*,
nor Stratocles,* nor Demetrius* with tender Haemus.*

100   The nation is born for comedy. You laugh—by a greater guffaw
he's shaken; he weeps if he's spotted the tears of a friend
(yet he feels no grief); if you seek a small fire in winter-time,
he grabs an overcoat; if you say 'I'm hot,' he sweats.
We are not, therefore, equals. Better is *he*, who is always, every

105   night and day, able to form his expression from someone else's
face: prepared to toss his hands, to give praise
if a friend burped nicely, if he pissed a straight jet,
if gold wine-mug, bottom up, released an audible gurgle.
What's more, nothing is holy or safe from his dick:

110   not the woman of the house, not the virgin daughter nor
the groom himself (still beardless), not the son (previously chaste).
If there's no one of these, he lays his friend's grandma.
What they're after is to know the household secrets, and thence be
    feared.
And, since talk of Greeks has started, pass over

115   the gymnasia* and hear a crime of a 'greater cloak.'*
The Stoic informer* killed Barea*, his friend and
student—the old man was brought up on that river-bank
at which the feather of the Gorgon-horse fell.*
There isn't room here for any Roman, where reigns

120   some Protogenes or Diphilus or Hermarchus
who, by fault of his race, never shares a friend—
he has him all to himself. For when he has trickled into easy ear
a small bit of his nature's and fatherland's poison,
I'm moved away from the threshold, periods are lost of long

125   service; nowhere is the jettisoning of a client of less importance.
    "Further, lest we flatter ourselves, what duty, or what
value for a poor man is there here, if he bothers to run toga-clad at
    night,
when the praetor prods the lictor on and

praecipitem iubeat dudum uigilantibus orbis,
ne prior Albinam et Modiam collega salutet?   130
diuitis hic seruo cludit latus ingenuorum
filius; alter enim quantum in legione tribuni
accipiunt donat Caluinae uel Catienae,
ut semel aut iterum super illam palpitet; at tu,
cum tibi uestiti facies scorti placet, haeres   135
et dubitas alta Chionen deducere sella.
da testem Romae tam sanctum quam fuit hospes
numinis Idaei, procedat uel Numa uel qui
seruauit trepidam flagranti ex aede Mineruam:
protinus ad censum, de moribus ultima fiet   140
quaestio. 'quot pascit seruos? quot possidet agri
iugera? quam multa magnaque paropside cenat?'
quantum quisque sua nummorum seruat in arca,
tantum habet et fidei. iures licet et Samothracum
et nostrorum aras, contemnere fulmina pauper   145
creditur atque deos dis ignoscentibus ipsis.
quid quod materiam praebet causasque iocorum
omnibus hic idem, si foeda et scissa lacerna,
si toga sordidula est et rupta calceus alter
pelle patet, uel si consuto uolnere crassum   150
atque recens linum ostendit non una cicatrix?
nil habet infelix paupertas durius in se
quam quod ridiculos homines facit. 'exeat' inquit,
'si pudor est, et de puluino surgat equestri,
cuius res legi non sufficit, et sedeant hic   155
lenonum pueri quocumque ex fornice nati,
hic plaudat nitidus praeconis filius inter
pinnirapi cultos iuuenes iuuenesque lanistae.'
sic libitum uano, qui nos distinxit, Othoni.
quis gener hic placuit censu minor atque puellae   160
sarcinulis inpar? quis pauper scribitur heres?

130
orders him to go in headlong haste when the childless are awake,*
lest his colleague greet first Albina* and Modia?*
Here the son of free-born citizens walks beside the slave of a rich man;
for as much as tribunes receive in a legion
he shells out to Calvina* or Catiena,*
just so he can hump on her once or twice. But *you*,

135
when the face of a dolled-up street-walker pleases you, freeze up
and hesitate to lure Chione* down from her high seat.
Present a witness at Rome as holy as was the host
of the Idaean divinity;* either Numa* or he who saved
fearful Minerva from burning shrine* could come forth to testify:

140
straight-away there will come questioning of his wealth, last and least about
his character. 'How many slaves does he feed? How many acres of field
has he? Off how many and how great snack-platters does he dine?'
As much as each person has saved in his treasure-box,
so much credit he has as well. You can swear by the altars of Samothrace,*

145
as well as by our own, and yet the poor man is believed to scorn
lightning-bolts and the gods (with the gods themselves forgiving him!).
What of the fact that this same man furnishes material and opportunities
for jokes to all, if his overcoat is filthy and ragged,
if his toga is a bit dirty and through split leather one shoe

150
gapes, or if, after a tear has been sewn together, it is
not just one repair-job that reveals the thick, new stitching?
Unhappy poverty has nothing harsher in it
than that it makes people ridiculous. 'Let him get out,' he says,
'if there's any respect, and let him rise from Knight-seat,*

155
whose capital does not meet legal requisite; and let sit here
pimps' boys and those born of whatever whore-house;
let the sparkling son of the town crier clap here among
the refined youths of a gladiator and the youths of a wrestling coach.'
Thus it pleased vain Otho,* who categorized us.

160
Here, what son-in-law won approval with savings account less and unequal
to the girl's cash-sacks? What poor man is declared heir?

quando in consilio est aedilibus? agmine facto
debuerant olim tenues migrasse Quirites.
haut facile emergunt quorum uirtutibus obstat
res angusta domi, sed Romae durior illis   165
conatus: magno hospitium miserabile, magno
seruorum uentres, et frugi cenula magno.
fictilibus cenare pudet, quod turpe negabis
translatus subito ad Marsos mensamque Sabellam
contentusque illic Veneto duroque cucullo.   170
pars magna Italiae est, si uerum admittimus, in qua
nemo togam sumit nisi mortuus. ipsa dierum
festorum herboso colitur si quando theatro
maiestas tandemque redit ad pulpita notum
exodium, cum personae pallentis hiatum   175
in gremio matris formidat rusticus infans,
aequales habitus illic similesque uidebis
orchestram et populum; clari uelamen honoris
sufficiunt tunicae summis aedilibus albae.
hic ultra uires habitus nitor, hic aliquid plus   180
quam satis est interdum aliena sumitur arca.
commune id uitium est: hic uiuimus ambitiosa
paupertate omnes. quid te moror? omnia Romae
cum pretio. quid das, ut Cossum aliquando salutes,
ut te respiciat clauso Veiiento labello?   185
ille metit barbam, crinem hic deponit amati;
plena domus libis uenalibus: accipe et istud
fermentum tibi habe. praestare tributa clientes
cogimur et cultis augere peculia seruis.
    "quis timet aut timuit gelida Praeneste ruinam   190
aut positis nemorosa inter iuga Volsiniis aut
simplicibus Gabiis aut proni Tiburis arce?
nos urbem colimus tenui tibicine fultam

When is he consultant of aediles? Battle-line formed,
long ago true Romans of slim means should have stormed out.
By no means easily do they make any headway, whose slender
165   household income stands in the way of their talents, but at Rome even
        more tough for them
is the attempt. The cost of a pitiful apartment is exorbitant, exorbitant
the bellies of slaves, exorbitant a modest supper.
It's embarrassing to dine off clay dishes, which you'd deny was
        disgraceful
if you were suddenly carried over to the Marsians and a Samnite table,*
170   and you'd be perfectly at ease there with a rough Venetian cowl.*
There is a great part of Italy, if we admit the truth, in which
nobody dons a toga unless he's dead. Even when the 'majesty'
of festival-days is cultivated in grassy theater,
and finally well-known comic after-piece returns to the stage
175   (when country-babe fears the gape of pale mask
as it's held in its mother's bosom),
you'll see there equal dress and the orchestra
and the public looking alike; as garment of illustrious office,
white tunics suffice for the high-ranking aediles.
180   *Here* there is dressy elegance of style beyond attainment, *here*
something more than is enough is periodically taken from someone
        else's treasure-chest.
That fault is shared by everyone: we live here in ambitious
poverty, all of us. Why do I delay you? In short, everything at Rome
has its price. What would you give to greet Cossus* sometime,
185   to have Veiento,* close-mouthed, turn back a glance at you?
That one's mowing a beard; this one's laying down the curl of a loved
        one;*
the house is full of cakes on sale: accept that baked treat*
and have it for yourself. We clients are forced to pay tribute*
and to augment the piggy-banks of cultivated slaves.*
190   "Who at cold Praeneste* fears, or ever feared, the collapse of
        buildings,
or among the thickly leaved ridges of Volsinii,* or
at unsophisticated Gabii* or steep-topped Tibur?*
We live in a city that is held up by scrawny pillar

magna parte sui; nam sic labentibus obstat
uilicus et, ueteris rimae cum texit hiatum,   195
securos pendente iubet dormire ruina.
uiuendum est illic, ubi nulla incendia, nulli
nocte metus. iam poscit aquam, iam friuola transfert
Vcalegon, tabulata tibi iam tertia fumant:
tu nescis; nam si gradibus trepidatur ab imis,   200
ultimus ardebit quem tegula sola tuetur
a pluuia, molles ubi reddunt oua columbae.
lectus erat Cordo Procula minor, urceoli sex
ornamentum abaci, nec non et paruulus infra
cantharus et recubans sub eodem marmore Chiron,   205
iamque uetus Graecos seruabat cista libellos
et diuina opici rodebant carmina mures.
nil habuit Cordus, quis enim negat? et tamen illud
perdidit infelix totum nihil. ultimus autem
aerumnae cumulus, quod nudum et frusta rogantem   210
nemo cibo, nemo hospitio tectoque iuuabit.
si magna Asturici cecidit domus, horrida mater,
pullati proceres, differt uadimonia praetor.
tum gemimus casus urbis, tunc odimus ignem.
ardet adhuc, et iam accurrit qui marmora donet,   215
conferat inpensas; hic nuda et candida signa,
hic aliquid praeclarum Euphranoris et Polycliti,
haec Asianorum uetera ornamenta deorum,
hic libros dabit et forulos mediamque Mineruam,
hic modium argenti. meliora ac plura reponit   220
Persicus orborum lautissimus et merito iam
suspectus tamquam ipse suas incenderit aedes.
si potes auelli circensibus, optima Sorae
aut Fabrateriae domus aut Frusinone paratur

in large part; for in such a manner the landlord props up slipping
    foundations
195   and, when he's covered up the gape of a long-standing fissure,
he orders his tenants to sleep safe and sound under imminent roof-fall.
One should live *there*, where there aren't any infernos, any
anxieties at night. Ucalegon* now asks for water, now removes
his petty possessions; now the third floor is smoking on you:
200   you've no idea what's happening; for if the panic starts from the bottom
    levels,
he'll fry last whom roof-tiling alone protects
from the rain—there where mild doves lay their eggs.
Cordus had a cot* too small for Procula,* a half-dozen tiny jars
his shelf's decoration, plus below that a minute
205   wine-tankard and a statue of a laid-back Chiron* under that same marble
shelf; and an aged box kept some Greek books
and the divine poems that uncultured mice used to gnaw.
Cordus had nothing, for who could deny that? And nevertheless that
entire 'nothing,' out of luck as he was, he has lost. The finishing touch
210   on his misfortune, however, is the fact that *no one*, as he is naked and
    begging for scraps,
will help him out with food, *no one* with hospitality and shelter.
If the great house of Asturicus* has fallen, the matron is disheveled,
the nobles wear black, the praetor puts off receipt of bail.
Then we bemoan the accidents of the city, *then* we hate fire.
215   *His* house is still on fire, and already somebody runs up to donate
    marbles,
to bear the expenses; this one will give bright nude statuary,
this one some illustrious piece of Euphranor* and Polyclitus,*
this or that ancient decoration of Asian gods;
this one will give books and book-cases with a Minerva-statue between
    them,
220   this one a quantity of silver. He replaces what he's lost with more and
    better,
that most wealthy of the childless, Persicus,* and he's now
rightly suspected of perhaps having burned down his house himself.
If you can be plucked away from the Circus-games, the best house in
    Sora*
or Fabrateria* or Frusino* can be had

quanti nunc tenebras unum conducis in annum.   225
hortulus hic puteusque breuis nec reste mouendus
in tenuis plantas facili diffunditur haustu.
uiue bidentis amans et culti uilicus horti
unde epulum possis centum dare Pythagoreis.
est aliquid, quocumque loco, quocumque recessu,   230
unius sese dominum fecisse lacertae.
    "plurimus hic aeger moritur uigilando (sed ipsum
languorem peperit cibus inperfectus et haerens
ardenti stomacho); nam quae meritoria somnum
admittunt? magnis opibus dormitur in urbe.   235
inde caput morbi. raedarum transitus arto
uicorum in flexu et stantis conuicia mandrae
eripient somnum Druso uitulisque marinis.
si uocat officium, turba cedente uehetur
diues et ingenti curret super ora Liburna   240
atque obiter leget aut scribet uel dormiet intus;
namque facit somnum clausa lectica fenestra.
ante tamen ueniet: nobis properantibus obstat
unda prior, magno populus premit agmine lumbos
qui sequitur; ferit hic cubito, ferit assere duro   245
alter, at hic tignum capiti incutit, ille metretam.
pinguia crura luto, planta mox undique magna
calcor, et in digito clauus mihi militis haeret.
nonne uides quanto celebretur sportula fumo?
centum conuiuae, sequitur sua quemque culina.   250
Corbulo uix ferret tot uasa ingentia, tot res
inpositas capiti, quas recto uertice portat
seruulus infelix et cursu uentilat ignem.
scinduntur tunicae sartae modo, longa coruscat
serraco ueniente abies, atque altera pinum   255
plaustra uehunt; nutant alte populoque minantur.

225   for what you now pay in annual rent for a dark hole.
Here is a little vegetable patch and a shallow well of water that does not
        have to be drawn by rope,
but with easy scoop is poured on the tender plants.
Live as hoe's lover and as overseer of a cultivated garden
from which you could throw dinner for a hundred Pythagoreans.*
230   It's something, in whatever place, in whatever corner,
to have made yourself the master of a single lizard.
     "Many a sick person dies here from lack of sleep (yet that very
queasiness arises from improperly prepared food that sticks to a
burning stomach); for what flop-houses admit sleep?
235   One sleeps in the city if he's got great wealth:
thence the head of the epidemic. The passage of wheeled carts in
the cramped winding of the streets and the curses directed at loitering
        cattle
will rip the sleep from Drusus* and sea-cows.*
If 'duty calls,' the rich man* will be carried, the mob giving way,
240   and he will cruise along above their faces in a massive Liburnian sedan-
        chair;*
and en route he'll either read or write or sleep inside,
since a sedan-chair with closed window facilitates sleep.
Nevertheless he will arrive ahead: in our way as we're rushing
comes first a wave of humanity; the crowd that follows in a great throng
        shoves against
245   our loins; this one knocks me with his elbow; another hits me with a
        hard pole;
yet this one bashes a wooden beam against my head, that one a ten-
        gallon keg.
Shins thick with mud, next from all sides by massive foot
I'm trodden, and a soldier's spiked heel sticks in my toe.
Don't you see with how much smoke the hand-out is thronged?*
250   There are *a hundred* 'banqueters,' and his own kitchen follows each
        one.
Corbulo* could hardly carry so many massive vessels, so many things
placed on his head—things that with unbent neck the unhappy
little slave carries as he fans the flames while he runs.
Tunics just mended are ripped apart; a long tree-trunk wobbles
255   on an approaching wagon; other carts are carrying pine-logs;
these bob back and forth on high and threaten the populace.

nam si procubuit qui saxa Ligustica portat
axis et euersum fudit super agmina montem,
quid superest de corporibus? quis membra, quis ossa
inuenit? obtritum uolgi perit omne cadauer   260
more animae. domus interea secura patellas
iam lauat et bucca foculum excitat et sonat unctis
striglibus et pleno componit lintea guto.
haec inter pueros uarie properantur, at ille
iam sedet in ripa taetrumque nouicius horret   265
porthmea nec sperat caenosi gurgitis alnum
infelix nec habet quem porrigat ore trientem.
    "respice nunc alia ac diuersa pericula noctis:
quod spatium tectis sublimibus unde cerebrum
testa ferit, quotiens rimosa et curta fenestris   270
uasa cadant, quanto percussum pondere signent
et laedant silicem. possis ignauus haberi
et subiti casus inprouidus, ad cenam si
intestatus eas: adeo tot fata, quot illa
nocte patent uigiles te praetereunte fenestrae.   275
ergo optes uotumque feras miserabile tecum,
ut sint contentae patulas defundere pelues.
ebrius ac petulans, qui nullum forte cecidit,
dat poenas, noctem patitur lugentis amicum
Pelidae, cubat in faciem, mox deinde supinus: 280
[ergo non aliter poterit dormire; quibusdam]*
somnum rixa facit. sed quamuis inprobus annis
atque mero feruens cauet hunc quem coccina laena
uitari iubet et comitum longissimus ordo,
multum praeterea flammarum et aenea lampas.   285
me, quem luna solet deducere uel breue lumen
candelae, cuius dispenso et tempero filum,

For if the axle sinks down that carries Ligurian boulders*
and pours its overturned mountain upon the lines of people,
what remains of their bodies? Who discovers the limbs, who the bones?

260 Each body of the crowd, rubbed out, disappears
in the manner of the soul. Meanwhile the household, unconcerned,
is now washing the plates, and with distended cheek stirs up the hearth-
      fire and makes a clatter
with greasy flesh-scrapers and arranges the hand towels with the full
      oil flask.
These various chores are being done in a hurry by the slave-boys, but
      he

265 now sits on river's bank and, newcomer as he is, fears
the morose ferryman;* he neither hopes for the alder-wood raft of the
muddy whirlpool, nor does the wretch have a half-cent to offer in his
      mouth.*
      "Have a look now at the other various dangers of night-time:
what a distance there is to the high roof-tops from which jug-fragment

270 bashes my skull, whenever from windows cracked and fractured
jars fall—with what weight they strike and
scar the pavement! You can be considered lazy
and unmindful of sudden accident if you venture out to dinner
without a will. As far as that goes, there are just as many chances for
      disaster as the

275 unsleeping windows that are open as you pass underneath.
Therefore you'd better hope and bear with you a sorry prayer:
that they be satisfied merely to pour out broad basins.
Drunk and belligerent, he who by chance has beaten nobody up,
pays the penalty; he suffers throughout the night as though he were

280 the son of Peleus mourning his friend.* He lies on his face, then soon
      on his back:
not otherwise therefore will he be able to sleep; for certain people
a fight brings on sleep. But however bold (given his age)
and however fevered with strong wine, he's wary of *this* man whom a
      crimson cloak
orders be avoided, and an extremely long row of companions,

285 not to mention abundant torch-flames and brass lamp.
Me he despises, whom the moon usually escorts or the tiny light
of a candle (the wick of which I eke out and conserve).

contemnit. miserae cognosce prohoemia rixae,
si rixa est, ubi tu pulsas, ego uapulo tantum.
stat contra starique iubet. parere necesse est;   290
nam quid agas, cum te furiosus cogat et idem
fortior? 'unde uenis' exclamat, 'cuius aceto,
cuius conche tumes? quis tecum sectile porrum
sutor et elixi ueruecis labra comedit?
nil mihi respondes? aut dic aut accipe calcem.   295
ede ubi consistas: in qua te quaero proseucha?'
dicere si temptes aliquid tacitusue recedas,
tantumdem est: feriunt pariter, uadimonia deinde
irati faciunt. libertas pauperis haec est:
pulsatus rogat et pugnis concisus adorat   300
ut liceat paucis cum dentibus inde reuerti.
nec tamen haec tantum metuas; nam qui spoliet te
non derit clausis domibus postquam omnis ubique
fixa catenatae siluit compago tabernae.
interdum et ferro subitus grassator agit rem: 305
armato quotiens tutae custode tenentur
et Pomptina palus et Gallinaria pinus,
sic inde huc omnes tamquam ad uiuaria currunt.
qua fornace graues, qua non incude catenae?
maximus in uinclis ferri modus, ut timeas ne   310
uomer deficiat, ne marra et sarcula desint.
felices proauorum atauos, felicia dicas
saecula quae quondam sub regibus atque tribunis
uiderunt uno contentam carcere Romam.
    "his alias poteram et pluris subnectere causas,   315
sed iumenta uocant et sol inclinat. eundum est;
nam mihi commota iamdudum mulio uirga

Recognize the prelude to the miserable fight,
if it's a 'fight' when you hammer away and only I am beaten.
290   He stands opposite me and orders me to stand still. To obey is necessary;
for what are you supposed to do when a lunatic compels you, and one
who's at the same time stronger? 'Where are you coming from?' he
            yells, 'With whose acid-wine,
with whose string-beans are you bloated? What shoemaker gobbled up
with you chopped leeks and the lips of a boiled goat?
295   You don't answer me? Either talk or get a heel-kick.
Tell me, where's your beggar's hang-out? In what synagogue do I look
            for you?'
If you try to say something or if you silently withdraw,
it amounts to the same thing: they beat you up either way; and then,
            they
take you to court fuming. This is the poor man's freedom:
300   beaten to a pulp he asks, and sliced up by fists he begs,
to be allowed to leave there with a few teeth.
Nor, moreover, should you fear these things only; for he who'll rip you
            off
in shut-up houses won't be absent, after every latch everywhere
of a chained-up shop has become silent.
305   Sometimes a mugger does the job suddenly with dagger-steel:
whenever both Pontine swamp*
and Gallinarian pine-grove* are held safe by armed guard,
from there to here they all run as though to a refuge.
In what furnace, on what anvil is there not heavy chain-production?
310   The greatest measure of iron is for fetters, so that you fear lest
plow-share be lost, lest hoe and rake be absent.
You would say that the ancestors of our great-grandfathers were happy,
and you would call happy the ages that formerly (under kings and
            tribunes)
saw a Rome content with just one jailhouse.
315   "To these I could connect many other reasons as well,
but the oxen call and the sun is sinking. I have to get going,
as for some time now the mule-driver has been motioning to me and
            shaking

adnuit. ergo uale nostri memor, et quotiens te
Roma tuo refici properantem reddet Aquino,
me quoque ad Heluinam Cererem uestramque Dianam   320
conuerte a Cumis. saturarum ego, ni pudet illas,
auditor gelidos ueniam caligatus in agros."

his stick. Farewell therefore—remember me, and whenever Rome
returns you to your Aquinum* as you're hastening to repose,
320   divert me as well to Helvine Ceres* and your Diana
from Cumae.* I'll come booted through the frigid fields
as listener to your satires, unless that embarrasses them!"

JUVENAL, *SATIRE* 6

credo Pudicitiam Saturno rege moratam
in terris uisamque diu, cum frigida paruas
praeberet spelunca domos ignemque Laremque
et pecus et dominos communi clauderet umbra,
siluestrem montana torum cum sterneret uxor   5
frondibus et culmo uicinarumque ferarum
pellibus, haut similis tibi, Cynthia, nec tibi, cuius
turbauit nitidos extinctus passer ocellos,
sed potanda ferens infantibus ubera magnis
et saepe horridior glandem ructante marito.   10
quippe aliter tunc orbe nouo caeloque recenti
uiuebant homines, qui rupto robore nati
compositiue luto nullos habuere parentes.
multa Pudicitiae ueteris uestigia forsan
aut aliqua exstiterint et sub Ioue, sed Ioue nondum   15
barbato, nondum Graecis iurare paratis
per caput alterius, cum furem nemo timeret
caulibus ac pomis et aperto uiueret horto.
paulatim deinde ad superos Astraea recessit
hac comite, atque duae pariter fugere sorores.   20
anticum et uetus est alienum, Postume, lectum
concutere atque sacri genium contemnere fulcri.
omne aliud crimen mox ferrea protulit aetas:
uiderunt primos argentea saecula moechos.
conuentum tamen et pactum et sponsalia nostra   25
tempestate paras iamque a tonsore magistro
pecteris et digito pignus fortasse dedisti.
certe sanus eras. uxorem, Postume, ducis?
dic qua Tisiphone, quibus exagitere colubris.
ferre potes dominam saluis tot restibus ullam,   30
cum pateant altae caligantesque fenestrae,

JUVENAL, *SATIRE* 6

(Satire's Woman)

I believe that Chastity lingered during Saturn's reign,*
and was seen for a long time in the lands when a cold cave
offered small houses and covered the hearth-fire and the Lar*
and both flock and masters with a common shade,

5   when mountain-wife* spread out woodsy bed
with leaves, thatch, and neighboring beasts'
hides, hardly similar to *you*, Cynthia*, nor to *you*, whose
shining little eyes dead sparrow disturbed*—
but rather bearing teats to be drunk by huge babes,

10   and often more hairy than her acorn-burping* husband.
To be sure, when the world was new and the sky was fresh,
people lived differently then who, born of shattered oak-tree
or fashioned from mud,* had no parents.
Perhaps many, or *some*, vestiges of old Chastity

15   existed even under Jove, but under a Jove not yet
bearded, with the Greeks not yet prepared to give oath
on another's head, when nobody feared a thief
of his cabbage and apples and one lived with open garden.
Then, gradually, Astraea* receded to the gods above

20   with her as companion, and the two sisters* fled together.
It's an old and well-established thing, Postumus,*
to shake another's bed and to hold in contempt the guardian spirit of
       sacred bed-post.
Soon the Iron Age* brought forth another crime;
the Silver Century* saw the first adulterers.

25   Nevertheless *you* are putting together an agreement, pact, and
betrothal in *our* times, and already by master-barber
you're being combed, and perhaps you've put the binding ring on her
       finger?
Certainly you *were* sane. Postumus, are *you* taking a wife?
Tell me, by what Tisiphone,* by what snakes are you being driven
       mad?

30   Can you bear any dominatrix when so many nooses are ready,
when high and dizzying windows lie open,

cum tibi uicinum se praebeat Aemilius pons?
aut si de multis nullus placet exitus, illud
nonne putas melius, quod tecum pusio dormit?
pusio, qui noctu non litigat, exigit a te   35
nulla iacens illic munuscula, nec queritur quod
et lateri parcas nec quantum iussit anheles.
　　　sed placet Vrsidio lex Iulia: tollere dulcem
cogitat heredem, cariturus turture magno
mullorumque iubis et captatore macello.   40
quid fieri non posse putes, si iungitur ulla
Vrsidio? si moechorum notissimus olim
stulta maritali iam porrigit ora capistro,
quem totiens texit perituri cista Latini?
quid quod et antiquis uxor de moribus illi   45
quaeritur? o medici, nimiam pertundite uenam.
delicias hominis! Tarpeium limen adora
pronus et auratrum Iunoni caede iuuencam,
si tibi contigerit capitis matrona pudici.
paucae adeo Cereris uittas contingere dignae,   50
quarum non timeat pater oscula. necte coronam
postibus et densos per limina tende corymbos.
unus Hiberinae uir sufficit? ocius illud
extorquebis, ut haec oculo contenta sit uno.
magna tamen fama est cuiusdam rure paterno   55
uiuentis. uiuat Gabiis ut uixit in agro,
uiuat Fidenis, et agello cedo paterno.
quis tamen adfirmat nil actum in montibus aut in
speluncis? adeo senuerunt Iuppiter et Mars?
　　　porticibusne tibi monstratur femina uoto   60
digna tuo? cuneis an habent spectacula totis
quod securus ames quodque inde excerpere possis?
chironomon Ledam molli saltante Bathyllo
Tuccia uesicae non imperat, Apula gannit,

when the nearby Aemilian bridge* offers itself to you?
Or, if no escape from so many pleases you,
don't you think *that* option better: that boy-toy sleep with you?
35   A boy-toy, who doesn't argue in the night, doesn't force from you
as he lies there small gifts; he does not complain because
you are sparing your effort and are not panting as much as he demands.
    Yet the Julian Law* pleases Ursidius:* to raise a sweet
heir is his plan, yet he'll lack large turtle-dove
40   and mullets' beards and the market-provisions of legacy-hunters.*
What do you think can't happen, if any woman is being joined
to *Ursidius*? If the one-time best known of adulterers
now offers his stupid face to the marriage-halter—
he, whom the box of Latinus, about to perish, so often concealed?*
45   What of the fact that a wife of out-dated character is being sought for
            him?
Physicians, puncture his excessively swollen vein!*
Delightful example of man-kind! Adorn the Tarpeian threshold*
as you throw yourself face-down, and slaughter a gilded calf for Juno,*
if a "lady" of unpolluted head befalls you.
50   Few, for that matter, are worthy to touch Ceres' head-bands,*
whose kisses their father would not fear. Tie a wreath
to your door-posts and stretch thick ivy-clusters across the thresholds!
One man is enough for Hiberina?* More quickly you'll extract *this*:
that this woman be content with one eye.
55   Great, however, is the repute of she who lives on paternal farm.
Let her live at Gabii* as she lived in the field;
let her live at Fidenae,* and I concede the validity of "paternal plot."
Just the same, who can confirm that nothing was ever done in the
            mountains
or in caves?* Have Jupiter* and Mars* aged to such an extent?
60   Is there a female in the galleries you can point out
worthy of your vow? Or do the public shows, in all their seats, have
that which you can love securely and which you could pick out from
            there?
With tender Bathyllus dancing the role of gyrating Leda,*
Tuccia doesn't control her gash's flow; Apula moans,*

sicut in amplexu, subito et miserabile longum.   65
attendit Thymele: Thymele tunc rustica discit.
ast aliae, quotiens aulaea recondita cessant,
et uacuo clusoque sonant fora sola theatro,
atque a plebeis longe Megalesia, tristes
personam thyrsumque tenent et subligar Acci.   70
Vrbicus exodio risum mouet Atellanae
gestibus Autonoes, hunc diligit Aelia pauper.
soluitur his magno comoedi fibula, sunt quae
Chrysogonum cantare uetent, Hispulla tragoedo
gaudet: an expectas ut Quintilianus ametur?   75
accipis uxorem de qua citharoedus Echion
aut Glaphyrus fiat pater Ambrosiusque choraules.
longa per angustos figamus pulpita uicos,
ornentur postes et grandi ianua lauro,
ut testudineo tibi, Lentule, conopeo   80
nobilis Euryalum murmillonem exprimat infans.
nupta senatori comitata est Eppia ludum
ad Pharon et Nilum famosaque moenia Lagi
prodigia et mores urbis damnante Canopo.
inmemor illa domus et coniugis atque sororis   85
nil patriae indulsit, plorantisque improba natos
utque magis stupeas ludos Paridemque reliquit.
sed quamquam in magnis opibus plumaque paterna
et segmentatis dormisset paruula cunis,
contempsit pelagus; famam contempserat olim,   90
cuius apud molles minima est iactura cathedras.
Tyrrhenos igitur fluctus lateque sonantem
pertulit Ionium constanti pectore, quamuis
mutandum totiens esset mare. iusta pericli
si ratio est et honesta, timent pauidoque gelantur   95
pectore nec tremulis possunt insistere plantis:
fortem animum praestant rebus quas turpiter audent.

65   suddenly and pathetically and long, as though in sexual embrace.
         Thymele's attentive: then "country-girl" Thymele learns.*
         Yet others, whenever stored stage-curtains are quiet,
         and the Fora alone sound (the theater empty and closed),
         and when the Megalesians* are far from the People's Games*—sad
70   they handle the mask, wand and loin-cloth of Accius.*
         Urbicus* compels laughter by his performances of the Atellan farce*
         of Autonoe;* penniless Aelia* cherishes this man.
         A comic-actor's dick-pin is loosened for these women for a great price;*
             there are those
         who prevent Chrysogonus* from singing. Hispulla* in tragic-actor
75   rejoices—or do you expect Quintilian to be loved?*
         You'll get a wife by whom the harp-plucker Echion*
         might become a father, or the flute-blowers Glaphyrus* and Ambrosius.*
         Let's plant long platforms along the narrow streets;
         let door-posts and gates be decorated with massive laurel-wreaths,
80   so that, Lentulus,* in his tortoise-rimmed cradle,
         your "noble child," might reveal for you the facial features of Euryalus
             the gladiator.*
         Wedded to a senator, Eppia* accompanied a gladiator-troop
         to Pharos,* the Nile and the famed walls of Lagus*
         (with even Canopus* condemning the unnatural character of the city).
85   She, unmindful of house, husband, and sister,
         conceded nothing to her homeland; perverse, she abandoned her crying
             children
         and, something that will astonish you even more, she left the games
             and Paris.*
         But although she had slept in great wealth, paternal comfort
         and finely quilted cradle as a little girl,
90   she disdained the sea; she had formerly disdained her reputation
         (the loss of which is most slight among posh armchairs).
         She withstood, then, Tyrrhian waves and the wide-sounding
         Ionian sea with firm heart, even though
         the sea-crossings were by necessity so frequent.
95   If the reason for a hazard is just and honest, they are fearful and freeze up
         with chilled heart; nor can they stand on shaking feet.
         Yet they show brave spirit in matters that they dare in disgrace.

si iubeat coniunx, durum est conscendere nauem,
tunc sentina grauis, tunc summus uertitur aer:
quae moechum sequitur, stomacho ualet. illa maritum   100
conuomit, haec inter nautas et prandet et errat
per puppem et duros gaudet tractare rudentis.
qua tamen exarsit forma, qua capta iuuenta
Eppia? quid uidit propter quod ludia dici
sustinuit? nam Sergiolus iam radere guttur   105
coeperat et secto requiem sperare lacerto;
praeterea multa in facie deformia, sicut
attritus galea mediisque in naribus ingens
gibbus et acre malum semper stillantis ocelli.
sed gladiator erat. facit hoc illos Hyacinthos;   110
hoc pueris patriaeque, hoc praetulit illa sorori
atque uiro. ferrum est quod amant. hic Sergius idem
accepta rude coepisset Veiiento uideri.
    quid priuata domus, quid fecerit Eppia, curas?
respice riuales diuorum, Claudius audi   115
quae tulerit. dormire uirum cum senserat uxor,
sumere nocturnos meretrix Augusta cucullos*   118
ausa Palatino et tegetem praeferre cubili*   117
linquebat comite ancilla non amplius una.
sed nigrum flauo crinem abscondente galero   120
intrauit calidum ueteri centone lupanar
et cellam uacuam atque suam; tunc nuda papillis
prostitit auratis titulum mentita Lyciscae
ostenditque tuum, generose Britannice, uentrem.
excepit blanda intrantis atque aera poposcit.   125
[continueque iacens cunctorum absorbuit ictus.]*
mox lenone suas iam dimittente puellas
tristis abit, et quod potuit tamen ultima cellam

It's rough to climb aboard a ship if a husband so asks:
then bilge-water is nasty, then the air above spins about—
100   she who's following her adulterer is strong of stomach. *That* one
pukes all over her husband; *this* one both lunches among the sailors
            and wanders
around the deck; plus she rejoices in tugging rough ropes.
By what beauty, moreover, did Eppia flare up, captured by what youth?
What did she see on account of which she endured to be called "game-
            girl?"
105   For "dear Sergius" had already begun to shave his neck
and to hope for a requiem with sliced off arm;
further, there were many unsightly lesions on his face, as though
it was rubbed away by a helmet, and in the middle of his nose a massive
wart, and a vigorous, foul fluid from constantly dripping eye.
110   But he was a gladiator. *This* makes them Hyacinthuses.*
This she preferred to sons and homeland, *this* to sister
and husband. It is sword-steel that they love. This same Sergius,
his staff of discharge accepted, would have begun to seem a Veiento.*
       Do you care what a private household did, what Eppia* did?
115   Look at the rivals of the gods; hear what things Claudius*
withstood! When his wife had perceived that her husband was sleeping,
118   this August hooker dared to take up night-time cowls
117   and to prefer to the Palatine* marriage-bed a whore-mat,
       and she would leave with no more than one maid-servant as her
            companion.
120   But with a blond wig hiding her black mane
she entered the whorehouse warm with long-used quilt
and an empty cell belonging to her alone. Then naked, with gold-tipped tits
she stood forth and displayed the lying advertisement "Wolf-lady";*
and she flaunted, noble Britannicus,* your birth-belly.
125   She coaxingly welcomed those entering and asked for bronze coin.
And, lying there continually, she absorbed the thrusts of all.
Soon, the pimp now dismissing his girls,
she left sadly; and moreover, after remaining as long as she could, her
            cell

clausit, adhuc ardens rigidae tentigine uoluae,
et lassata uiris necdum satiata recessit,   130
obscurisque genis turpis fumoque lucernae
foeda lupanaris tulit ad puluinar odorem.
hippomanes carmenque loquar coctumque uenenum
priuignoque datum? faciunt grauiora coactae
imperio sexus summumque libidine peccant.   135
    "optima sed quare Caesennia teste marito?"
bis quingena dedit. tanti uocat ille pudicam,
nec pharetris Veneris macer est aut lampade feruet:
inde faces ardent, ueniunt a dote sagittae.
libertas emitur. coram licet innuat atque   140
rescribat: uidua est, locuples quae nupsit auaro.
    "cur desiderio Bibulae Sertorius ardet?"
si uerum excutias, facies non uxor amatur.
tres rugae subeant et se cutis arida laxet,
fiant obscuri dentes oculique minores,   145
"collige sarcinulas" dicet libertus "et exi.
iam grauis es nobis et saepe emungeris. exi
ocius et propera. sicco uenit altera naso."
interea calet et regnat poscitque maritum
pastores et ouem Canusinam ulmosque Falernas—   150
quantulum in hoc!—pueros omnes, ergastula tota,
quodque domi non est, sed habet uicinus, ematur.
mense quidem brumae, cum iam mercator Iason
clausus et armatis obstat casa candida nautis,
grandia tolluntur crystallina, maxima rursus   155
murrina, deinde adamas notissimus et Beronices
in digito factus pretiosior. hunc dedit olim
barbarus incestae dedit hunc Agrippa sorori,
obseruant ubi festa mero pede sabbata reges
et uetus indulget senibus clementia porcis.   160

she closed, still burning with swollen cunt's horniness.
130   And she departed, worked over by men yet still not satisfied;
and foul with grimy cheeks and filthy with lamp's smoke
she carried whorehouse's stink to the state couch.
Should I speak of love-potions, chants, and cooked-up poison
given to a stepson? More grievous things they do compelled
135   by their sex's mandate, and they sin most of all out of lust.
        "But why is Caesennia,* by her own husband's testimony, the best?"
She gave him twice five-hundred. At such a price he calls her chaste.
He's not thin from the quiver of Venus; nor lit by her lamp does he
        burn—
thence the torches burn: the arrows come from her dowry.
140   Freedom is bought. Openly it's permitted that she give a nod and
write return love-letters; the rich woman who marries a greedy man is
        unmarried.
        "Why does Sertorius* burn with desire for Bibula?"*
If you shake out the truth, what's loved is the face, not the wife.
Let three wrinkles spring up and dry skin relax;
145   let her teeth become dark and her eyes smaller:
"Collect your bags," a freedman will say, "and get out!*
Now you're a burden to us and you often blow snot. Get out
quick and hurry up! Another's coming with a dry nose."
Meanwhile she's hot favorite and reigns supreme and asks her husband
150   for shepherds (and Canusian sheep*) and Falernian grapevines*—
how little there is in this!—she asks for all the boys, whole workhouses,
and whatever's not at home (but if a neighbor has it) must be purchased.
Indeed, in the month of winter-cold,* when now the salesman Jason*
is shut in and a white stall* obstructs his armed sailors,
155   massive crystal pieces are taken away, then the most massive
of fluorspar, then a most well-known diamond*—
one made more pricy by Berenice's finger.* Once a barbarian* gave
        this
to incest-girl; that is to say Agrippa* gave it to his sister,
where bare-footed "kings" observe festival sabbaths
160   and long-standing clemency indulges pigs into their old age.

"nullane de tantis gregibus tibi digna uidetur?"
sit formonsa, decens, diues, fecunda, uetustos
porticibus disponat auos, intactior omni
crinibus effusis bellum dirimente Sabina,
rara auis in terris nigroque simillima cycno,   165
quis feret uxorem cui constant omnia? malo,
malo Venustinam quam te, Cornelia, mater
Gracchorum, si cum magnis uirtutibus adfers
grande supercilium et numeras in dote triumphos.
tolle tuum, precor, Hannibalem uictumque Syphacem   170
in castris et cum tota Carthagine migra.
"parce, precor, Paean, et tu, dea, pone sagittas;
nil pueri faciunt, ipsam configite matrem"
Amphion clamat, sed Paean contrahit arcum.
extulit ergo greges natorum ipsumque parentem,   175
dum sibi nobilior Latonae gente uidetur
atque eadem scrofa Niobe fecundior alba.
quae tanti grauitas, quae forma, ut se tibi semper
inputet? huius enim rari summique uoluptas
nulla boni, quotiens animo corrupta superbo   180
plus aloes quam mellis habet. quis deditus autem
usque adeo est, ut non illam quam laudibus effert
horreat inque diem septenis oderit horis?
    quaedam parua quidem, sed non toleranda maritis.
nam quid rancidius quam quod se non putat ulla   185
formosam nisi quae de Tusca Graecula facta est,
de Sulmonensi mera Cecropis? omnia Graece:
[cum sit turpe magis nostris nescire Latine.]*
hoc sermone pauent, hoc iram, gaudia, curas,
hoc cuncta effundunt animi secreta. quid ultra?   190
concumbunt Graece. dones tamen ista puellis,
tune etiam, quam sextus et octagensimus annus
pulsat, adhuc Graece? non est hic sermo pudicus

"Does no one, from such great flocks, seem to you worthy?"
Let her be shapely, seemly, rich, and fertile; ancient
ancestors let her line up in the halls; let her be more untouched
than every war-breaking Sabine with hair let loose,*
165   a rare bird in the lands, most like a black swan—
who could bear a wife in whom all qualities exist? I prefer
and would rather have Venustina* than you, Cornelia,* mother
of the Gracchi,* if you bring along with your great virtues
a massive arrogance and count in your dowry triumphal processions.
170   Take away, I pray, your Hannibal* and Syphax* conquered
in camp, and get out of here with all of Carthage.*
"I pray you, Paean,* be sparing, and you, goddess, set aside your arrows!*
The children did nothing; transfix the mother herself!"*
So yelled Amphion,* yet Paean drew his bow.
175   He took therefore the herds of offspring as well as the parent herself,
as Niobe* seemed to herself more noble than Latona's lineage*
and likewise more fertile than the white sow.*
What dignity, what beauty, is of so great value that it should always
be reckoned a fault against you? For the pleasure of this rarity and
        greatness
180   is no good whenever a debased woman with haughty attitude
possesses more bitter aloe than honey. Moreover, who is dedicated
to such a degree that, her whom he takes out in public full of praise,
he does not shudder at and hate for seven hours of the day?
        Some things are indeed petty, yet should not be tolerated by husbands.
185   For what is more despicable than the fact that no woman thinks herself
beautiful unless she has become a little Greek from a Tuscan,*
from pure child of Sulmo* to one of Cecrops?* Everything in Greek—
although it's even more base for our girls not to know Latin.
In this language they express their fears; in this they pour out their
        anger, joys, cares;
190   in this all the secrets of their soul. What else?
They screw in Greek. Nevertheless you might grant those faults to mere
        girls,
but even *you*, whom an eighty-sixth year
is battering, still carry on in Greek? This type of speech is not clean
in uetula. quotiens lasciuum interuenit illud

ζωὴ καὶ ψυχή, modo sub lodice relictis   195
uteris in turba. quod enim non excitet inguen
uox blanda et nequam? digitos habet. ut tamen omnes
subsidant pinnae, dicas haec mollius Haemo
quamquam et Carpophoro, facies tua conputat annos.
    si tibi legitimis pactam iunctamque tabellis   200
non es amaturus, ducendi nulla uidetur
causa, nec est quare cenam et mustacea perdas
labente officio crudis donanda, nec illud
quod prima pro nocte datur, cum lance beata
Dacicus et scripto radiat Germanicus auro.   205
si tibi simplicitas uxoria, deditus uni
est animus, summitte caput ceruice parata
ferre iugum. nullam inuenies quae parcat amanti.
ardeat ipsa licet, tormentis gaudet amantis
et spoliis; igitur longe minus utilis illi   210
uxor, quisquis erit bonus optandusque maritus.
nil umquam inuita donabis coniuge, uendes
hac obstante nihil, nihil haec si nolet emetur.
haec dabit affectus: ille excludatur amicus
iam senior, cuius barbam tua ianua uidit.   215
testandi cum sit lenonibus atque lanistis
libertas et iuris idem contingat harenae,
non unus tibi riualis dictabitur heres.
"pone crucem seruo." "meruit quo crimine seruus
supplicium? quis testis adest? quis detulit? audi;   220
nulla umquam de morte hominis cunctatio longa est."
"o demens, ita seruus homo est? nil fecerit, esto:

in an old hag. Whenever that lascivious phrase is interjected,

195   "life and soul"*—what's just been left under the bed-sheet

you are using in public company. For what prick doesn't

a flattering and good-for-nothing voice excite? It has fingers. However,

     so that all

your "feathered arrows" droop, even though you say these things more

     seductively than Haemus*

or even Carpophorus,* your face numbers up your years.

200   If you're not destined to love the one bonded to you by law

and joined to you by document, there seems to be no cause to marry;

nor is there reason for you to waste a wedding-feast and must-cakes

that have to be given to peptic guests when the ceremony's ending, nor

     that

which is given as first night's reward, when on well-endowed platter

205   Dacian and German shine on inscribed gold coin.*

If you have that uncomplicated urge for a wife, and devoted to one

     woman

is your mind, submit your head with neck ready

to bear the yoke. You'll find no woman who spares her lover.

Granted that she herself might burn with passion, she still rejoices in

     her lover's torments

210   and losses. Therefore far less useful to him is

a wife, whoever will be a good husband, the kind one should wish for.

You'll never give anything as a gift with your wife unwilling; you'll

     sell

nothing with her in your way; nothing will be bought if she doesn't

     want it so.

She will define your feelings: that friend is to be shut outside,

215   now rather old, whose youthful beard your door saw.

While for pimps and fighting coaches there's freedom of drawing up a

     will,

and the same right befalls those of the arena,

dictated to you will be not just one rival as heir.

"Crucify the slave!" "By what crime did the slave earn

220   punishment? Who's at hand as witness? Who accused him? Hold a

     hearing!

No postponement is ever too lengthy concerning a person's death."

"You idiot! So a slave is a person? Suppose he's done nothing; so be it:

hoc uolo, sic iubeo, sit pro ratione uoluntas."
imperat ergo uiro. sed mox haec regna relinquit
permutatque domos et flammea conterit; inde   225
auolat et spreti repetit uestigia lecti.
ornatas paulo ante fores, pendentia linquit
uela domus et adhuc uirides in limine ramos.
sic crescit numerus, sic fiunt octo mariti
quinque per autumnos, titulo res digna sepulcri.   230
     desperanda tibi salua concordia socru.
illa docet spoliis nudi gaudere mariti,
illa docet missis a corruptore tabellis
nil rude nec simplex rescribere, decipit illa
custodes aut aere domat. tum corpore sano   235
aduocat Archigenen onerosaque pallia iactat.
abditus interea latet et secretus adulter
inpatiensque morae silet et praeputia ducit.
scilicet expectas ut tradat mater honestos
atque alios mores quam quos habet? utile porro   240
filiolam turpi uetulae producere turpem.
     nulla fere causa est in qua non femina litem
mouerit. accusat Manilia, si rea non est.
conponunt ipsae per se formantque libellos,
principium atque locos Celso dictare paratae.   245
     endromidas Tyrias et femineum ceroma
quis nescit, uel quis non uidit uulnera pali,
quem cauat adsiduis rudibus scutoque lacessit
atque omnis implet numeros dignissima prorsus
Florali matrona tuba, nisi si quid in illo   250
pectore plus agitat ueraeque paratur harenae?
quem praestare potest mulier galeata pudorem,

I want this; *I* so order; let *my* will be just cause!"
She is emperor, therefore, over her husband. But soon she leaves behind
 these domains,
225 and she completely changes houses and wears out her veils. From there
she flies back and seeks again her own traces on the scorned bed.
She abandons doors just before decorated, the hanging
awnings of the house and boughs still green on the threshold.
Thus the number grows; thus eight husbands come about
230 through a span of five autumns, a thing worthy of her epitaph.
  You'll have to forget about household harmony with your mother-
  in-law alive and well.
She teaches her to rejoice in the loot taken from stripped-bare husband;
she teaches her to respond to letters sent by adulterous lover
(and in no crude or uncomplex fashion); *she* deceives
235 guards or buys them off. Then, with healthy body,
she summons Archigenes* and tosses off the "heavy blankets."
Meanwhile the adulterer lies hidden and,
impatient of the delay, silently jacks off.
You don't suppose, do you, that the mother might pass on an upright
 character
240 different from that of herself? What's more, it's convenient
for a corrupt old hag to produce a corrupt "little daughter."
  Almost no legal case is there in which a woman didn't
start the litigation. Manilia* is accuser, if not defendant.
They themselves put together and set up the briefs by themselves,
245 prepared to dictate to Celsus* opening statement and precedents.
  Of jackets of Tyrian hue* and feminine wrestling oil*
who does not know? Or who has not seen the wounds of the post,
which she makes hollow* with continuous practice-sword and injures*
 with shield,
and she follows all the prescribed steps, although she's an utterly
 worthy
250 lady of Flora's horn*—unless there's something in that
breast of hers that more agitates her and she's preparing for the true
 arena?
What shame can a helmeted woman show,

quae fugit a sexu, uires amat? haec tamen ipsa
uir nollet fieri; nam quantula nostra uoluptas!
quale decus, rerum si coniugis auctio fiat,   255
balteus et manicae et cristae crurisque sinistri
dimidium tegimen! uel si diuersa mouebit
proelia, tu felix ocreas uendente puella.
hae sunt quae tenui sudant in cyclade, quarum
delicias et panniculus bombycinus urit.   260
aspice quo fremitu monstratos perferat ictus
et quanto galeae curuetur pondere, quanta
poplitibus sedeat quam denso fascia libro,
et ride positis scaphium cum sumitur armis.
dicite uos, neptes Lepidi caeciue Metelli   265
Gurgitis aut Fabii, quae ludia sumpserit umquam
hos habitus? quando ad palum gemat uxor Asyli?
     semper habet lites alternaque iurgia lectus
in quo nupta iacet; minimum dormitur in illo.
tum grauis illa uiro, tunc orba tigride peior,   270
cum simulat gemitus occulti conscia facti,
aut odit pueros aut ficta paelice plorat
uberibus semper lacrimis semperque paratis
in statione sua atque expectantibus illam,
quo iubeat manare modo. tu credis amorem,   275
tu tibi tunc, uruca, places fletumque labellis
exorbes, quae scripta et quot lecture tabellas
si tibi zelotypae retegantur scrinia moechae!
sed iacet in serui complexibus aut equitis. dic,
dic aliquem sodes hic, Quintiliane, colorem.   280
haeremus. dic ipsa. "olim conuenerat" inquit
"ut faceres tu quod uelles, nec non ego possem
indulgere mihi. clames licet et mare caelo
confundas, homo sum." nihil est audacius illis

one who flees from her sex, loves physical strength? This same one,
    however,
wouldn't wish to become a man; for so minuscule is our pleasure!
255   What pride, if there should happen an auction of your wife's things:
belt, fighting-gloves, plumes, and the guard of her left shin
(half-length covering)! Or if she instigates different types
of battles, lucky are you, with your girl selling her greaves.
These are the ones who sweat in thin gauze garment, whose
260   delicate nature even a silken wrap irritates.
Look with what a groan she carries out the blows she's shown,
and by what a weight of helmet she's bent over; see what a great
bandage* sits on her shins, how thick with tree-bark*—
and then laugh when, weapons set down, she takes up a piss-pot.
265   You tell us, grand-daughters of Lepidus* or of blind Metellus,*
or of Fabius Gurges,* what gladiator-girl ever took on
these appearances? When did the wife of Asylus* groan at a practice-
    post?
    The bed always has quarrels and back-and-forth altercations
in which a bride lies; one sleeps very little in it.
270   Then she's a burden to her husband, then worse than tigress bereft of
    kittens,
when, conscious of a secret misdeed, she feigns grief.
She either hates the slave-boys or cries about an invented mistress,
her tears always abundant and always ready
in their particular place, and waiting on her,
275   ready to drip in the fashion she commands. You think it love;
then you, crawling insect, are happy with yourself, and the weeping
    with your lips
you dry—you, who would read such writings and so many notes,
if the book-box of your "jealous" wife-adulteress were opened for you!
But she lies in the embraces of a slave or a knight. Marshal,
280   marshal some argument here if you will, Quintilian!*
I'm stuck. Marshal it yourself. "It had been long ago agreed," she says,
"that you do what you want, and so too that I be able
to gratify myself. You can shout and confuse the sea with the sky—
I'm human." There's nothing more brazen than those

deprensis: iram atque animos a crimine sumunt.   285
    unde haec monstra tamen uel quo de fonte requiris?
praestabat castas humilis fortuna Latinas
quondam, nec uitiis contingi parua sinebant
tecta labor somnique breues et uellere Tusco
uexatae duraeque manus ac proximus urbi   290
Hannibal et stantes Collina turre mariti.
nunc patimur longae pacis mala, saeuior armis
luxuria incubuit uictumque ulciscitur orbem.
nullum crimen abest facinusque libidinis ex quo
paupertas Romana perit. hinc fluxit ad istos   295
et Sybaris colles, hinc et Rhodos et Miletos
atque coronatum et petulans madidumque Tarentum.
prima peregrinos obscena pecunia mores
intulit, et turpi fregerunt saecula luxu
diuitiae molles. quid enim uenus ebria curat?   300
inguinis et capitis quae sint discrimina nescit
grandia quae mediis iam noctibus ostrea mordet,
cum perfusa mero spumant unguenta Falerno,
cum bibitur concha, cum iam uertigine tectum
ambulat et geminis exsurgit mensa lucernis.   305
i nunc et dubita qua sorbeat aera sanna
Maura, Pudicitiae ueterem cum praeterit aram,*   308
Tullia quid dicat, notae collactea Maurae.*   307
noctibus hic ponunt lecticas, micturiunt hic
effigiemque deae longis siphonibus implent   310
inque uices equitant ac Luna teste mouentur,
inde domos abeunt: tu calcas luce reuersa
coniugis urinam magnos uisurus amicos.
nota bonae secreta deae, cum tibia lumbos
incitat et cornu pariter uinoque feruntur   315
attonitae crinemque rotant ululantque Priapi
maenades. o quantus tunc illis mentibus ardor

285   when they're caught: they take their anger and courage from their
        misdeed.

       From where, however, or out of what source do you expect to find
         these monsters?

    Humble fortune set forth chaste Latin women

    once upon a time; nor did toil permit small roofs to be contaminated by
        vices,

    and brief periods of sleep, and hands hardened and worn out

290   by Tuscan fleece, and next to the city

    Hannibal* and husbands standing at the Colline tower.*

    Now we are suffering the evils of an extended peace—more savage
        than arms,

    luxury has lain upon us and avenges a conquered world.

    No misdeed and crime of lust is absent since the time when

295   Roman poverty perished. Hither has flowed to these

    hills Sybaris,* hither both Rhodes* and Miletus*

    and Tarentum,* garlanded and wanton and drunken.

    Obscene money first introduced foreign morals,

    and with base excess effeminate riches have shattered the centuries.

300   For what concerns has a drunken Venus?*

    She doesn't know the distinctions of head and prick

    who, now in the middle of the night, devours massive oysters,

    when unguents mixed with undiluted Falernian* foam up,

    when one drinks from shell-vessel, when now overhead the ceiling

305   moves round and the table rises up with double-vision's lamps.

    Go now and try to figure out why with a sneer Maura* sniffs the air,

308   when she goes past the long-standing altar of Chastity,*

307   what Tullia* says to her well-known sister Maura.*

    Nights, here they set down their litters; here they piss

310   and they fill the goddess' image with long jets

    and in turn they "ride-horse"; they move with the moon as witness;

    from there they leave for home. You, the daylight having returned,
        tread

    the urine of your wife as you are about to see your "great friends."

    Well-known are the secrets of the Good Goddess,* when flute excites
        loins

315   and equally by horn-music and by wine are carried away

    Priapus' Maenads,* frenzied, and they twirl their locks and scream.

    Then, oh what a passion there is in those minds

concubitus, quae uox saltante libidine, quantus
ille meri ueteris per crura madentia torrens!
lenonum ancillas posita Saufeia corona   320
prouocat et tollit pendentis praemia coxae,
ipsa Medullinae fluctum crisantis adorat:
palma inter dominas, uirtus natalibus aequa.
nil ibi per ludum simulabitur, omnia fient
ad uerum, quibus incendi iam frigidus aeuo   325
Laomedontiades et Nestoris hirnea possit.
tunc prurigo morae inpatiens, tum femina simplex,
ac pariter toto repetitus clamor ab antro
"iam fas est, admitte uiros." dormitat adulter,
illa iubet sumpto iuuenem properare cucullo;   330
si nihil est, seruis incurritur; abstuleris spem
seruorum, uenit et conductus aquarius; hic si
quaeritur et desunt homines, mora nulla per ipsam
quo minus inposito clunem summittat asello.
atque utinam ritus ueteres et publica saltem   335
his intacta malis agerentur sacra; sed omnes
nouerunt Mauri atque Indi quae psaltria penem
maiorem quam sunt duo Caesaris Anticatones
illuc, testiculi sibi conscius unde fugit mus,
intulerit, ubi uelari pictura iubetur   340
quaecumque alterius sexus imitata figuras.
et quis tunc hominum contemptor numinis, aut quis
simpuuium ridere Numae nigrumque catinum
et Vaticano fragiles de monte patellas
ausus erat? sed nunc ad quas non Clodius aras?   345
[audio quid ueteres olim moneatis amici,*
"pone seram, cohibe." sed quis custodiet ipsos*
custodes? cauta est et ab illis incipit uxor.]*
iamque eadem summis pariter minimisque libido,
nec melior silicem pedibus quae conterit atrum   350
quam quae longorum uehitur ceruice Syrorum.
    ut spectet ludos, conducit Ogulnia uestem,
conducit comites, sellam, ceruical, amicas,
nutricem et flauam cui det mandata puellam.

for screwing, what wailing, with their lust vaulting, what a great
torrent of seasoned wine down their dripping legs!
320   Garland set aside, Saufeia* challenges the slave-girls of pimps,
and she takes away the prizes for the "swaying buttocks."*
She herself adores the wavy motion of gyrating Medullina:*
victory palm's between the mistresses, virtue equal to birth.*
Nothing is simulated there in play; everything happens
325   for real, by which can be fired up the now age-frozen
son of Laomedon* and the hirneated organ of Nestor.*
Then the burning, impatient of the delay, then pure female,
all at once from the whole grotto is repeated the shout
"Now the time's right! Send in the men!" The adulterer is sleeping—
330   she commands a young man to hurry, having grabbed his cloak.
If there's nothing, there's an assault on the slaves; should you remove
        hope
of slaves, there comes even a hired water-boy. If this one
is sought and humans are absent, there's no delay on her part
in positioning her buttock beneath a donkey placed on top of her.
335   And would that long-standing rituals and at least public
holy-observances were carried out untouched by these evils; but all
know—Moors and Indians—which "cithara-girl" introduced a penis*
greater than are the two Anti-Catos of Caesar*
to that place, out of which a mouse flees, aware of its testicles,
340   the place where a representation is ordered veiled,
if it depicts the shapes of the other sex.
And who of mankind then was despiser of divinity, or who
had dared to poke fun at the bowl of Numa* and the black basin
and fragile dishes* from the Vatican mountain?*
345   But now, at which altars is there not a Clodius?*
I hear what you once advised, old friends:
"Put a lock on the door; enclose her." But who will guard
the guards themselves? She's shrewd, my wife, and she starts from
        them.
And now there is the same lust alike in the highest and the lowest;
350   nor is she better who wears out dark pavement with her feet
than she who is carried on the neck of tall Syrians.*
      In order to observe the games, Ogulnia* rents a dress;
she rents companions, a sedan-chair, a head-pillow, girlfriends,
a nurse, and a blond girl to whom she can give her orders.

haec tamen argenti superest quodcumque paterni   355
leuibus athletis et uasa nouissima donat.
multis res angusta domi, sed nulla pudorem
paupertatis habet nec se metitur ad illum
quem dedit haec posuitque modum. tamen utile quid sit
prospiciunt aliquando uiri, frigusque famemque   360
formica tandem quidam expauere magistra:
prodiga non sentit pereuntem femina censum.
ac uelut exhausta recidiuus pullulet arca
nummus et e pleno tollatur semper aceruo,
non umquam reputant quanti sibi gaudia constent.   365
     in quacumque domo uiuit luditque professus*   O 1
obscenum et tremula promittit et omnia dextra,*
inuenies omnis turpes similesque cinaedis.*
his uiolare cibos sacraeque adsistere mensae*
permittunt, et uasa iubent frangenda lauari*   O 5
cum colocyntha bibit uel cum barbata chelidon.*
purior ergo tuis laribus meliorque lanista,*
in cuius numero longe migrare iubetur*
Psyllus ab †Euhoplo.† quid quod nec retia turpi*
iunguntur tunicae, nec cella ponit eadem*   O 10
munimenta umeri †pulsatamque arma† tridentem*
qui nudus pugnare solet? pars ultima ludi*
accipit has animas aliusque in carcere neruos.*
sed tibi communem calicem facit uxor et illis*
cum quibus Albanum Surrentinumque recuset*   O 15
flaua ruinosi lupa degustare sepulchri.*
horum consiliis nubunt subitaeque recedunt,*
his languentum animum †seruant† et seria uitae,*
his clunem atque latus discunt uibrare magistris,*
quicquid praeterea scit qui docet. haud tamen illi*   O 20
semper habenda fides: oculos fuligine pascit*
distinctus croceis et reticulatus adulter.*
suspectus tibi sit, quanto uox mollior et quo*

355   This woman moreover, whatever is remaining of paternal silver,
even very new vessels, gives as a gift to smooth athletes.
For many, domestic resources are slim, yet no woman considers
the shame of her poverty; nor does she budget according to that limit
which this has given her and the end it's imposed. Nevertheless, what
        is useful

360   men sometimes see ahead of time, and both cold and hunger
they indeed dread, the ant as their model;*
wasteful woman does not perceive expiring savings.
And as though from exhausted treasure-box grew recurring coin,
and it were taken out of an ever-growing heap,

365   she does not ever re-calculate how much her joys add up to.

O 1*   In whatever house there lives and plays a teacher of
obscenity—and one promising all things with quivering right hand,
you'll find everyone base and exactly like sexual perverts.
The violation of food and the right to sit down at holy table to these

O 5   is allowed, and they order the washing of vessels that should be smashed
when "Gourd-face"* or when "Bearded-swallow"* has drunk.
Therefore more pure than your household gods, and better, is the place
        of the gladiator-trainer,
in whose collection "Lisper"* is ordered to get far away
from "Big-tool."* What of the fact that neither net-man to base

O 10   tunic-wearer is joined, nor in the same storage-room does he place his
arm-guards, weapons, and stabbing fork,
who is accustomed to fight nude? The most distant part of the gladiator
        troop
receives these souls, and a different type of fetter in jail.
But your wife makes you share the wine-glass with them—

O 15   them with whom Alban and even Surrentine wine*
blond hooker of abandoned grave-yard would refuse to partake.
By the counsels of these, women act as brides and suddenly leave;
to these they release their aching mind and life's serious concerns;
with these as instructors they learn to vibrate buttock and hips—

O 20   whatever else he who teaches knows. By no means, however,
should you always have faith in him: he grooms his eyes with charcoal,
distinguished by yellow clothes and hair-net—he the adulterer.
Let him be suspect to you, the more soft his voice and the

saepius in teneris haerebit dextera lumbis.*
hic erit in lecto fortissimus; exuit illic*   O 25
personam docili Thais saltata Triphallo.*
quem rides? aliis hunc mimum! sponsio fiat:*
purum te contendo uirum. contendo: fateris?*
an uocat ancillas tortoris pergula? noui*
consilia et ueteres quaecumque monetis amici,*   O 30
"pone seram, cohibe." sed quis custodiet ipsos*
custodes, qui nunc lasciuae furta puellae*
hac mercede silent? crimen commune tacetur.*
prospicit hoc prudens et ab illis incipit uxor.*   O 34
      sunt quas eunuchi inbelles ac mollia semper   366
oscula delectent et desperatio barbae
et quod abortiuo non est opus. illa uoluptas
summa tamen, quom iam calida matura iuuenta
inguina traduntur medicis, iam pectine nigro.   370
ergo expectatos ac iussos crescere primum
testiculos, postquam coeperunt esse bilibres,
tonsoris tantum damno rapit Heliodorus.
mangonum pueros uera ac miserabilis urit*   373 A
debilitas, follisque pudet cicerisque relicti.*   373 B
conspicuus longe cunctisque notabilis intrat
balnea nec dubie custodem uitis et horti   375
prouocat a domina factus spado. dormiat ille
cum domina, sed tu iam durum, Postume, iamque
tondendum eunucho Bromium committere noli.
      si gaudet cantu, nullius fibula durat
uocem uendentis praetoribus. organa semper   380
in manibus, densi radiant testudine tota
sardonyches, crispo numerantur pectine chordae
quo tener Hedymeles operas dedit: hunc tenet, hoc se
solatur gratoque indulget basia plectro.
quaedam de numero Lamiarum ac nominis Appi   385
et farre et uino Ianum Vestamque rogabat,
an Capitolinam deberet Pollio quercum

more often his right hand adheres to his slender hip-bones.

O 25   This man will be most robust in bed; there Thais,*
having danced, strips the mask from the expert "Triple-phallus."*
Whom are you fooling? This charade's for others! Let there be a wager:
I assert that you are pure man. I so assert: do you confess?
Or does the torturer's mat need to summon the slave-girls? I know

O 30   the counsels and whatever things you advise, old friends:
"Put a lock on the door; enclose her." But who will guard
the guards themselves, who now keep silent the secrets of the lascivious
            girl
with her as their payment? A crime in common is covered up.

O 34   Shrewd, a wife foresees this and she starts from them.

366   There are some women whom effeminate eunuchs and their soft
kisses always delight, and their hopelessness of a beard,*
and the fact that there's no need for abortion. That pleasure
is the highest, however, when, now mature with hot youth,

370   genitals are given over to the physicians, their pubic fringe now black.
Therefore the awaited (and first encouraged to grow)
testicles, after they've begun to be two pounds,
Heliodorus* snatches away (to only the barber's loss*).

373A   The boys of slave-traders a real and pathetic debility scars;
373B   they are ashamed of the sack and the remaining chick-pea.
Visible from far away and noticeable to all he enters

375   the baths, and no doubt vine and garden's guard*
he challenges—he who's been made a eunuch by his mistress. Let him
            sleep
with his mistress, but you, Postumus,* your now firm and now
shave-ready Bromius* do not entrust to a eunuch!
        If she delights in song, the dick-pin of no one remains fixed

380   who sells his voice to the praetors. Instruments always
are in her hands;* on the whole tortoise-shell sparkle thick
rings of sardonyx; the chords are struck with the vibrating quill
with which tender Hedymeles* gave performances. This she holds; with
            this
she consoles herself and she grants kisses to the pleasure-giving pick.

385   A certain woman of the number of Lamiae and Appius' name*
beseeched Janus* and Vesta* with meal and wine to see
whether or not Pollio* should hope for the Capitoline oak-crown*

sperare et fidibus promittere. quid faceret plus
aegrotante uiro, medicis quid tristibus erga
filiolum? stetit ante aram nec turpe putauit   390
pro cithara uelare caput dictataque uerba
pertulit, ut mos est, et aperta palluit agna.
dic mihi nunc, quaeso, dic, antiquissime diuom,
respondes his, Iane pater? magna otia caeli;
non est, quod uideo, non est quod agatur apud uos.   395
haec de comoedis te consulit, illa tragoedum
commendare uolet: uaricosus fiet haruspex.
    sed cantet potius quam totam peruolet urbem
audax et coetus possit quae ferre uirorum
cumque paludatis ducibus praesente marito   400
ipsa loqui recta facie siccisque mamillis.
haec eadem nouit quid toto fiat in orbe,
quid Seres, quid Thraces agant, secreta nouercae
et pueri, quis amet, quis diripiatur adulter;
dicet quis uiduam praegnatem fecerit et quo   405
mense, quibus uerbis concumbat quaeque, modis quot.
instantem regi Armenio Parthoque cometen
prima uidet, famam rumoresque illa recentis
excipit ad portas, quosdam facit; isse Niphaten
in populos magnoque illic cuncta arua teneri   410
diluuio, nutare urbes, subsidere terras,
quocumque in triuio, cuicumque est obuia, narrat.
nec tamen id uitium magis intolerabile quam quod
uicinos humiles rapere et concidere loris
†exortata† solet. nam si latratibus alti   415
rumpuntur somni, "fustes huc ocius" inquit
"adferte" atque illis dominum iubet ante feriri,
deinde canem. grauis occursu, taeterrima uultu
balnea nocte subit, conchas et castra moueri
nocte iubet, magno gaudet sudare tumultu,   420

and promise it to his lyre's strings. What more would she have done
were her husband ill, what, if the physicians were grim concerning
390   her tiny son? She stood before the altar and did not think it base
to veil her head on behalf of a lyre, and the dictated words
she carried through, as is the custom, and she grew pale as the lamb
        was opened.
Tell me now, I ask, tell, most ancient of the gods,
do you respond to these, father Janus? Heaven has lots of free time;
395   there's nothing, as far as I can see, there's nothing to be done among
        you.
This woman consults you about comedians; that one will wish
to commend a tragedian: the seer will grow varicose.*
    But let her sing rather than fly through the whole city
boldly, and be the type who can bear men's gatherings
400   and, when her husband is present with leaders in generals' cloaks,
she herself is able to converse with straight face and dried-up tits.
This same woman knows what's happening over the entire globe,
what the Chinese, what the Thracians are up to, the secrets of the
        stepmother
and the boy, who's in love, which adulterer is currently the rage.
405   She can say who made the widow pregnant and in what
month, with what words each woman screws, in how many positions.
The comet threatening the Armenian or Parthian king
she sees first; report and recent rumors she
receives at the gates; certain ones she makes up. That the Niphates*
410   has gone onto the populace and all the farmland there is held by massive
flood, that cities are tottering, lands sinking—
this she relates at whatever cross-road to whomever she meets.
Nor, however, is that vice more intolerable than the fact that
she is accustomed to seize and lacerate with whips her humble neighbors
415   if she's been roused from sleep. For if by barking her deep
slumbers are shattered, "Cudgels here quick," she says;
"bring them!" And with them she orders first the master beaten,
then the dog. Dreadful to meet, most hideous in aspect,
she goes down to the baths at night; her camp and perfume-shells
420   she orders to be moved at night; she rejoices to sweat in massive
        tumult,

cum lassata graui ceciderunt bracchia massa,
callidus et cristae digitos inpressit aliptes
ac summum dominae femur exclamare coegit.
conuiuae miseri interea somnoque fameque
urguentur. tandem illa uenit rubicundula, totum   425
oenophorum sitiens, plena quod tenditur urna
admotum pedibus, de quo sextarius alter
ducitur ante cibum rabidam facturus orexim,
dum redit et loto terram ferit intestino.
marmoribus riui properant, aurata Falernum   430
peluis olet; nam sic, tamquam alta in dolia longus
deciderit serpens, bibit et uomit. ergo maritus
nauseat atque oculis bilem substringit opertis.
    illa tamen grauior, quae cum discumbere coepit
laudat Vergilium, periturae ignoscit Elissae,   435
committit uates et comparat, inde Maronem
atque alia parte in trutina suspendit Homerum.
cedunt grammatici, uincuntur rhetores, omnis
turba tacet, nec causidicus nec praeco loquetur,
altera nec mulier: uerborum tanta cadit uis,   440
tot pariter pelues ac tintinnabula dicas
pulsari. iam nemo tubas, nemo aera fatiget:
una laboranti poterit succurrere Lunae.
inponit finem sapiens et rebus honestis;
nam quae docta nimis cupit et facunda uideri   445
crure tenus medio tunicas succingere debet,
caedere Siluano porcum, quadrante lauari.
non habeat matrona, tibi quae iuncta recumbit,
dicendi genus, aut curuum sermone rotato
torqueat enthymema, nec historias sciat omnes,   450
sed quaedam ex libris et non intellegat. odi
hanc ego quae repetit uoluitque Palaemonis artem
seruata semper lege et ratione loquendi
ignotosque mihi tenet antiquaria uersus
nec curanda uiris. opicae castiget amicae   455

when her arms, worn out by heavy barbell have fallen,
and the skilled masseur has dug his fingers into her clit
and forced the mistress' upper thigh to shout orgasm.
Meanwhile the wretched dinner-guests by both sleep and hunger
425   are tormented. Finally she arrives slightly blushed, thirsting
for that entire wine-skin which is stretched with full measure
and has been moved before her feet, out of which another sixth-measure
is drawn before food, destined to stimulate a rabid appetite,
until it returns and, intestine purged, hits the ground.
430   Rivers of vomit race over the marble tiles; of Falernian* the gold
basin reeks; for thus, just like a long snake that fell into
a deep barrel, she drinks and regurgitates. Thus her husband
is nauseous and with closed eyes he suppresses his bile.
      But that woman is worse yet who, when she's begun to recline at
      table,
435   praises Vergil,* forgives Elissa* destined to perish,
pits bards against each other and compares them; here Maro
she suspends,* and in the other part of the balance, Homer.*
Grammarians yield; rhetoricians are conquered; the entire
crowd is silent; neither lawyer nor herald can speak,
440   nor another woman: so great a force of words falls,
you would say that so many basins and bells all together
were being clashed. Now let no one wear out trumpets, no one bronze;
one woman shall be able to rescue the laboring moon.
The wise man imposes a limit even to honorable pursuits;
445   for she who desires to seem too learned and fluent
ought to gird up as far as mid-knee her tunics,*
slaughter a pig for Silvanus, take a bath for a quarter.*
Let not the lady to whom you're wedded, as she reclines,
possess a high-fashion of speaking, or, with twisted speech, hurl
450   a winding argument; nor let her know all the histories;
but there should be certain things from the books she does not know. I
      hate,
for my part, the woman who goes over and unrolls Palaemon's art,*
the law of grammar* always preserved, as well as proper manner of
      speaking,
and who, in out-dated fashion, imposes on me unknown verses—
455   verses of no concern to men. Let her correct a doltish girlfriend's

uerba: soloecismum liceat fecisse marito.
    nil non permittit mulier sibi, turpe putat nil,
cum uiridis gemmas collo circumdedit et cum
auribus extentis magnos commisit elenchos.
[intolerabilius nihil est quam femina diues.]*   460
interea foeda aspectu ridendaque multo
pane tumet facies aut pinguia Poppaeana
spirat et hinc miseri uiscantur labra mariti.
ad moechum lota ueniunt cute. quando uideri
uult formonsa domi? moechis foliata parantur,   465
his emitur quidquid graciles huc mittitis Indi.
tandem aperit uultum et tectoria prima reponit,
incipit agnosci, atque illo lacte fouetur
propter quod secum comites educit asellas
exul Hyperboreum si dimittatur ad axem.   470
sed quae mutatis inducitur atque fouetur
tot medicaminibus coctaeque siliginis offas
accipit et madidae, facies dicetur an ulcus?
    est pretium curae penitus cognoscere toto
quid faciant agitentque die. si nocte maritus   475
auersus iacuit, periit libraria, ponunt
cosmetae tunicas, tarde uenisse Liburnus
dicitur et poenas alieni pendere somni
cogitur, hic frangit ferulas, rubet ille flagello,
hic scutica; sunt quae tortoribus annua praestent.   480
uerberat atque obiter faciem linit, audit amicas
aut latum pictae uestis considerat aurum
et caedit, longi relegit transuersa diurni
et caedit, donec lassis caedentibus "exi"
intonet horrendum iam cognitione peracta.   485
praefectura domus Sicula non mitior aula.
nam si constituit solitoque decentius optat
ornari et properat iamque expectatur in hortis
aut apud Isiacae potius sacraria lenae,
disponit crinem laceratis ipsa capillis   490
nuda umeros Psecas infelix nudisque mamillis.

words: a husband should be permitted a slip of syntax.
          Nothing does a woman not allow herself, she thinks nothing base,
when she has placed around her neck green gems and when
she's entrusted massive pearls to her stretched-out ears.
460   Nothing is more intolerable than a wealthy woman.
Meanwhile, filthy in aspect and cause of much laughter
is her face as it swells with bread-paste or reeks with thick Poppaean
mask* (by which the lips of her wretched husband are made gooey).
They come to their adulterer with skin cleansed. When does she wish
465   to seem pretty at home? For adulterers face-oils* are prepared;
for these is purchased whatever you, slim Indians, send here.*
Finally she uncovers her face* and removes the first layers;
she begins to be recognized, and is caressed with that milk*
on account of which she leads she-ass companions* with her
470   if she's sent away as an exile to the Hyperborean pole.*
But that which is over-spread with changed layers and caressed
by so many medications and receives lumps of dough cooked-up
and moist—is it to be called a "face" or an ulcer?
          It's worth knowing specifically what, during the whole
475   day, they accomplish and carry on about. If at night her husband
has lain facing away from her, the wool-girl perishes, the
cosmeticians put off their tunics, Liburnian chair-carrier* is said
to have come late, and he's compelled to pay the penalty for another's
          sleep.
This man has sticks cracked on him; that one is made red with a thong,
480   this one with a whip; some women pay annual salaries to torturers.
She flogs, and while so doing daubs her face, listens to girlfriends
or considers the broad gold of an embroidered garment
and she beats, as she re-reads the breadth of the long day-report
and she beats, until, the beaters exhausted, "Get out!"
485   she thunders in a horrible shout, the inquisition now completed.
"Prefect" of home, she is no softer than the Sicilian court.*
For if she has decided, and desires to be fixed-up more nicely than
          usual
and she hastens and is now being waited for in the gardens
(or rather beside the shrine of Isis* the procuress),
490   with torn hair unlucky Psecas loses her locks*
nude-shouldered and with naked breasts.*

"altior hic quare cincinnus?" taurea punit
continuo flexi crimen facinusque capilli.
quid Psecas admisit? quaenam est hic culpa puellae,
si tibi displicuit nasus tuus? altera laeuum   495
extendit pectitque comas et uoluit in orbem.
est in consilio materna admotaque lanis
emerita quae cessat acu; sententia prima
huius erit, post hanc aetate atque arte minores
censebunt, tamquam famae discrimen agatur   500
aut animae: tanta est quaerendi cura decoris.
tot premit ordinibus, tot adhuc conpagibus altum
aedificat caput: Andromachen a fronte uidebis,
post minor est, credas aliam. cedo si breue parui
sortita est lateris spatium breuiorque uidetur   505
uirgine Pygmaea nullis adiuta coturnis
et leuis erecta consurgit ad oscula planta.
     nulla uiri cura interea nec mentio fiet
damnorum. uiuit tamquam uicina mariti,
hoc solo propior, quod amicos coniugis odit   510
et seruos, grauis est rationibus. ecce furentis
Bellonae matrisque deum chorus intrat et ingens
semiuir, obsceno facies reuerenda minori,
mollia qui rapta secuit genitalia testa
iam pridem, cui rauca cohors, cui tympana cedunt   515
plebeia et Phrygia uestitur bucca tiara.
grande sonat metuique iubet Septembris et austri
aduentum, nisi se centum lustrauerit ouis
et xerampelinas ueteres donauerit ipsi,
ut quidquid subiti et magni discriminis instat   520
in tunicas eat et totum semel expiet annum.
hibernum fracta glacie descendet in amnem,

"Why's this ringlet protruding?" Bull-whip punishes*
incessantly for curl's crime and lock's misdeed.
What did Psecas do wrong? Is it the girl's fault here,

495   if your own nose has displeased you? Another is on the left;
she draws out and combs the hair-strands and twists then into a circle.
In the council is a maternal maid, moved up to the wool department,
one who's earned her way out of hairdresser's pin. The first opinion
will be hers; after her those lesser in age and craft

500   will express their opinions, just as though a dilemma of reputation were
         being resolved
or of life: so great is the concern for seeking beauty.
With so many rows she presses her head; with so many levels she
builds it high: you'll see an Andromache* from the front;
from the rear she's smaller—you'd think it another person. Imagine if
         she's

505   been given the fate of short stature and she seems shorter
than a Pygmy maiden (aided by no elevator boots)
and she lightly rises up for kisses on stretched-out foot.
      No care has she meanwhile of her husband; nor will there be mention
of his losses. She lives as though she's her husband's neighbor,

510   nearer to him in this alone: that she hates her mate's friends
and slaves, and she's a burden to his finances. Behold!
The chorus of mad Bellona* and mother of the gods enters, and a massive
half-man, a countenance demanding the respect of a lesser obscenity,
one who, pot-sherd taken in hand, cut off his soft genitals

515   long ago, one to whom the raucous throng, to whom timbrels yield
and whose plebeian cheek is dressed in Phrygian tiara.
Greatly he intones and orders September's and the south-wind's
arrival to be feared, unless she shall have purged herself with a hundred
         eggs
and made a gift to him himself of some old clothes the color of dried
         leaves,

520   so that whatever sudden and great crisis is impending
may enter into the garments and simultaneously expiate the whole year.
The ice having been broken, she'll descend into the wintry river;

ter matutino Tiberi mergetur et ipsis
uerticibus timidum caput abluet, inde superbi
totum regis agrum nuda ac tremibunda cruentis　　　　525
erepet genibus; si candida iusserit Io,
ibit ad Aegypti finem calidaque petitas
a Meroe portabit aquas, ut spargat in aede
Isidis, antiquo quae proxima surgit ouili.
credit enim ipsius dominae se uoce moneri.　　　　530
en animam et mentem cum qua di nocte loquantur!
ergo hic praecipuum summumque meretur honorem
qui grege linigero circumdatus et grege caluo
plangentis populi currit derisor Anubis.
ille petit ueniam, quotiens non abstinet uxor　　　　535
concubitu sacris obseruandisque diebus
magnaque debetur uiolato poena cadurco
et mouisse caput uisa est argentea serpens;
illius lacrimae meditataque murmura praestant
ut ueniam culpae non abnuat ansere magno　　　　540
scilicet et tenui popano corruptus Osiris.
cum dedit ille locum, cophino fenoque relicto
arcanam Iudaea tremens mendicat in aurem,
interpres legum Solymarum et magna sacerdos
arboris ac summi fida internuntia caeli.　　　　545
implet et illa manum, sed parcius; aere minuto
qualiacumque uoles Iudaei somnia uendunt.
spondet amatorem tenerum uel diuitis orbi
testamentum ingens calidae pulmone columbae
tractato Armenius uel Commagenus haruspex;　　　　550
pectora pullorum rimabitur, exta catelli
interdum et pueri; faciet quod deferat ipse.
Chaldaeis sed maior erit fiducia: quidquid
dixerit astrologus, credent a fonte relatum
Hammonis, quoniam Delphis oracula cessant　　　　555
et genus humanum damnat caligo futuri.

she'll submerge herself three times in the morning Tiber and in the very

swirls she'll cleanse her frightened head; thence over the "Proud

525 King's" entire field,* naked and trembling, on bleeding

knees, she'll crawl. If gleaming Io* shall so have ordered,

she will go to the end of Egypt and from warm

Meroe* will carry the petitioned waters in order to sprinkle them in the shrine

of Isis, which rises up next to the ancient sheep-pen.

530 For she believes that she's being advised by the voice of the goddess herself.

Behold the soul and mind with which the gods speak at night!

Thus this one merits special and supreme honor

who, surrounded by linen-clad flock and bald-headed herd,*

runs along as Anubis, mocker of the bewailing populace.*

535 He seeks forgiveness, whenever a wife does not abstain

from sexual intercourse on sacred days and those that must be observed,

and a great penalty is due the violated bed-cover

and the silver serpent has been seen to have moved its head;*

the tears of *that* one and his thought-over whispers hold forth

540 that Osiris will not deny pardon from guilt

(to be sure, having been bribed by a large goose and thin pastry).

When he has made way, with basket and hay set aside,

trembling Jewess begs in her ear in secret,*

interpreter of Jerusalem's laws and great priestess

545 of the tree* and faithful liaison of highest heaven.

She too fills her hand, but more sparingly; for minuscule coin

the Jews sell whatever dream-prophesies you like.

A tender lover or childless rich man's

massive will an Armenian or Syrian seer will promise you,*

550 once he's looked over the lung of a still-warm dove;*

chickens' breasts he'll pry into, the guts of a puppy,*

sometimes too of a boy;* he will do something he can inform on himself.

But there will be greater trust in Chaldaeans:* whatever

an astrologer will have said, they will believe related from the fount

555 of Ammon,* since the oracles at Delphi are idle

and a blind fog of future events damns the human race.

praecipuus tamen est horum, qui saepius exul.*   557
inde fides artis, sonuit si dextera ferro   560
laeuaque, si longe castrorum in carcere mansit.
nemo mathematicus genium indemnatus habebit,
sed qui paene perit, cui uix in Cyclada mitti
contigit et parua tandem caruisse Seripho.
consulit ictericae lento de funere matris,   565
ante tamen de te Tanaquil tua, quando sororem
efferat et patruos, an sit uicturus adulter
post ipsam; quid enim maius dare numina possunt?
haec tamen ignorat quid sidus triste minetur
Saturni, quo laeta Venus se proferat astro,   570
quis mensis damnis, quae dentur tempora lucro:
illius occursus etiam uitare memento,
in cuius manibus ceu pinguia sucina tritas
cernis ephemeridas, quae nullum consulit et iam
consulitur, quae castra uiro patriamque petente   575
non ibit pariter numeris reuocata Thrasylli.
ad primum lapidem uectari cum placet, hora
sumitur ex libro; si prurit frictus ocelli
angulus, inspecta genesi collyria poscit;
aegra licet iaceat, capiendo nulla uidetur   580
aptior hora cibo nisi quam dederit Petosiris.
si mediocris erit, spatium lustrabit utrimque
metarum et sortes ducet frontemque manumque
praebebit uati crebrum poppysma roganti.
diuitibus responsa dabit Phryx augur et inde*   585
conductus, dabit astrorum mundique peritus
atque aliquis senior qui publica fulgura condit.
plebeium in circo positum est et in aggere fatum.
quae nudis longum ostendit ceruicibus aurum

557   The foremost of these, moreover, is he who is more often in exile.

560   Thence comes faith in the art, if manacle-iron has rattled on right
       and left hand, if one has remained long in military-jail.
       No numerologist, if uncondemned, shall have "talent,"
       but he who has almost perished, whom it almost befell to be sent to the
          Cyclades,
       and nevertheless to have lacked the small Seriphos.

565   She consults about the over-due funeral of her jaundiced mother,
       having, however, (your Tanaquil*) previously done so about you, when
       she might carry her sister to the grave and her uncles, whether her
          adulterous lover shall live
       past herself; for what greater thing can the divinities bestow?
       This woman, however, doesn't know what Saturn's grim star* threatens,

570   under what constellation fruitful Venus* offers herself,
       what month is assigned to losses, what times to gain.
       Remember certainly to avoid meeting *that* one,
       in whose hands you perceive, like fat amber-balls, worn-down
       ephemerals, one who consults no one and now

575   is consulted, who, when her husband is seeking camp and fatherland
       will not go along if called back by Thrasyllus' numbers.*
       When it suits her fancy to be taken to the first mile-stone, the right hour
       is taken from a book; if, after rubbing it, her delicate eye's
       corner itches, she asks for ointment after the horoscope's been looked
          at.

580   She can be lying sick in bed; no hour for taking food seems
       better than that which Petosiris* has given.
       If she'll be of moderate means, she will wander over the stadium-space*
          on either side
       of the turning-posts* and will draw lots; and both forehead and hand*
       she'll offer to the seer as he asks for frequent lip-smacking.*

585   A Phrygian augur will give answers to the rich, thence*
       hired;* so too will one experienced in the stars and cosmos,
       and some older character who disposes of the public's lightning-bolts.*
       Plebeian fate is established in the Circus and on the rampart.*
       She who displays long necklace-gold on nude shoulders

consulit ante falas delphinorumque columnas   590
an saga uendenti nubat caupone relicto.
    hae tamen et partus subeunt discrimen et omnis
nutricis tolerant fortuna urguente labores,
sed iacet aurato uix ulla puerpera lecto.
tantum artes huius, tantum medicamina possunt,   595
quae steriles facit atque homines in uentre necandos
conducit. gaude, infelix, atque ipse bibendum
porrige quidquid erit; nam si distendere uellet
et uexare uterum pueris salientibus, esses
Aethiopis fortasse pater, mox decolor heres   600
impleret tabulas numquam tibi mane uidendus.
transeo suppositos et gaudia uotaque saepe
ad spurcos decepta lacus, saepe inde petitos
pontifices, salios Scaurorum nomina falso
corpore laturos. stat Fortuna inproba noctu   605
adridens nudis infantibus: hos fouet omni
inuoluitque sinu, domibus tunc porrigit altis
secretumque sibi mimum parat; hos amat, his se
ingerit utque suos semper producit alumnos.
    hic magicos adfert cantus, hic Thessala uendit   610
philtra, quibus ualeat mentem uexare mariti
et solea pulsare natis. quod desipis, inde est,
inde animi caligo et magna obliuio rerum
quas modo gessisti. tamen hoc tolerabile, si non*
et furere incipias ut auunculus ille Neronis,   615
cui totam tremuli frontem Caesonia pulli
infudit. quae non faciet quod principis uxor?
ardebant cuncta et fracta conpage ruebant
non aliter quam si fecisset Iuno maritum
insanum. minus ergo nocens erit Agrippinae   620
boletus, siquidem unius praecordia pressit
ille senis tremulumque caput descendere iussit
in caelum et longa manantia labra saliua:
haec poscit ferrum atque ignes, haec potio torquet,

590   inquires before the wooden pillars and dolphins' columns*
       whether she should marry the rag-seller, the inn-keeper left behind.
            These women, however, both undergo childbirth's crises
       and tolerate all the nurse's labors when fortune imposes,
       yet scarcely any woman with-child lies in gilded bed.
595   So great are the arts of *this* one, so great powers have her drugs,*
       she who sterilizes and offers the service of killing humans in the belly.*
       Rejoice, wretch, and you yourself offer her to drink*
       whatever it will be;* for if she were willing to stretch
       and torment her womb with jumping baby boys, you would be
600   perhaps an Ethiopian's father. Then a heir of the wrong color
       would fill out your last will—one you shouldn't see in dawn's light.
       I pass over spurious offspring and the joys and vows often
       deceived at the dirty cess-pools,* the often thence-sought
       priests, "Leapers"* destined to carry the names of Scauri
605   with false body.* Unjust Fortune stands there at night
       smiling upon the naked infants: these she caresses, and in her whole
       bosom she fondles them; then she extends them to lofty houses
       and readies a secret farce for herself; these she loves; on these she
       forces herself and she always leads them forth as her own nurslings.
610   This one brings to her magic chants, this one sells her Thessalian
       love-potions,* with which she'll be able to vex the mind of her husband
       and beat his rump with shoe-sole.* That you're idiotic comes from
               that;
       from that comes mind's fogginess and massive oblivion of the things
       you just did. This, however, is tolerable, if you do not
615   begin also to rave like that uncle of Nero,*
       for whom Caesonia poured an entire forehead-philter of trembling foal.*
       What woman will not do what the emperor's wife has done?
       All was ablaze and, world's cohesiveness shattered, all was collapsing
       no differently than if Juno had made her husband*
620   insane. Less harmful, therefore, shall be Agrippina's
       mushroom,* considering that it checked the heart-throbs of one
       old man* and bade his shaking head to voyage
       to heaven with its lips slobbering with long streams of drool.
       This potion of Caesonia demands sword-iron and fires; it tortures;

haec lacerat mixtos equitum cum sanguine patres.   625
tanti partus equae, tanti una uenefica constat.
    oderunt natos de paelice; nemo repugnet,
nemo uetet, iam iam priuignum occidere fas est.
uos ego, pupilli, moneo, quibus amplior est res,
custodite animas et nulli credite mensae: 630
liuida materno feruent adipata ueneno.
mordeat ante aliquis quidquid porrexerit illa
quae peperit, timidus praegustet pocula papas.
fingimus haec altum satura sumente coturnum
scilicet, et finem egressi legemque priorum   635
grande Sophocleo carmen bacchamur hiatu,
montibus ignotum Rutulis caeloque Latino?
nos utinam uani. sed clamat Pontia "feci,
confiteor, puerisque meis aconita paraui,
quae deprensa patent; facinus tamen ipsa peregi."   640
tune duos una, saeuissima uipera, cena?
tune duos? "septem, si septem forte fuissent."
credamus tragicis quidquid de Colchide torua
dicitur et Procne; nil contra conor. et illae
grandia monstra suis audebant temporibus, sed   645
non propter nummos. minor admiratio summis
debetur monstris, quotiens facit ira nocentes
hunc sexum et rabie iecur incendente feruntur
praecipites, ut saxa iugis abrupta, quibus mons
subtrahitur cliuoque latus pendente recedit: 650
illam ego non tulerim quae conputat et scelus ingens
sana facit. spectant subeuntem fata mariti
Alcestim et, similis si permutatio detur,
morte uiri cupiant animam seruare catellae.
occurrent multae tibi Belides atque Eriphylae   655
mane, Clytemnestram nullus non uicus habebit.
hoc tantum refert, quod Tyndaris illa bipennem

625   it lacerates fathers mixed with the blood of knights.
      So great stands the power of mare's offspring, so great the power of
           one poisoner.
         They hate those born of a mistress; let no one oppose it;
      let no one forbid it—now, now it's right to kill off a stepson.*
      I warn you all, wards, for whom there stands a rather full store of wealth:
630   guard your souls and trust in no dinner-table!
      Dark-colored pastries seethe with maternal poison.
      Let someone chew beforehand whatever she offers
      who gave birth to you; let your fearful tutor pre-taste your drinks.
      Do you suppose I'm fashioning these ideas with my satire assuming
           the high stage-boot
635   of tragedy,* and that I have transgressed limit and law of precedent*
      as I rage my massive poem with Sophoclean gape,*
      a poem unknown to Rutulian hills and Latin sky?*
      Would that I were groundless. But Pontia* shouts "I did it!
      I confess, and I prepared aconite* for my own children,
640   a fact obvious now detected—yet I myself accomplished the crime!"
      You, you most vicious viper, killed two with a single dinner?
      You killed two? "Seven, if by chance there had been seven."
      Let us believe whatever is related in tragedies about the fierce Colchian*
      and Procne;* I try nothing to the contrary. Even those women
645   used to dare great monstrosities in their times, yet
      not on account of money. Less wonderment is due the highest
      monstrosities whenever anger makes this sex harmful
      and with madness firing up their liver, they are carried away
      headlong, like rocks torn from ridges under which the mountain
650   is eroded and its side recedes leaving steep cliff.
      Her I cannot stand who plans and commits an enormous crime
      perfectly sane. They watch Alcestis undergoing the fate of her husband*
      and, if a similar shift of fortune were given to them,
      they would desire to save a puppy's soul by their husband's death.
655   Many Belides* will confront you and Eriphyles*
      in the morning; no neighborhood will not have a Clytemnestra.*
      This only, however, makes the difference: that daughter of Tyndareus*

insulsam et fatuam dextra laeuaque tenebat;
at nunc res agitur tenui pulmone rubetae,
sed tamen et ferro, si praegustarit Atrides   660
Pontica ter uicti cautus medicamina regis.

held a tasteless and idiotic two-headed axe* in right and left hands;
but now the deed is done with the slim lung of a toad;*
660   but, however, also with sword-steel, if "Atrides"* has pre-tasted,
cautious as he is, the medicines of the thrice-conquered Pontic king.*

NOTES ON LUCILIUS, FRAGMENTS

2   **Oh the cares of human beings! Oh how much emptiness there is in things!:** This fragment forms the basis for the opening of Persius' program piece. Persius evidently quotes the line *verbatim*, a device that points to his self-establishment as satirist within the Lucilian tradition (see Persius, *Satire* 1.1). Some evidence suggests that Lucilius originally placed these words in the mouth of a god in a satire entitled "A Council of the Gods."

3–4   **The letter *r*, which an angry dog says more plainly than a human being:** The significance of *r* ("the dog-letter," so called after the sound made by a growling canine) here relates to the "growl" of satire (compare Persius, *Satire* 1.109–110 and keyed note).

36–37   **What's the appearance — poison:** Well illustrated by this fragment is Lucilius' typical harsh personal invective.

70   **Live, gluttons, devourers; live, you bellies!:** Evidently an attack on overeaters, this line is echoed by Persius, prologue 11 in his attack on poets whose motivation springs from their stomach. Criticism of gluttons is a standard satirical topic.

87–93   **You have preferred — hence an enemy!:** The entire passage is said to have been voiced by one of Lucilius' characters, the praetor Scaevola.

87   **Albucius:** Titus Albucius, an associate of Scaevola. On encountering Albucius at Athens, Scaevola makes fun of his philhellenism.

90   **praetor:** This class of official was responsible for hearing legal cases concerning the right of persons and of property; eventually the duties of the praetor were extended to include those of a military commander and of a provincial governor.

92–93   **Chaere:** A traditional Greek greeting equivalent to "hello" or "good-day."

92   **lictors:** These were attendants of the consuls; the lictors carried the *fasces* (bundles of rods bound together), which were a symbol of the consuls' power as heads of state.

567–573 Surely you don't think — one tooth projecting a bit?: This fragment on women, despite the mention of blemishes that even women of beauty must have, contrasts with Juvenal's picture of women as depraved freaks of nature in *Satire* 6.

569   Amphitryon's wife Alcmena: Alcmena, daughter of Electryon, was the wife of Amphitryon. She was the mother of Iphiclus by Amphitryon and of his twin-brother by Jupiter. The story of her rape by Jupiter is told in Plautus' *Amphitryo*.

570   Helen: Wife of Menelaus of Sparta, Helen was renowned for her beauty. She was carried off by Paris to Troy, which was then besieged for ten years before finally falling to the Greek forces led by Agamemnon. The Trojan war is the subject of Homer's *Iliad*.

570–571 I don't want to say it — choose any bisyllabic word you like: Here Lucilius feigns not wanting to say a word such as *moecha* ("adulteress").

713–714 You should undertake this task — sing the deeds of Cornelius: Like his followers Horace (*Satire* 2.1.10–12) and Persius (prologue), Lucilius suggests that epic poetry treating historical topics is a potentially lucrative pursuit—more so than satire. On Popillius and Cornelius, see the note on line 714 below.

714   Popillius ... Cornelius: Popillius Laenas and Publius Cornelius Scipio Aemilianus were historical figures in the Roman campaigns against the Numantines in Spain. Popillius was defeated by the Numantines in 138 B.C.E., while Scipio Aemilianus ended the resistance of the Numantines to Roman imperialism in 133 B.C.E. by destroying the town of Numantia.

1145–1151 But, as it is, from morning until night — as if everyone were everyone's enemies: This fragment on the urban rat race is reminiscent of Juvenal's elaborate sketch of urban "disease" in *Satire* 3.

1196–1208 Virtue, Albinus — those of ourselves: These lines convey some of the basic tenets of Stoicism applied to human conduct.

1196   Albinus: This figure may be Aulus Postumius, who was defeated by Jugurtha in 110 C.E., or possibly his brother Spurius Postumius, who was consul in the same year.

NOTES ON HORACE, *SATIRE* 1.9

1   **Sacred Way:** The *Via Sacra*, "Sacred Way," so called for the religious temples that lined it. This road connected the Roman forum with the Palatine and Oppian hills.

11   **Bolanus:** Although this particular Bolanus is unknown, he seems here to exemplify the short-tempered type and thus able to rid himself easily of such a bothersome person as the pest.

18   **Tiber . . . Gardens of Caesar:** The Tiber river flowed through Rome, while the gardens referred to had been donated by Julius Caesar to the Roman public.

22–23   **Viscus . . . Varius:** These figures were prominent on the contemporary literary scene. It was Varius (along with Vergil) who arranged the initial introduction of Horace to Maecenas, a well-to-do patron of the arts and himself a writer, on whom see the note on line 43 below.

25   **Hermogenes:** He is mentioned at a number of other points in Horace's *Satires*. Here he is apparently noted for his singing ability, which, given the disparaging references elsewhere in the *Satires* to his artistic accomplishments (for example, *Satire* 1.10.18, 80, 90), suggests a lack of artistic taste on the part of the pest.

29–30   **Sabine hag, her divine jar shaken:** The Sabines were famed in antiquity for magic and witchcraft. The hag's "divine jar" would have contained "lots," one of which would have fallen out as it was shaken.

35   **Vesta's temple:** A temple devoted to the worship of Vesta (Greek Hestia), the Roman goddess of the hearth and household.

43   **Maecenas:** Gaius Maecenas, a man of equestrian rank, was one of the closest friends and advisers of Augustus, in whose armies he fought and under whom he achieved enormous wealth and power, although he held no official title. He had a reputation for great extravagance, but is best known as the patron of many of the principal literary figures of the Augustan age, including Horace, Vergil, and Propertius. Some fragments of his own works survive. The pest hopes to secure an introduction to Maecenas through Horace.

61   **Fuscus Aristius:** He is evidently a real friend of Horace, as he is the addressee of other poems (*Ode* 1.22; *Epistle* 1.10).

66   **my liver burned with bile:** The liver was the seat of passion in the view of the ancients, while bile was indicative of strong anger.

69–70   **thirtieth Sabbath . . . circumcised Jews:** Fuscus' words are to be construed as a joke; there was apparently no such thing as the "thirtieth Sabbath." Circumcision was not normally practiced by Romans—hence its association with Judaism in particular.

73–74   **left me under the knife:** What Horace means here is that he is like a sacrificial animal about to be slaughtered (by the persistence of the pest).

76–77   **I put forth my ear:** The Roman custom was for a solicitor of a court-witness to touch the ear of the one he wished to testify. Thus Horace offers himself as a willing participant against the pest.

78   **Apollo saved me:** One of Apollo's traditional religious functions was to protect poets; Horace's final words are a humorous acknowledgment of the god's traditional role.

NOTES ON HORACE, *SATIRE* 2.1

2   **to stretch my work beyond the law:** Horace creates an intentional pun. In the legal context of the satire (with Trebatius as lawyer), "law" suggests "what is allowed by written decree." That Horace's composition seems "beyond the law," however, suggests, in another sense, that he is violating the rules of generic composition; his satire breaks the conventional limits set by literary critics.

4   **Trebatius:** Gaius Trebatius Testa, a contemporary of Cicero, was a distinguished legal figure, who was prominent under both Julius Caesar and Augustus.

7   **after being oiled:** Oiling oneself was customary before and/or after engaging in any sort of athletic activity. That Trebatius suggests a triple oiling recalls the magic number three in many rituals (here to bring on sleep).

8   **Tiber:** The river Tiber ran through Rome.

11   **Caesar's exploits:** The Caesar referred to here is the emperor Augustus. What Trebatius advises is that Horace write of Augustus as national hero and his deeds and achievements. Horace, however (like Persius and Juvenal), objects to mercenary poetry, which he would consider heroic epic/history to be.

12–15   **Although I desire it — as he slips from his horse:** These lines comprise Horace's apology (*recusatio*) for not writing poetry dealing with epic themes.

12   **father:** A commonly used term of respect often used to address an elder.

14–15   **lances . . . Gauls . . . Parthian:** The lances called attention to the Roman army, whose legions carried them into battle. The Gauls were long-standing enemies of Rome who plagued the northern provinces of the empire, and Octavian/Augustus made several successful campaigns against them. The Parthians were also a constant threat to Rome. Their resistance in the East was carried out in large part by their horsemen.

17   **Lucilius . . . Scipio:** Gaius Lucilius was an acquaintance of Publius Cornelius Scipio Aemilianus, the most prominent general of his generation; compare the note on lines 65–66 below.

18–19   **Flaccus' words . . . attentive ear of Caesar:** Horace (Quintus Horatius Flaccus) here refers to himself in the third person and makes a pun on his *cognomen* Flaccus, which means "floppy-eared," in contrast to the "attentive ear of Caesar."

22   **Pantolabus . . . Nomentanus:** Pantolabus is the Greek nickname of an unknown character; it means "he who takes everything," that is, food. Nomentanus is likewise unknown.

24   **Milonius:** An unknown character, whose drunkenness is imagined as causing him to have double-vision.

26   **Castor . . . he born from the same egg:** Castor and his twin brother Pollux (referred to here as "he born from the same egg") were mythological figures, sons of Leda by Jupiter, who seduced her while disguised as a swan. Among other qualities, Castor was famed for his horsemanship, Pollux for his prowess as a boxer.

28–29   **to wrap words in meter-feet in the manner of Lucilius:** to compose verse satire (as opposed to prose) in the Lucilian fashion, specifically dactylic hexameter.

34   **of dual nature as I am — Lucanian or Apulian:** Horace, as a former resident of Venusia, relates himself to two primitive Italian tribes of that region. Lucania and Apulia were regions in southern Italy.

35–39   **for a Venusian colonist — strike up any war:** Here Horace refers to the Roman practice of establishing colonies in recently conquered areas to serve as a sort of perimeter defense.

36   **Samnites:** The Samnites were among the principal enemies of Rome during her period of expansion in Italy in the fourth and third centuries B.C.E.; the Latin text reads *Sabelli*, "a fierce race of men," a term referring to the people of Italic origin who spoke Oscan.

39–40   **stylus . . . it shall protect me like a sword:** The stylus was the pointed writing instrument of the Romans. It was used either to carve letters into wax-coated tablets or, dipped in ink, to write on parchment. Here Horace plays on the physical resemblance between the pointed stylus and a sword. Both are "weapons."

47   **Cervius:** An unknown, but he appears to have been an informer.

48   **Canidia's enemy . . . Albucius' poison:** Canidia is a sorceress or witch mentioned elsewhere by Horace; compare Horace, *Satire* 2.8.95 and keyed note. Albucius is unknown.

49   **Turius . . . massive evil:** Turius is evidently a crooked judge and the "massive evil" is most likely a monetary fine.

53   **Scaeva:** A genuine Roman name, but it also has the literal meaning of "left-handed," which Horace exploits in the following line.

60   **whatever the color of my life:** That is, whether Horace encounters good fortune (and his life takes on a light "color") or whether he finds misfortune of some kind (and his life is of a dark hue).

62   **may strike you with a chill:** This refers to the metaphor of "the cold shoulder."

63   **in this manner:** This refers specifically to the genre of satire, with its personal invective.

65–66   **Laelius . . . he who took his well-earned name from defeated Carthage:** Laelius is Gaius Laelius the younger (*circa* 190–125 B.C.E.), a close friend and associate of Publius Cornelius Scipio Aemilianus, the Scipio referred to in line 17 above; "he who took his well-earned name from defeated Carthage" is Scipio himself. Both Scipio Aemilianus and his grandfather by adoption, Publius Cornelius Scipio, were awarded the honorary name "Africanus," the latter for his defeat of the Carthaginians under Hannibal at the battle of Zama in 202 B.C.E., the former for the eventual destruction of Carthage in 146 B.C.E.

67   **Metellus:** Quintus Caecilius Metellus Macedonicus, another prominent general of the time of Lucilius, was a political opponent of Scipio Aemilianus and Gaius Laelius.

68   **Lupus:** Lucius Cornelius Lentulus Lupus was a prominent political figure in the mid-second century B.C.E. and was, like Metellus Macedonicus, an opponent of Scipio Aemilianus.

69   **he seized upon — the populace a whole tribe at a time:** Lucilius directed his satire indiscriminately, sparing no man, whatever his social standing might be.

73   **to trifle with him:** That is, to joke and satirize with Lucilius.

74   **vegetables boiled:** Vegetables and simple garden fare were the foods espoused by Roman satirists as indicative of the honest, simple, and rustic life that was seen as typical of the early Romans.

81   **sacred laws:** The laws originally set up in the Roman forum in the form of the "Twelve Tables."

82–83   **If anyone composes bad poems — there is right to action and legal judgment:** The law that Trebatius cites forbids the composition of poems that are "bad" in the sense that they slander someone. Horace undercuts Trebatius' argument by construing "bad" as "poorly composed."

NOTES ON HORACE, *SATIRE* 2.8

1   **Nasidienus' dinner:** Unknown, Nasidienus is evidently wealthy (perhaps we are even to imagine him a millionaire), yet extravagant and pretentious. The discursive structure of this satire is centered around the narrative of Nasidienus' dinner-guest, Fundanius (on whom see Introduction, p. 7), as he relates to Horace the evening's events.

6   **Lucanian:** Lucania was a region of southern Italy known for its sausages and other delicacies.

9   **Coan wine:** Wine from Cos, a Greek island off the coast of Asia Minor.

11   **the maple table with a purple cloth of wool:** The table of maple-wood was an unusual elegance; while purple fabric, as the towel here, was a sign of excessive luxury and is frequently mentioned as such by Roman satirists.

13–14   **like an Attic maiden, with her sacred objects of Ceres:** Horace refers to the young girls known as "basket-bearers" (Greek *kanephoroi*), who bore on their heads the sacred objects used in festivals of various deities at Athens, including Demeter (Ceres) and Athene (Minerva). The point of the simile is the absurd solemnity of the slaves as they go about their serving.

14–15   **Hydaspes ... Caecuban wine ... Alcon ... Chian devoid of sea-water:** Hydaspes is a famous Indian river, therefore suitable as a name for the archetypal foreign slave. This river was the site of one of Alexander the Great's victories in 326 B.C.E. Caecuban wine came from Caecubum in Latium and was regarded as among the finest of Italian wines. Chian, from the island of Chios, was accorded similar esteem among the wines of Greece and is here appropriately served by a slave with a Greek name, Alcon. That Nasidienus' Chian is "devoid of sea-water" is a sign of its quality, as sea water was often used as a preservative with Greek wines.

16   **Maecenas ... Alban ... Falernian:** Gaius Maecenas, on whom see the note on Horace, *Satire* 1.9.43, may well have been the guest of honor. Alban and Falernian wines ranked just below Caecuban (on

which see the note on lines 14–15 above) among those of Italy; compare the note on Juvenal, *Satire* 1.70.

19   **Fundanius:** A contemporary writer of New Comedy in the style of the Greek comic playwright Menander. That the dinner is narrated by him hints at a comic spectacle in the making.

20–23   **I was at the top — Porcius below:** The standard Roman dining arrangement was known as a *triclinium*, which comprised a single large table surrounded by three separate couches. There were normally three diners situated on each couch; each took his or her position on the couch barefoot and assumed a prone posture. The seating arrangement of the participants reflects their status. The three couches were described as "top," "middle," and "bottom," as were the three places on each. Normally the host took the place at the "top" of the "bottom" couch (4), but Nasidienus has assigned Nomentanus to this position so he can look after and explain the food to Maecenas, who assumes the traditional place of honor at the "bottom" of the "middle" couch (1). The narrator Fundanius sits at the "top" of the "top" couch (9). The full seating arrangement is as follows:

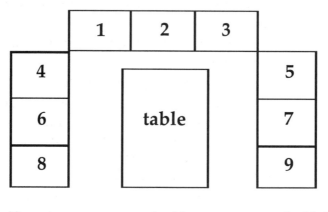

4 = Nomentanus	1 = Maecenas	5 = Varius
6 = Nasidienus (the host)	2 = Vibidius	7 = Viscus
8 = Porcius	3 = Servilius Balatro	9 = Fundanius

20   **Thurian:** Thurii (Thuria), a Roman town on the Gulf of Taranto, was founded on the site of the former Greek colony of Sybaris, the citizens of which were notorious for their excessive luxury and vice.

21   **Varius:** Lucius Varius Rufus, a member of Maecenas' literary circle. He wrote various types of poetry, including tragedy, but only fragments survive. Varius was a friend of Vergil and was involved in the preparation of the unfinished *Aeneid* for publication. He and Vergil introduced Horace to Maecenas.

21–22   **Vibidius . . . Servilius Balatro:** Unknown figures; Balatro literally means "jester" or "buffoon" and may be a nickname.

23   **Nomentanus . . . Porcius:** Parasites of the host Nasidienus. Porcius is a genuine Roman name, but here reflects the character's behavior; it implies "Mr Pig."

40   **Allifanian cups:** Allifae was a town in Samnium near the border shared with Campania. The wine-cups produced in Allifae were inordinately large.

45–47   **olive oil of the first Venafran pressing . . . this side of the sea:** Venafrum was a town south-east of Rome famous for its olive oil, while "this side of the sea" means Italian, rather than foreign, especially Greek.

49–50   **vinegar that has changed by acidity the Methymnean grape:** The point of the reference is the quality of Nasidienus' vinegar. Methymna, a town on the Greek island of Lesbos, was esteemed for its wine.

52   **Curtillus:** Otherwise unknown, he was apparently either the cook of Nasidienus or like Nasidienus, a gourmet.

56   **Campanian:** Campania was the region of Italy just south of Latium, in which Rome was located.

58   **Rufus:** This is the host himself (Nasidienus Rufus).

92–93   **the feastmaster told of their origins and nature:** The "nature" of the food served is a matter of preoccupation on the part of Nasidienus and of irritation on the part of the guests. The wording of the original text suggests that the host lectures on the food as though he were dealing with a complex philosophical exposition.

95   **Canidia:** This Canidia is mentioned by Horace elsewhere (*Epodes* 5, 17; *Satire* 1.8) as a hideous and deadly witch.

NOTES ON PERSIUS, PROLOGUE

1–14: Some manuscripts of Persius place these lines after the *Satires* themselves and some editors have printed them in that position, that is, as an epilogue rather than a prologue.

1–6   **I neither washed my lips — by adherent ivy:** The reference in these lines is to the traditional poetic inspiration that was often claimed by poets as sent to them by the Muses. The initial lines of the prologue mock the epic poetry of Ennius especially; see Introduction, p. 2).

1   **horse-fount:** A rather derogatory reference to Hippocrene, the spring that myth held as having its origin in the winged horse Pegasus, which supposedly created it by a stab from its hoof.

2   **dreaming on two-headed Parnassus:** Mount Parnassus, notable for its twin peaks, held another spring sacred to the Muses—the Castalian spring. To have dreamed on Parnassus therefore implied divine poetic inspiration. Hesiod's *Theogony* (*circa* 700 B.C.E.) described how the poet had been inspired by the Muses on another of their mountains, Helicon, and this idea had been taken up by the Greek poet Callimachus (third century B.C.E.) and the early Roman epic poet Ennius (239–169 B.C.E.), both of whom claimed to have been inspired by dreams involving Helicon. Persius probably has such claims in mind here.

4   **daughters of Mount Helicon . . . pallid Pirene:** The "daughters of Mount Helicon" (Greek Heliconiades) refers to the Muses. Mount Helicon was the home of the Hippocrene, on which see the note on line 2 above. Pirene, in Corinth, was another spring that had "musical" associations. It is called "pallid" because poets themselves ostensibly turned pale from intense study.

8   **Chaere!:** A traditional Greek greeting, on which see the note on Lucilius, fragment 92–93.

14   **Pegasian nectar:** "Sweet" poetry that stemmed from divine inspiration.

NOTES ON PERSIUS, *SATIRE* 1

1 **Oh the cares of human beings! Oh how much emptiness there is in things!:** Compare Lucilius, fragment 2 and keyed note.

4 **Polydamas . . . the Trojan ladies . . . Labeo:** "Polydamas" and "the Trojan ladies" are taken from Homer's *Iliad* (22.100, 105), where they stand as unfavorable critics. Labeo is likely one Attius Labeo, who was known in Persius' time as a translator of Homeric epic. That Persius should seek their approval of his poetry is sarcastically posited as an absurd idea.

13 **we write—that one verses, this one free of meter:** The references are to poetry and prose respectively.

16 **sardonyx birthday-ring:** The sardonyx (ring) symbolizes pretense and perversion. Sex, food and poetry are all interrelated in Persius' attack on the pretentious and effeminate poetasters of his day.

20 **massive Tituses:** "Tituses" most likely is used generically here for "Romans." That they are "massive" implies two aspects: they are ironically perverse, since they are sexually aroused in a passive way by the poetry they hear; while physical brawn implies stupidity and critical inability.

24–25 **ferment . . . fig-tree . . . shatter the liver and spring forth:** The rising of yeast ("ferment") and the fig-tree, which was proverbial for its roots' power in shattering rock as it grew, both stand metaphorically for a poet's innate passion to produce. The image of these forces bursting from the liver is deliberately grotesque.

29 **you have stood as the dictation-exercises of a hundred curly headed boys:** The works of certain authors might find their way into children's classrooms as material for study and recitation. Some viewed this as a claim to fame, while others, such as Persius here and Horace (for example, *Satire* 1.10.74ff.), thought it a disgrace.

30 **Romulids:** "Romulids" ("sons of Romulus") is a grandiose mock-epic name for Romans. That they are "stuffed" implies their gluttonous nature, which itself reflects critical inability.

42–43 **worthy of cedar, to leave behind poems fearing neither mackerel nor incense:** The parchment on which good literature was written was naturally valued and kept safe, sometimes preserved in boxes of cedar; while the pages of poor literature were sometimes converted to scrap-paper, for instance, to wrap fish and incense.

50 *Iliad* **of Attius:** See the note on line 4 above.

72–73 **Palilia smoky with hay. . . Remus . . . Quintius . . . plow-shares:** The Palilia was the festival held in honor of Pales, the tutelary god of shepherds, on 21 April, the date celebrated as the anniversary of the founding of Rome; the participants at this festival leaped over a fire of hay—hence "smoky with hay." Remus, who lived a rural life, was the mythical co-founder (along with Romulus) of Rome. (On Aeneas as the traditional founder of Rome, see the note on Juvenal, *Satire* 6.177.) Quintius, whose full name was Lucius Quinctius Cincinnatus, was called to Rome from his "plow-shares" to become dictator in 458 B.C.E.

76–78 **Brisaean Accius . . . Pacuvius . . . warty Antiope:** Lucius Accius (170–85 B.C.E.), famous for his many tragedies and other works, is termed "Brisean" because of his two-fold connection with the god Dionysus (Briseus). He wrote a tragedy on the female followers of Dionysus' cult (*Bacchae*); but the adjective also implies that his poetry is "drunken" (that is, inspired by the god of wine). Marcus Pacuvius (*circa* 220–130 B.C.E.), another early Roman tragedian, composed a tragedy on Antiope that portrayed her sufferings. Both Accius and Pacuvius were attacked by Lucilius as verbicides.

82 **Trossulus:** The name is generic for any pretentiously fashionable or ostentatious (young) person.

93 **Berecyntius Attis:** Attis, whose standard epithet was "Berecyntian," was associated with the orgiastic rites of Cybele.

96 **'Arms, the man' . . . just foam and swollen:** "Arms and the man" (*arma virumque*) are the famous opening words of Vergil's *Aeneid*, regarded since ancient times as one of the greatest works of Latin literature. That the interlocutor finds these words "just foam and swollen" shows his absolute lack of critical judgment.

99–102 **Mimmalonian . . . Bassarid . . . Maenad . . . "euhion":** These names are associated with the cult of Bacchus, the god of wine. "Mimallonian" is unparalleled; both "Bassarid" and "Maenad" are female celebrants of the orgiastic, sometimes violent, rites of the wine-god Bacchus as depicted in Greek literature. "Euhion" is the cry with which Bacchus was invoked—hence also an epithet of the god.

109–110 **dog-letter:** the letter *r*, called the "dog-letter" because of its similarity to the growl of a dog. Both Lucilius (compare Lucilius, fragment 3–4 and keyed note) and Persius use it in reference to the snarling nature of satire.

114 **Lucilius:** The first major author of satire, on whom see Introduction, pp. 5–6.

115 **Lupus . . . Mucius:** Lucius Cornelius Lentulus Lupus and Publius Mucius Scaevola were important political figures in the mid-second century B.C.E. On Lentulus Lupus compare the note on Horace, *Satire* 2.1.68; Mucius Scaevola was a supporter of Tiberius Gracchus (on which see the note on Juvenal, *Satire* 6.167–168) and an opponent of Lucilius' patron Scipio Aemilianus (on which see the notes on Lucilius, fragment 714 and Horace, *Satire* 2.1.65–66).

116 **Flaccus:** Quintus Horatius Flaccus (Horace), on whom see Introduction, pp. 6–8.

123–124 **Cratinus . . . Eupolis . . . the great old man:** Cratinus, Eupolis, and Aristophanes ("the great old man") were considered the three greatest writers of Attic Old Comedy. Eleven plays of Aristophanes survive complete and there are many fragments from the work of all three. The social comment and apparent personal invective characteristic of the Old Comedy were seen by the Roman satirists as anticipating their own genre.

126 **Thence:** That is, by the mental, spiritual, and ideological preparation given the reader through the appreciation of Old Comedy.

130 **he as aedile . . . Arretium:** An aedile had various urban responsibilities, including the upkeep of the roads, the distribution of water, the maintenance of weights and measures, the control of the price of corn and other commodities, and the organization of games; in addition, the aedile had some judicial functions related to the aforementioned duties. Arretium (modern Arezzo) was in Etruria.

133 **Nones-girl . . . Cynic's beard:** A "Nones-girl" was either a prostitute who started work at the ninth hour or a slave-girl enjoying her special holiday on the Nones (seventh day) of July. A beard was a distinguishing characteristic of philosophers, including the Cynics, who espoused a disdain for social customs and material possessions.

134   To these I give the play-schedule in the morning, after lunch
Callirhoe: What is probably suggested here is that Persius dismisses
those unsuited to intellectually stimulating literature (such as satire)
and ironically suggests that they check the day's listing of plays early
on and then attend one of these later in the day. *Callirhoe*, which in
Greek means "beautifully flowing," would then be the title of a play
that appealed to the mindless public.

NOTES ON PERSIUS, *SATIRE 3*

1–2   **Clear morning — narrow cracks with light:** The setting of this satire seems to be one of late-morning repose. The "dramatic plot" of the poem involves a complex mixture of voice and a dissuasive discourse on sloth and philosophical retardation. The satirist seems to shift between two attitudes—that of the narrator and that of the lazy student. A third voice is also present, one we may term the "censorious companion."

3   **untamed Falernian:** A highly regarded Italian wine; compare the notes on Horace, *Satire* 2.8.16 and Juvenal, *Satire* 1.70. The epithet "untamed" presumably means that the wine was not mixed with water, as was the usual custom.

4   **the sun-dial's fifth line is touched by shadow:** That is, at the "fifth hour," roughly 11:00 a.m.

5   **Unhealthy Sirius:** Sirius (*Canis Maior* or the "Dog-Star") is called "unhealthy" because its arrival signaled the advent of hot weather.

8   **bile:** Considered by the ancients a physiological index of anger (as here) or depression.

9   **Arcadia:** This region in the Peloponnese (Greece) was well-known for its farm animals, especially donkeys. It was used in pastoral poetry as the archetypal rural setting.

10   **bicolor writing-sheet with hairs removed:** The "writing-sheet" referred to here is an animal hide. One side of the hide would have been treated to improve its qualities of ink absorption; the other would have been cleaned of hairs by friction with pumice.

13   **cuttlefish:** Persius uses "cuttlefish" (by metonymy) to mean the black, inky fluid derived from the animal. In this case, the cuttlefish's ink is too thick for clear writing and must be diluted.

21–22   **the pot sounds flawed — with its unchanged clay:** The slack student is likened to a vessel improperly formed by the potter and not yet hardened by heat-treatment. The metaphor had precedent in Roman comedy and was evidently not uncommon.

28   **Etruscan pedigree:** This reference to an Etruscan origin may refer to Persius himself, who came originally from Volterra. The theme of priding oneself on one's lineage is quite common in Roman satire as a means of attacking those who pretend, yet lack, real virtue.

29   **you greet your censor dressed in the trabea:** The "trabea" was a formal garment that one put on for special occasions only. What is referred to here is a ceremony of inspection, wherein members of the socio-economic class of *equites* ("knights") were assessed by the emperor or one of his agents, in this case a censor; if a person of the equestrian class seemed in some way not worthy of it, he could be deprived of his privileges. The censor was an official of great importance and authority with numerous civic functions, including conducting various censuses of citizens and their property, superintending public works and buildings, and keeping an eye on public morals.

31   **Natta:** The character Natta is mentioned by Horace as well at *Satire* 1.6.124, where he stands as an example of a filthy person who is so careless and stingy that he oils his body not with pure olive oil but with the grimy oil he has stolen from lamps.

39   **Or did the bronze of Sicilian bullock groan more:** The reference here is to the legendary "Bull of Phalaris." Phalaris of Acragas (Agrigentum = modern Agrigento in Sicily) was a sixth-century B.C.E. tyrant who was said to have placed his victims inside a hollow, bronze bull to be baked to death; the screams of the dying would perversely mimic the bellowing of a real bull. The bull's first victim was said to have been its inventor.

40   **the sword dangling from gold-paneled ceiling:** Persius here refers to the story of Damocles, who was tortured by the Syracusan tyrant, Dionysius I (*circa* 430–367 B.C.E.), who made him sit with a sword poised above his head. The sword was attached to the ceiling by only a strand of hair and so caused constant dread.

44–45   **to dab my eyes with olive oil . . . mighty words of Cato:** Since olive oil was considered a treatment for eye-ailments, the speaker here admits that he used to pretend sickness in order to avoid school. The "mighty words of Cato" would have been part of a class-room lesson in oratory in which the student either repeated the words of a famous historical figure or else gave a fabricated speech to such a character. The Cato mentioned here was Marcus Porcius Cato

Uticensis (95–46 B.C.E.), who was active on the republican side in the civil war between Gaius Pompeius and Julius Caesar and who committed suicide at Utica in North Africa after Caesar's victory in the battle of Thapsus.

48–50   **the advantageous 'six' . . . the ruinous 'one' . . . neck of narrow jar:** The "six" and the "one" refer to throws of the dice. Apart from dice-playing, top-spinning, and a game involving the tossing of objects into a narrow-necked jar were common school-boy past-times. Here such games of course symbolize mindless pursuits.

53   **wise portico . . . trouser-wearing Medes:** The "wise portico" is the *Stoa Poikile* ("Painted Stoa"), which was located in Athens. It symbolizes Stoic philosophy in general here, since it was at this portico that Zeno, the original founder of Stoicism, expounded his principles. The *Stoa Poikile* was so named because of its famous wall-paintings, one of which depicted the famous battle of Marathon, in which the Athens and her allies had defeated a large Persian army; thus the "trouser-wearing Medes" were Persian soldiers.

54–55   **and the things for which — barley grits:** Students of Stoic philosophy had short hair and followed a simple and modest diet as an outward reflection of their inner pursuit of a lifestyle that shunned luxury and ostentation.

56–57   **the letter that has drawn apart Samian branches . . . hill on the right-hand path:** Pythagoras (born at Samos; lived *circa* 580–500 B.C.E.) posited the Greek letter upsilon (Y) as symbol of the human course of life. According to this symbolism, a maturing person ascended the "trunk" of the tree-shaped letter and was confronted with the divergent branches. To follow the left branch was to embark on a dissolute and morally unsound mode of existence, while to follow the right branch (the "hill on the right-hand path") was to choose the difficult life-long quest for philosophical wisdom.

63   **hellebore:** Used as a medicine to alleviate the symptoms of both edema and insanity.

65   **Craterus:** This name seems to be used here as a generic reference to physicians.

74   **fat Umbrians:** The Umbrians were known for their prosperity. The Latin phrase *pinguibus Vmbris* ("fat Umbrians") is a pun on *pinguibus umbris* ("fat shades"), thus being intended as a playful oxymoron.

75   **pepper and hog-legs:** These are foods of low or modest repute. The *Lex Cincia* forbade the payment of advocates, but gifts of food were often given for legal services that were provided by patrons for their clients, especially at birthdays and at festivals.

78   **I know's:** The Latin text reads *sapio*, a word that furnishes a double entendre with its meanings of "I know" and "I taste," thus emphasizing the centurion's bestial appetite as well as his ignorance.

79   **Arcesilas . . . Solons:** Arcesilas of Pitane (*circa* 315–241 B.C.E.) was a prominent philosopher of his time and head of the Academy, the philosophical school founded in Athens by Plato. Solon was an Athenian statesman of the first half of the sixth century B.C.E. who was credited with radically reforming both the political geography and the legal system of Athens in an attempt to resolve internal conflicts. Solon is somewhat inappropriate as an example of an impractical philosopher. Persius may intend this to reveal the ignorance of the goatish centurion through his own words, although Solon was responsible for a body of reflective poems, often referring to his political reforms, and was regarded as a sage by writers from Herodotus onwards.

91   **on the third night his veins are flowing steadily:** The patient seems to think he has recovered, but he should have waited longer before considering himself cured.

93   **Surrentine:** A light wine recommended for invalids from the region of Sorrento; compare the notes on Horace, *Satire* 2.8.16 and Juvenal, *Satire* 1.70.

105–106 **new Romans . . . donning caps on their heads:** The deceased patient emancipated his slaves either in his will or just prior to his death—hence "new Romans" (Latin *Quirites*, on which see the notes on Persius, *Satire* 4.8 and Juvenal, *Satire* 3.60). Freedmen wore skull-caps on shaved heads.

107–108 **Take my pulse — touch the tips of my toes and fingers:** Persius' exhortation to the addressee to examine him physically has an apparent moral application to the addressee himself.

118   **mad Orestes:** The Furies drove Orestes insane for murdering his mother to avenge his father's death; he was typically portrayed in antiquity as the classic archetype of a madman.

NOTES ON PERSIUS, *SATIRE* 4

1   **Do you handle the interest of the populace?:** This line (in the original Latin) carries a double entendre: in addition to "handling the populace's interest," it suggests (in a sexual sense) "pulling the public's thing," that is, its sexual organ.

1–2   **the bearded teacher whom dire sip of hemlock removed:** Socrates of Athens, who was sentenced to death in 399 B.C.E. for alleged corruption of youth and blasphemy of the traditional pantheon.

3   **little pupil of great Pericles:** The reference is to the youthful Alcibiades (*circa* 450–404 B.C.E.), whom Pericles (*circa* 495–429 B.C.E., a famous Athenian statesman) raised and who became a well-known politician and general; he is Socrates' addressee in this satire. Especially emphasized are the aspiring politician's inexperience and lack of self-knowledge.

8   **Romans:** The Latin *Quirites* (Latin for "sons of Quirinus"—hence "Romans") is a formal and poetic equivalent for *Romani* ("Romans") and also implies descent from old Roman stock. Quirinus was a mythological and religious figure from early Roman history and was later equated with Romulus, Rome's mythical co-founder (along with Remus) and first king, so that *Quirites* came to suggest "true Romans," its use at Juvenal, *Satire* 3.60. (On Aeneas as the traditional founder of Rome, see the note on Juvenal, *Satire* 6.177.) The word in the mouth of the Greek Alcibiades (or Socrates) is of course incongruous, a witty twist of context by Persius.

13   **black theta:** The "black theta" (Greek letter pronounced *th*], signifying *thanatos* (Greek for "death"), was the judge's mark denoting the death penalty.

16   **Anticyras:** Medicinal doses of the herb hellebore were called "Anticyras" after the geographical region from which they originated. The hellebore concoction was used as a treatment for insanity.

20   **Dinomache:** Mother of Alcibiades, she was of an illustrious family: both her father Megacles and her grandfather Cleisthenes were members of the Athenian aristocracy.

21 **Baucis:** An old woman who along with her husband Philemon hospitably received Jupiter and Mercury in mortal guise when every other home was barred against them; for the full story see Ovid, *Metamorphoses* 8.618–724, especially 631–719. Although Baucis is a mythical figure, her name here seems to be generic for any vegetable-selling old woman.

25–26 **Vettidius ... Cures:** This Vettidius may be the same one mentioned by Juvenal, *Satire* 3.169, although he is otherwise unknown. Cures was in the Sabine region and those who lived there apparently had a reputation for excessive frugality.

51 **Cerdo:** Best taken as a generic name with the connotation "the average man in the street." *Cerdo* as noun means "a (lowly) craftsman."

52 **Reside with yourself:** This command recalls the well-known Delphic maxim "Know Thyself." The point of the satire, however, is that very few people are willing to explore their own faults, as self-knowledge is both difficult to attain and hard to accept.

NOTES ON JUVENAL, *SATIRE* 1

1 **Am I always a listener only?:** Literary figures frequently performed their works at formal recitations.

2 **annoyed by the *Theseid* of rasping Cordus:** A *Theseid* would be an epic poem recounting the myths of Theseus. It is exactly the type of work to which Juvenal and other satirists object; compare lines 52–54 below and keyed note. This Cordus seems not to be the one mentioned by Juvenal at *Satire* 3.203, 208. He simply represents a typically poor poet.

3 **recited to me dramas:** The Latin *fabula togata* was a dramatic performance treating specifically Roman subjects in Italian setting, as opposed to Greek. The *fabula palliata* was, on the other hand, a comic play that was an adaptation of an original Greek drama.

4–5 ***Telephus . . . Orestes*:** Telephus was a king of Mysia who, when his country was mistakenly attacked by the Greeks, who thought it was Troy, received from Achilles a wound that according to an oracle could be healed only by the one who had inflicted it. Telephus went to Argos, where Achilles and others were gathering for the famous expedition to Troy, and drew attention to his plight by threatening Orestes, the infant son of Agamemnon. He was healed with rust from the spear of Achilles, the one who had inflicted his wound, and guided the Greeks to Troy. His story was the subject of a Greek tragedy by Euripides. Orestes was the son of Agamemnon and Clytemnestra. To avenge his father's murder, he killed his mother and her lover Aegisthus, thereby incurring the wrath of the Furies, the goddesses who avenged crimes against blood relations. Orestes and his sister Electra, who assisted him, appear in a number of surviving Greek and Roman tragedies. Both Telephus and Orestes were evidently popular subjects; thus the massive works *Telephus* and *Orestes* are named after them.

7–9 **wood of Mars . . . Cave of Vulcan . . . Aeolean cliffs:** Mars' grove in Colchis was said to house the "Golden Fleece," which Jason stole with the help of Medea; see line 10 and keyed note below. Vulcan's smithy was supposedly in a cave on a small island north of Sicily.

Aeolus, governor of the winds, likewise resided on the islands around Sicily.

9   **Aeacus:** As one of the three mythological judges of the Underworld, Aeacus decided the fate of the soul of one departed.

10   **another swipes the gold of pilfered petty hide:** The reference is to the Golden Fleece from the well-known myth of Jason and the Argonauts; see note on lines 7–9 above. Juvenal's indignant sarcasm is especially manifest here. The quest for the Golden Fleece is the subject of a surviving epic of the late first century C.E. (that is, during the middle years of Juvenal's life)—the *Argonautica* of Gaius Valerius Flaccus. It would be wrong, however, to see Juvenal's remarks as directed at this poem in particular, since his point is the very frequency with which the myth is used by contemporary poets.

11   **Monychus:** Monychus figured in the mythological account of the battle of the Lapiths and the Centaurs (of which he was one), which occurred when the Centaurs, who were part-man and part-horse and who were not used to drinking wine, attempted to abduct the bride and other women at the wedding feast of the Lapith Pirithous. Monychus' weapons were tree trunks.

12–13   **so always shout Fronto's plane-trees — incessant reciter:** Fronto is typical of any wealthy Roman who sponsored poetry performances at his estate.

15–16   **I too gave advice to Sulla:** Lucius Cornelius Sulla Felix (*circa* 138–78 B.C.E.) was a prominent general and a major figure in Rome's constitutional development. He used the army to gain power and attempted to use it to restore the dominance of the senatorial classes, not without considerable opposition. This apparently autobiographical reference by Juvenal is to the standard Roman school-room exercise of delivering hypothetical advisory speeches to famous characters of Roman history.

20   **the great son of Aurunca:** That is, Gaius Lucilius (*circa* 180–102 B.C.E.), the prototypical Roman satirist, who was born at Suessa Aurunca in the southwestern Italian region of Campania.

22–23   **Mevia stabs an Etruscan boar and grasps spears nude-titted:** This attack on Mevia (of no historical significance) hints at a major theme of *Satire* 6—the inversion of gender roles in a perverse Rome.

26   **Crispinus of Canopus:** Crispinus typifies the foreigner, in this case
Egyptian, who has moved from slavery to wealth. Juvenal attacks
Egyptians especially in *Satire* 15, where he accuses them of being
irreligious cannibals. The city of Canopus was on the delta of the Nile
river. Its reputation in antiquity was for moral depravity and fantastic
luxury.

27   **Tyrian capes:** Garments dyed with Tyrian colors were an ostenta-
tious shade of purple as well as expensive.

30   **it is difficult *not* to write satire:** This claim indicates succinctly the
satirical stance of the speaker (better termed the literary *persona*). He is
portrayed as being so overwhelmed by indignation at what he observes
about him that poetic inspiration comes upon him almost unsolicited.

35   **Massa . . . Carus:** Informers under the emperorship of Domitian (81–
96 C.E.). Professional informers were spies who extorted payment from
persons or gained the favor of those in power based on what they
observed or imagined; such informers played especially on the fears
of powerful people.

36   **Latinus . . . Thymele:** Latinus was, under Domitian, an actor of mimes
and perhaps a part-time informer. Thymele was his co-actor, evidently
used by Latinus as a sexual bribe. On Latinus compare Juvenal, *Satire*
6.44 and keyed note.

43   **let him turn pale:** The gigolo supposedly turned pale through excessive
sexual activity. The ejaculation of blood was thought by some to result
from this.

44   **an orator about to speak at Lugudunum's altar:** Lugudunum (more
commonly spelt Lugdunum) is the modern-day Lyon in France, origi-
nally a Roman colony in Gaul. According to Suetonius, *Caligula* 20,
the emperor Caligula sponsored oratorical contests here, in which the
orators who most failed to impress were required to delete their writings
with either a sponge or their tongue; if one refused, he was beaten with
sticks or submerged in a river.

45   **my dry liver burns:** Here (and very often in Greek myth and literature)
the "liver" stands as seat of the passions (compare English "heart");
compare Horace, *Satire* 1.9.66 and keyed note.

49–50 **Marius . . . drinks from the eighth hour . . . victorious province,
lament:** This Marius was governor in Africa from 97 to 98 C.E. and

was condemned to exile on charges of extortion. The "eighth hour" was 2.00 p.m.; etiquette dictated that drinking should not commence until the evening meal, which normally started at the ninth hour, that is, 3.00 p.m. The province is "victorious" because it won its case against Marius, yet it "laments" because Marius goes unpunished.

51   **worthy of the Venusian lamp:** The reference is to Quintus Horatius Flaccus, who was born in the Apulian city of Venusia. The "lamp" refers both to satire's role of revealing things and to Horace's gentle satirical touch. See Introduction, pp. 6–8.

52–53   **Hercules . . . Diomedes . . . Labyrinth's "moo":** Both Hercules, the most famous and most popular of Greek and Roman mythological heroes, and Diomedes, presumably here one of the heroes of the Trojan war, are once again typical of trite literary topics. The Cretan Labyrinth housed the Minotaur, a creature part-man and part-bull (hence the "moo"), which was slain by the Athenian hero Theseus.

54   **sea smashed by boy and the flying craftsman:** These refer to the well-known story of Daedalus, the craftsman, and his son Icarus, who attempted to escape from Crete on wings with his father but was killed when he flew too high and the sun melted the wax that held his wings together.

59   **horse-stalls:** The Latin word *praesepe* ("horse-stall") was used to denote "brothel" as well as "stall"; thus there is a pointed double-entendre here.

60   **Automedon:** The charioteer of the Greek hero Achilles.

61   **Flaminian Way:** The *Via Flaminia*, "Flaminian Way," was built *circa* 220 B.C.E. Over 200 miles long, it was the main road north of Rome.

63   **fill up massive wax-sheets:** This refers to the use of the wax-coated tablets (notebooks) onto which letters were etched with a stylus. One's writing could be erased easily by smoothing out the wax with the larger end of the stylus.

66   **sprawled-out Maecenas:** This Maecenas was the patron of Horace and other Augustan writers, on whom see Horace, *Satire* 1.9.43 and keyed note. In contrast to Horace's picture of him as a tasteful and cultured literary man and friend, Juvenal presents him as extremely self-indulgent and even effeminate.

70   **Calenian:** Two types of wine were especially popular in Rome at this time: Calenian, named after the *Calenus Ager* (modern Calvi), and Falernian (named after the *Falernus ager*, a region associated with the modern Carinola). Better and more expensive wines were Alban, named from Alba Longa, an ancient settlement near Rome, and Surrentine, named after the town Surrentum (modern Sorrento) in Campania. Compare the note on Horace, *Satire* 2.8.16.

71   **Lucusta:** An expert poisoner, we are told by Suetonius, who was employed by the emperor Nero (reigned 54–68 C.E.).

73   **minute Gyara:** Gyara is a small island in the Aegean Sea that served as a locus of exile in ancient times (and in modern times as well).

78   **child-adulterer:** The Latin *praetextatus adulter* suggests an adulterer who wears the *toga praetexta*, a symbol of boyhood (as opposed to manhood). At the age of sixteen one shed the *toga praetexta* and *bulla* (a gold or leather amulet, protection against the evil eye) and adopted the dress symbolic of maturity, that is, of manhood—the *toga virilis*.

80   **Cluvienus:** This Cluvienus is unknown; he probably was a contemporary poet who did not enjoy much esteem, but it is possible that he was another critic of Roman society in the Juvenalian mould.

81–84 **From the time when Deucalion . . . the mountain. . . malleable stones . . . Pyrrha:** Deucalion and his wife Pyrrha are said in Greek myth to have repopulated the earth after a divinely sent universal deluge. They took refuge in a boat and when the flood subsided were grounded on Mount Parnassus ("the mountain"). Compare the Biblical account of Noah and his Ark. Thus "from the time when Deucalion" signifies here "from the origin of modern man"; "malleable stones" recalls one mythical version of the origin of humankind—that men and women emerged from the stones that Deucalion and his wife had thrown over their shoulders after being told by the goddess Themis to throw the "bones of their mother" (that is, mother earth) behind them.

85–86 **whatever people do — is the stuffing of my little book:** Juvenal's actual satirical program (the themes treated in the *Satires*) is not really so wide-ranging as this declaration promises.

88   **gulf of Greed:** The word "gulf" (Latin *sinus*) embraces a plurality of meanings, especially if "Greed" is personified (as here). Apart from the meanings "pocket" and "purse," other meanings are at work as well: "net" (thus the "net of Greed"), "sail" ("Greed in full sail") and "vagina" (common slang; thus the image of "Greed with gaping gash"). Juvenal has taken advantage of the semantic ambiguity of *sinus*; we may imagine any or all of the above connotations.

95–96 **paltry picnic basket sits outside the doorway for the toga'd mob to grab:** The Latin *sportula* ("picnic basket") was a customary donation of food or (later) money given by a patron to his client. The important contrast is between one who will selfishly devour seven courses, not bothering to have dinner guests, and the general populace, who have to scramble for morsels handed out at the rich person's doorstep.

100 **Sons of Troy:** Latin *Troiugenas*, an ironic reference to the (imagined) descendants of Rome's traditional founder, Aeneas, who escaped from Troy after its take-over by the Greeks—see especially book 2 of Vergil's *Aeneid*. (On Romulus and Remus as mythical co-founders of Rome, see the note on Juvenal, *Satire* 6.177.) At any rate, these descendants would be members of the oldest and wealthiest Roman families. The irony lies in the fact that they, as well as the traditionally poorer citizens, show up for free food. The emphasis may be on greed masked by feigned impoverishment or, as the freedman's speech that follows suggests, on the real impoverishment of those who by virtue of their birth supposedly have the greatest claim to Rome's wealth.

101 **Give the praetor his, then the tribune his:** There is further irony here, since even powerful political figures are present who, were it not for their excessive greed, would theoretically not require the paltry subvention of the *sportula*. On the functions of a praetor, see the note on Lucilius, fragment 90. Although real tribunician power eventually became vested in the emperor, originally the main duties of a tribune were to present bills at the assembly of the plebs, to defend the lives, rights, and property of the plebeians, and to assert the right of veto against legislation put before the various assemblies of the people; furthermore, a tribune was able to bring a criminal prosecution against an individual.

103–105 **Why should I be afraid — even if I myself denied it:** This is the first of several open attacks on foreigners, a group, including Greeks, that is blamed throughout the *Satires* for various urban ills. In this case the freedman supposedly came to Rome as a slave from somewhere near modern Iraq, where his ears were pierced in "oriental" fashion—hence the "tender holes in my ear" in line 104.

106   **million:** The sum cited by the ex-slave is specifically 400,000 *sesterces*, the amount required for admission to the socio-political rank of *eques* ("Knight").

106   **wider purple stripe:** Members of the senatorial class sported on their toga the *clavus latus* ("broad stripe"), conspicuous marker of their rank.

107   **Laurentum's field:** Laurentum was a region on the coast of Latium.

107   **Corvinus:** He represents the member of an old Roman family who is reduced to working as a hired hand, while freedman foreigners command the real wealth.

109   **Pallas . . . Licinus:** Freedmen of the early Principate who had achieved enormous wealth. The type was a common target for ridicule, the most famous example being Trimalchio in Petronius' *Satyricon*.

110   **sacred office:** The tribunes of the plebs were sacrosanct.

111   **white feet:** The soles of the imported slave up for sale were chalked.

116   **Concord, who clacks, her nest greeted:** Noisy storks installed nests on the roofs of some temples, such as that of the Temple of Concord.

121   **hundred coins:** A "hundred coins" (Latin *quadrantes*) was an especially paltry sum. Here the *sportula* is a gift of money.

128   **the forum and Apollo the expert lawyer:** Apollo was associated with the more developed institutions of civilization, including law, especially the approval of legal codes. As early as Greek mythology he was an agent of litigation, a symbol of legal proceedings (see, for instance, the Greek tragedy *Eumenides* by Aeschylus). In the Augustan forum at Rome there was a statue of Apollo, who naturally became witness to so many lawsuits that he was as skillful as any lawyer.

130   **Egyptian Arabarches:** The term Arabaches meant "Lord of Arabs," yet denoted "customs official." Juvenal may be referring specifically to the Roman prefect of Egypt in 66–70 c.e., Tiberius Julius Alexander.

154   **Mucius:** On this figure see the note on Persius, *Satire* 1.115.

155   **Tigellinus:** This was a notorious figure who served as prefect of the elite praetorian guard under Nero and who was responsible for the executions of many real and supposed enemies of the emperor; thus he stands here as a prime example of the politically powerful, yet corrupt, public figure.

155–157 you'll light up in that pyrotechnic — you'll carve a wide groove along the middle of the sand-lot: Christians and other offenders of the Roman government might be burned and their corpses pulled about the arena—this as a public spectacle.

162–163 Aeneas and the fierce Rutulian . . . Achilles: Here Juvenal renews his attack on the trite irrelevancies of myth and epic. It is in book 12 of Vergil's *Aeneid* that the Trojan exile and Roman founder Aeneas (see the note on Juvenal, *Satire* 6.177) kills the Italian prince Turnus, the "Rutulian" (from his tribe, the *Rutuli*). Achilles' death at the hands of Paris, who shot him in the heel with an arrow, is likewise irrelevant in the satirist's view.

164   Hylas, much sought after while he chased a jug: The myth concerning Hylas is typical, in Juvenal's view, of over-worked literary topics. Hercules dropped out of the Argonautic expedition for the Golden Fleece when he lost his male lover Hylas, who was pulled into a spring by some nymphs on an island. There are extant treatments of the story by the Greek poets Theocritus and Apollonius Rhodius and the Latin poet Valerius Flaccus. In referring to an episode from the Argonautic myth, Juvenal is again returning to the specific examples he had used to attack mythological narrative at the opening of the satire; compare lines 7–10.

168–169 ponder over with yourself — regret comes too late to the helmeted: These lines bring to the fore imagery that is markedly military in nature. The satirist is likened to an armed soldier entering a war against absurdity.

171   those whose ash is hidden by the Flaminian and Latin ways: Tombs lined the major roadways of Rome, such as the Flaminian and Latin Ways and so what Juvenal suggests here is that, in order to avoid adverse reaction by powerful persons, he will satirize only the dead. This suggestion, however, is quite tongue-in-cheek, since Juvenal's characters (dead or alive) naturally symbolize members of the contemporary population. Juvenal's implication of real danger for the outspoken satirist, however, hints that freedom of speech at Rome was itself quite a limited proposition.

NOTES ON JUVENAL, *SATIRE 3*

3   **Cumae . . . Sibyl:** Cumae was an ancient (even in Juvenal's day) colony founded by Greeks to the north of the Bay of Naples on the south-western coast of Italy. Its mythical and literary significance lies in the idea that a prophetess of Apollo (called the Sibyl) lived in a cave under the town's acropolis.

4   **Baiae's gateway:** Baiae, near Cumae, was popular from the first century B.C.E. to the third century C.E. as a holiday resort and because of its hot volcanic springs. Many wealthy Romans, including emperors, owned houses in the area.

5   **Prochyta . . . Subura:** Prochyta was a small island off the Italian coast near Cumae. The Subura, which lay between the Viminal and Esquiline hills in eastern Rome, was by Juvenal's time the bustling "red-light district" of downtown Rome, noted for its dirt and noise and as the haunt of prostitutes.

9   **"poets" reciting:** The theme of "poets reciting" as irritant was set forth first by Juvenal in *Satire 1*. Here it marks a humorous climax to a series of real (serious) urban ills.

11   **moist Capena:** The *Porta Capena* was a gateway through the southern wall of Rome that led to the Appian Way, one of the principal routes leading southward from Rome—thus symbolic of Umbricius' final exit. (On Umbricius see the note on line 21 below.) Juvenal refers to the *Porta Capena* as "moist" because water from an overhanging aqueduct, the *Via Marcia*, "Marcian Way," seeped onto it.

12   **Numa used to get together with his night-time girl:** The second king of Rome, Numa Pompilius, a quasi-historical figure who traditionally succeeded Romulus, was believed to have reigned from 715 to 673 B.C.E. He was credited with establishing many Roman religious traditions and was thought to have met near the *Porta Capena* a mystical nymph, Egeria ("his night-time girl"), for religious edification. Juvenal's wording suggests humorously, however, that these meetings were erotic in nature.

15   **For each *tree* has been ordered to donate goods to the populace:** For the theme of beggars loitering under trees, compare Juvenal, *Satire* 6.542–547 and the note on Juvenal, *Satire* 6.543; on the Jews meeting among the trees near the *Porta Capena*, compare the note on Juvenal, *Satire* 6.544–545.

16   **Camenae:** These were water-deities who were thought to inhabit a grove near the *Porta Capena* and who were believed to have inspired Numa; Egeria, on whom see line 12 and keyed note above, was one of their number. They were the Roman answer to the Greek Muses, goddesses of such cultural pursuits as music and poetry. The image of Jews displacing Roman goddesses reflects the larger theme of Umbricius' complaint—that is, foreigners displacing native Roman citizens. (On Umbricius see the note on line 21 below.)

21   **Umbricius:** It is difficult to ascertain if this character is an actual historical figure, although there is inscriptional evidence of an Umbricius at Puteoli. Whether Umbricius is a historical or fictitious figure, it is possible that Juvenal chose the name for its semantic force in Latin of "shade, shadow." The significance of the name is ambiguous: given the theme of the poem, the name suggests the refuge that the character is seeking from the rottenness of Rome; since the character is not without fault, as shown by his display of anger and envy, his name could be thought of as "Mr Shady."

25   **Daedalus shed exhausted wings:** Daedalus figured incidentally in several well-known Greek myths. An extraordinary craftsman, he built the Labyrinth to enclose the Cretan Minotaur; it was also his artificial cow that allowed Pasiphäe to have sexual intercourse with a bull, resulting in the birth of the Minotaur. Daedalus also crafted some wings with wax and feathers, enabling him and his son Icarus to escape by air from Crete, following which he is said to have landed at Cumae and here to have taken off his artificial wings; his son Icarus was killed *en route* when he flew too close to the sun, causing his wings to melt, and fell into the sea.

27   **there remains *something* for Lachesis to spin:** Lachesis was one of the three Parcae (Greek Moirai), or Fates. They are generally depicted in art and literature as haggish and unyielding. Lachesis ("Measurer"), determined a mortal's longevity by drawing a symbolic thread from the spool held by Clotho ("Spinner"); one's fate was then fixed by Atropos ("Inflexible"), who cut off the measured thread.

29–30 **Artorius . . . Catulus:** These characters are not known; they are posited by Umbricius as representative examples of unscrupulous social-climbers.

33 **to offer venal head under the spear of control:** The idiom "to offer venal head" is either to auction off one's goods under (false) declaration of bankruptcy or to sell slaves at auction. The "spear" was both symbol of conquering force (hence "control") and conspicuous marker of an auction in progress.

36 **turned thumb:** The spectators signaled a "thumbs down" if they wanted a defeated gladiator to be let off alive; "thumbs up" was the signal that the fighter deserved to be killed—this in contrast to our modern-day popular form of expression.

44–45 **frog's guts I've never inspected:** Umbricius presumably means that he has not practiced divination, but the reference could be to magic spells or poisoning.

48 **a crippled corpse useless with its right hand:** Someone unable to take bribes because he is crippled with a mutilated right hand.

53 **Verres:** The infamous governor of Sicily (73–71 B.C.E.) prosecuted by Cicero for corruption.

54–55 **Tagus (and whatever gold it rolls into the sea):** The Tagus was a river of the Iberian peninsula, believed to bear gold in its sands.

60 **sons of Quirinus:** Latin *Quirites* ("sons of Quirinus") marks the contrast between foreigner and (true) Roman. Quirinus was a mythical/religious figure, one of the symbols of pre-Roman history. Since Quirinus had by Juvenal's day become amalgamated as symbol with the mythical co-founder of Rome (Romulus), the expression *Quirites* suggests "true Romans," that is, descended from the earliest Romans. (On Aeneas as the traditional founder of Rome, see the note on Juvenal, *Satire* 6.177.)

61 **Achaeans:** Greeks in general, since the word formerly, as, for example, in Homer's *Iliad*, could denote a specific Greek tribe; in the mouth of Umbricius it has a sarcastic overtone.

62 **Syrian Orontes has flowed down into the Tiber:** The chief river of Syria on which the city of Antioch stood. Juvenal cites the region and river here to represent the Near East, whose language and customs he portrays disparagingly as flowing into the Tiber as refuse.

66   **barbarian:** Denotes specifically non-Roman, that is, foreign.

67–68   **run-to-dine jacket . . . Nike-prizes . . . perfumed:** The expressions "run-to-dine jacket," "Nike-prizes" (from Greek Nike, "Victory") and "perfumed" are, in the Latin text, deliberate and pointed Graecisms (Greek words incorporated into Latin). These words serve, therefore, to stress Greek invasion upon Roman customs.

69–70   **Sicyon . . . Amydon . . . Andros . . . Samos . . . Tralles . . . Alabanda:** Sicyon was a Greek city in the Peloponnese and to the west of Corinth. Amydon was in Macedonia. Andros and Samos are Greek islands of the Aegean. Tralles and Alabanda were inland cities of western Asia Minor. This listing of names is an example of the so-called "foreign lands theme," of which many examples may be found in ancient literature. The point of the references is their cumulative effect, which is in this case to suggest the abundance of foreigners, especially from the Greek world, at Rome. It may be noted that Juvenal draws two names each from the Greek mainland, the Aegean and Asia Minor, the three principal regions of Greek habitation.

71   **Esquiline . . . the hill named after a sprig:** There were seven hills of Rome: Capitoline, Palatine, Aventine, Quirinal, Caelian, and the two mentioned here—Esquiline and Viminal ("named after a sprig"; from Latin *vimen*).

74   **more fluent than Isaeus:** The Isaeus mentioned here (not to be confused with the Athenian orator of the fourth century B.C.E.) was a Syrian rhetorician who visited Rome in around 100 C.E. and was popular for his extempore orations.

79   **Moor . . . Sarmatian . . . Thracian:** The Moors were inhabitants of Mauretania used here to refer in general to Africans, while the Sarmatians lived in the region between the Vistula and the Don in Poland and south-west Russia; the Thracians, who lived just outside the Greek world, represent the inhabitants beyond the imperial borders to the north.

80   **who donned feathers:** Daedalus, on whom see the note on line 25 above.

85   **Sabine berry ... Aventine:** The Sabine berry was the Italian olive. The Aventine was the southernmost of the seven hills of Rome; compare the note on line 71 above.

89   **Hercules as he holds Antaeus high off the ground:** In Greek mythology, Antaeus was a son of the sea-god Poseidon and Ge ("Earth"). He ruled a kingdom in North Africa and challenged all visitors to wrestling matches, which he always won even if he was thrown, since he drew his strength from the earth. The hero Heracles (Latin Hercules) overcame Antaeus by raising him from the ground with his great strength and then crushing him to death.

93–94   **Thais ... wife ... Doris:** Thais (the prostitute), the "wife" and Doris (the maid) are stock characters in Greek New Comedy and in the Roman comedy that was modeled on it. On Thais as a historical figure, see the note on Juvenal, *Satire* 6. O 25–26.

98–99   **Antiochus ... Stratocles ... Demetrius ... Haemus:** These figures were Greek comic actors who made names for themselves on the Roman stage.

113:   This self-contained line, with its commentary on the Greek's motives, seems to break the context somewhat. It may actually be an intrusion into the original text. Such intrusions in some cases resulted from the incorporation of ancient scribes' marginalia, which might often be written in the same meter as the text itself.

115   **gymnasia ... crime of a 'greater cloak':** The gymnasium, a fundamental feature of Greek social life, represented for some (conservative) Romans moral corruption, since these "exercise houses" were often associated with nudity and homosexuality. The word *gymnasium* (Greek *gymnasion*) actually derives from the Greek *gymnos* ("naked"). A "crime of a 'greater cloak'" is a vivid colloquial metaphor referring either to a more serious crime or the stature of the person committing it.

116   **Stoic informer ... Barea:** In 66 C.E., the Stoic philosopher Publius Egnatius Celer gave false evidence to secure the conviction of his former pupil, Quintus Marcius Barea Soranus, on charges of conspiracy against the emperor Nero.

117–118   **river-bank at which the feather of the Gorgon-horse fell:** The Gorgon-horse is Pegasus, who was born, according to mythical tradition, from the severed head of the Gorgon Medusa after she was killed by

Perseus. A feather was said to have fallen from Pegasus' wings onto the bank of the river Cydnus in Tarsus.

129 **to go in headlong haste when the childless are awake:** The childless were the targets of zealous *captatores* ("legacy-hunters"), who waited on and flattered childless old people in the hope of benefiting from their wills or even being adopted by them.

130 **Albina . . . Modia:** These figures are unknown.

133 **Calvina . . . Catiena:** These may be "high-class" women, but it seems more likely that they are merely expensive prostitutes.

136 **Chione:** This (cheap) prostitute's name, which also appears in the work of Juvenal's friend Martial, is Greek and suggests the meaning "Snowy."

137–138 **the host of the Idaean divinity:** The Near Eastern mother-goddess Cybele, the "Great Mother"; "Idaean" refers to Ida, a mountain in Phrygia, not far from Troy, where the goddess was worshipped. Her "host" was Publius Cornelius Scipio Nasica who in 204 B.C.E. was judged the most worthy man to conduct to Rome from Asia Minor a black stone sacred to the goddess, which was obtained to secure Cybele's aid against the invading Carthaginians under Hannibal.

138 **Numa:** A legendary king of early Rome famous for his piety; compare the note on line 12 above and Juvenal, *Satire* 6.343 and keyed note.

138–139 **he who saved fearful Minerva from burning shrine:** Tradition held that in 241 B.C.E. Lucius Caecilius Metellus sacrificed his eyesight to save Minerva's statue from the Temple of Vesta, which had caught fire.

144 **You can swear by the altars of Samothrace:** It was believed that if one lied after swearing on the "altars of Samothrace," one would be subject to divine retribution; compare the modern practice of "swearing on the Bible."

154 **let him rise from Knight-seat:** The "Knight-seat" refers to a block of superior seats in the Roman theaters that by a law proposed in 67 B.C.E. by the tribune Lucius Roscius Otho (the "Otho" of line 159) was reserved for the relatively wealthy class of *equites* ("Knights"), while the poorer classes could use only inferior seating. The law caused considerable trouble in 63 B.C.E.

159 **vain Otho:** See the note on line 154 above.

169   **the Marsians and a Samnite table:** Both the Marsians and the Samnites were tribal groups of non-Roman Italians. The Marsians prompted the so-called "Social war" of 90–88 B.C.E. in a bid for Roman citizenship. The Samnites fought during this same period in an attempt to halt growing Roman socio-political and economic domination in central Italy. What is stressed above all in the satire is the relative simplicity and unpretentiousness of the country in respect to the city of Rome.

170   **rough Venetian cowl:** A hood either of the type worn by the Veneti, a tribe living near Venice, or "blue" or "bluish-green" in color, from Latin *ueneto*.

184–185   **Cossus . . . Veiento:** Veiento was a much-feared informer of the period of Domitian (reigned 81–96 C.E.) and Cossus, though otherwise unknown, was presumably another. Their names here are used to signify arrogant, stern aristocrats.

186   **That one's mowing a beard; this one's laying down the curl of a loved one:** These are slaves who have to be paid handsomely to perform their duties. One slave is cutting a beard, either his own or someone else's, while another is trimming the curls of a boyfriend as an offering to Venus.

187–189   **the house is full of cakes on sale — to augment the piggy-banks of cultivated slaves:** Cakes are provided at this feast, but the clients must pay for them. The low social status of the clients is suggested by the fact that they are compelled to pay the slaves for the cakes as a form of tribute.

190–192   **Praeneste . . . Volsinii . . . Gabii . . . Tibur:** Praeneste (modern Palestrina) is approximately thirty-seven kilometers east of Rome. Volsinii was located in Etruria, noted for its surrounding cliffs. Gabii, some twenty kilometers southwest of Rome, was the fabled site of the education of Romulus and Remus. Tibur (modern Tivoli) is about twenty-nine kilometers north-east of Rome. All are cited as typical examples of rural Italian towns of long standing.

198   **Ucalegon:** This character is from Vergil's *Aeneid* (2.311–312), where his house in Troy is burned down by the invading Greeks. There is some parody in Juvenal's adoption of this name, since here Ucalegon is not the epic figure of the Trojan war but a typical poverty-stricken and desperate Roman.

203   Cordus had a cot ... Procula: Cordus represents a typically modest
Roman with very few possessions. He is probably not to be identified
with the poet mentioned by Juvenal at *Satires* 1.2. Procula, it seems,
was either a dwarf or a prostitute, in which case Cordus' bed is so
modest that not even a prostitute would enter it.

205   Chiron: Chiron, a well-known mythological figure, was the unusually
civilized centaur (half-horse, half-man) who was said to have educated
other major mythological figures, including Achilles, Jason, and
Asclepius, the latter a son of Apollo and famous healer.

212   house of Asturicus: Mansions were named after their builders or
previous long-time owners, a practice that still occurs today. This
Asturicus may have been a Roman senator; nothing more of him is
known, but he stands as symbol of ostentatious wealth.

217   Euphranor ... Polyclitus: Euphranor and Polyclitus were respec-
tively fourth and fifth century B.C.E. Greek sculptors. Euphranor was
especially famous for his "Spear-carrier," which he appears to have
sculpted to illustrate the principles set forth in his (lost) book on sculp-
tural technique and proportion. This book of Euphranor was extremely
influential in subsequent Greek and Roman figure sculpture; he also
wrote on proportion and technique. Sculptural works by these and other
such artists were precious and high-priced.

221   Persicus: Of this Persicus nothing is known for certain. He may have
lived in the "house of Asturicus" mentioned in line 212. He may be
Asturicus himself—most Romans had three names. He may simply be
another example of a wealthy citizen who has lost his house.

223–224 Sora ... Fabrateria ... Frusino: Sora, Fabrateria, and Frusino are
further examples of countryside villages, where rents were naturally
less expensive than those of Rome. All were located near Aquinum,
the traditional birth-place of Juvenal himself.

229   Pythagoreans: Since Pythagoreans were vegetarians, Umbricius is
advocating the cultivation of vegetables that make one self-sufficient.
Leeks, onions, and beans are frequently mentioned by Roman satirists,
often in pointed contrast to more exotic and expensive foods, for
instance, oysters and lobsters, symbolic of perverse luxury.

238   Drusus ... sea-cows: Drusus is the emperor Claudius, who reigned
from 41 to 54 C.E. He is the subject of the satirical *Apocolocyntosis*
("Pumpkinification") attributed to Seneca (*circa* 4 B.C.E.–65 C.E.).

Claudius was notorious for falling asleep at inappropriate times; "sea-cows" (marine seals) were likewise viewed as inordinately drowsy.

239–240 rich man . . . Liburnian sedan-chair: "Liburnian" suggests that the "sedan-chair" resembles, in appearance and function, a warship, the *liburna*, invented by the Liburni, a sea-faring people of the Adriatic. Thus the "rich man" is able to slice through the crowds of ordinary people just as a ship slices through the sea.

249   with how much smoke the hand-out is thronged: The "hand-out" (*sportula*) is here a portion of heated food. Recipients carry a portable charcoal stove to keep the food warm.

251   Corbulo: Gnaeus Domitius Corbulo, a Roman military officer who served under Claudius and Nero, was known for his massive physique and extraordinary strength.

257   Ligurian boulders: Blocks of marble, so called here after the region from which they were quarried.

266–267 morose ferryman . . . a half-cent to offer in his mouth: The "morose ferryman" is, in this underworld vignette, Charon. Myth held that a dead person's spirit must pay Charon for transfer across the river Styx; without "a half-cent to offer" as payment, usually placed in the mouth of the deceased, a spirit was supposedly forced to linger on the wrong side of the river, as here.

280   son of Peleus mourning his friend: The "son of Peleus" is Achilles, while the "friend" referred to here was Patroclus, who was killed in the Greek siege of Troy when he chose to fight in Achilles' armor in order to restore morale to the Greek forces that were suffering severely due to his friend's withdrawal. Achilles, disturbed by Patroclus' death, was said to have tossed and turned unable to sleep, just like the drunken bully described in lines 278–281. The scene is described in Homer, *Iliad* 24.1–13.

**281:   **This line, like line 113, is probably an insertion based on a marginal note.

306–307 Pontine swamp . . . Gallinarian pine-grove: The "Pontine swamp" was a vast semi-flooded area on the coast near Rome. The "Gallinarian pine-grove" was located near Cumae, Umbricius' destination. These regions were notorious as the hideouts of criminals and bandits and were apparently purged periodically by Roman troops.

319   **Aquinum:** Juvenal's native town (compare the note on line 226 above), which, if we accept Umbricius' words at face value, the poet might have visited on occasion.

320–321 Helvine Ceres . . . your Diana from Cumae: References signifying the temples of Ceres (Greek Demeter) and Diana (Greek Artemis), goddesses of corn and the wood respectively. The Temple of Ceres was presumably built by a Helvius, but the reference may be a reference to Ceres as the patron-goddess of the Helvii, a distinguished family in the region. On Cumae see the note on line 3 above.

NOTES ON JUVENAL, *SATIRE* 6

1 **Saturn's reign:** Reference to the reign of Saturn implies a Golden Age, when mankind was pure and simple. Saturn (Latin *Saturnus*) was an Italian deity who was later identified with the Greek god Cronus, who was ruler of the gods until his son Zeus deposed and exiled him. The early Greek poet Hesiod (*circa* 700 B.C.E.), in his poem *Works and Days*, posits an evolution of mankind in five stages in which the progression is from good to bad; the stages are represented in five ages described as the Golden Age, Silver Age, Bronze Age, Heroic Age, and Iron Age. Ovid (43 B.C.E.–17 C.E.), in *Metamorphoses* 1, likewise outlines an Age-based degeneration of mankind, yet he omits Hesiod's Heroic Age.

3 **Lar:** The Lar was the tutelary deity of a house; most commonly the Lares, whose images stood in a small chapel (*lararium*) or on the hearth in a little shrine (*aedes*).

5 **mountain-wife:** Compare the note on lines 7–8 below.

7–8 **Cynthia ... whose shining little eyes dead sparrow disturbed:** Both Cynthia and the one "whose shining little eyes dead sparrow disturbed" are the "girlfriends" celebrated by Roman love poets—Cynthia being that of Propertius (*circa* 50–16 B.C.E.) and Lesbia that of Catullus (*circa* 84–54 B.C.E.), who wrote a famous poem (Catullus 3) on the death of her pet sparrow. As supposedly elegant and emotionally disturbing women, these are set up in pointed contrast to the simple "mountain-wife" mentioned in line 5.

10 **acorn-burping:** Acorns here symbolize simplicity, modesty, even honesty. Extravagant foods are consumed, on the other hand, by gluttonous and overly luxurious moderns.

12–13 **born of shattered oak-tree or fashioned from mud:** The reference to mankind's origin from oak or mud recalls two versions of mythical creation. One version held that Prometheus fashioned the first human from a mixture of earth and water. The other version prefers (oak-) tree or rock as man's origin; compare the note on Juvenal, *Satire* 1.81–84.

185

19   Astraea: This female figure, who was eventually identified with the constellation Virgo ("the Virgin"), was supposedly the last of the divine presences to abandon earth during the Iron Age.

20   the two sisters: These are the Chastity mentioned in line 14 and Astraea in line 19.

21   Postumus: The unknown Postumus is the figure to whom this satire is ostensibly addressed (as a dissuasion from marriage).

23–24   Iron Age . . . Silver Century: On these ages see the note on line 1 above.

29   Tisiphone: Tisiphone is one of the mythical Furies (also known as Erinyes) who dwelled in the Underworld and punished people especially for crimes against blood-relatives. Those hounded by the Furies are tortured by snakes, whips, or burning torches. The two other Furies are Allecto and Megaera.

32   Aemilian bridge: The Aemilian bridge spanned the river Tiber, affording one the opportunity for suicide by drowning.

38   Julian Law . . . . Ursidius: To discourage adultery and to promote marriage, the bearing of legitimate children, and traditional "family values," Augustus imposed the Julian Law in 18 B.C.E. This law was re-established by Domitian and Juvenal here suggests that it encouraged marriage as well as discouraged adultery. Ursidius, like Postumus, is an unknown figure.

40   legacy-hunters: *Captatores* ("legacy-hunters") might offer to a childless person such extravagant and expensive foods as doves and bearded mullets with the hope of insinuating themselves into the legal testament of the childless.

44   whom the box of Latinus, about to perish, so often concealed: Latinus was an actor evidently well-known for playing fictional adulterers who might hide in a box (or elsewhere) to escape a jealous husband's punishment; compare Juvenal, *Satire* 1.36 and keyed note. Ursidius' real-life exploits are described as mirroring Latinus' fictional ones.

46   puncture his excessively swollen vein: The implication is that Ursidius is insane, since an excess of blood manifested in swollen veins was held to be symptomatic of insanity; the treatment was to drain away the excess blood.

47–48   Tarpeian threshold . . . Juno: The official state Temple of Jupiter Capitolinus on the Capitoline hill is here called "Tarpeian" after the rocky outcrop near it known as the Tarpeian rock. Juno, wife of Jupiter, was considered, among her other functions, to be the patron goddess of the marriage ceremony.

50   Ceres' head-bands: The August festival of Ceres required from its participants a nine day period of sexual abstinence; thus the implication here is that very few women at Rome can go without sexual activity for so long. Likewise, their mouths would be polluted from oral sex; the sexual theme of the "unclean mouth" (*os impurum*) is quite common in Roman satirical invective.

53   Hiberina: The name Hiberina suggests a woman of Spanish origin (Latin *Hiberia* = Spain), but nothing more is known of this character.

56–57   Gabii . . . Fidenae: Gabii and Fidenae here represent small rustic towns quite unlike Rome in cosmopolitan sophistication; compare Juvenal, *Satire* 3.192 and keyed note.

58–59   nothing was ever done in the mountains or in caves . . . Jupiter . . . Mars: The reference is to the mythical hypersexuality of the gods Jupiter and Mars. Jupiter especially, like his Greek equivalent Zeus, is frequently depicted as raping mortal girls and nymphs in rural settings, often appearing in the form of an animal. Mars was the Roman god of war; the adultery of his Greek counterpart Ares with Aphrodite (Latin Venus), goddess of sexual love, was famous from Homer, *Odyssey* 8.266–366. The joke seems somewhat misplaced, yet it serves to reconfirm the less than serious tone of the narrative persona.

63   Bathyllus dancing the role of gyrating Leda: Bathyllus, the name of a celebrated dancer of the first century B.C.E. with whom Maecenas (on whom see the note on Horace, *Satire* 1.9.43) apparently had a homosexual relationship, came to be a generic name for any effeminate stage-dancer. Here such an actor portrays the mythical woman Leda, with whom Jupiter supposedly had sexual intercourse after he had taken the physical form of a swan.

64–66   Tuccia doesn't control her gash's flow; Apula moans . . . Thymele learns: Tuccia, Apula, and Thymele as names are insignificant. The first two represent young women who derive (excessive) sexual excitement merely by seeing the seduction of Leda acted out; the third represents an inexperienced girl who sees the scene and learns the vices of the other two.

69   **Megalesians ... People's Games:** Megalesians were public festivals held in early April in honor of the Phrygian goddess Cybele and involved theatrical presentations. The People's Games began in early November. The six-month period in between these ceremonies thus supposedly disturbed the apparently actor-infatuated women of Rome.

70–71   **Accius ... Urbicus:** These are otherwise unknown actors, the type with whom overzealous women apparently became obsessed.

71–72   **performances of the Atellan farce ... Autonoe ... Aelia:** An Atellan farce was a crudely performed stage play belonging to an old Italian comic tradition. This one has as its subject the mythical figure Autonoe, daughter of Cadmus, king of Thebes. Aelia, like Tuccia, Apula, and Thymele above, is unknown.

73   **comic actor's dick-pin is loosened for these women for a great price:** A "dick-pin" (Latin *fibula*) was a sort of "safety-pin" sometimes inserted through the foreskin of a professional singer's penis. The common belief was that sexual activity was detrimental to one's voice. Juvenal suggests that the *fibula* might, however, be temporarily removed for a woman willing to pay.

74   **Chrysogonus ... Hispulla:** The name of the singer Chrysogonus is Greek; it suggests "Golden-born." There were several historical Hispullas; which, if any, Juvenal had in mind here is uncertain.

75   **do you expect Quintilian to be loved?:** This Quintilian is certainly the well-known writer and orator Marcus Fabius Quintilianus (*circa* 35–95 C.E.), author of the extant *Institutio Oratoria* ("Oratorical Education"); compare Introduction, p. 1. Juvenal sarcastically suggests that women will ignore the scholarly type altogether in preference to any actor.

76–77   **Echion ... Glaphyrus ... Ambrosius:** Echion, Glaphyrus, and Ambrosius are all pointed Graecisms. The names suggest respectively "hold," "elegant" or "hollow," and "sweet" or "divine"—as *ambrosia*, the mythical food of the gods.

80–81   **Lentulus ... Euryalus the gladiator:** The name, while here unspecific, suggests an individual from a wealthy and aristocratic family; thus the irony is strengthened by the suggestion that a Lentulus shall be cuckolded by a lowly gladiator (Euryalus).

82–84 **Eppia . . . Pharos . . . walls of Lagus . . . Canopus:** Although Eppia is not known to be a historical figure, the scandal surrounding her abandonment of family to follow a gladiator (Sergius in line 105) may indeed have been factual and well known. Pharos was the Egyptian island containing the lighthouse marking the port of Alexandria. Lagus was the father of the founder of the Ptolemaic dynasty, Ptolemy Sotor; thus the "walls of Lagus" refer to the Egyptian capital Alexandria. On Canopus see Juvenal, *Satire* 1.26 and keyed note.

87 **Paris:** Actors, especially pantomimes, frequently adopted the name Paris. This Paris may be the famous close associate of Domitian (emperor 81–96 C.E.), executed in 83 C.E. for an alleged sexual affair with the emperor's wife.

110 **Hyacinthuses:** Hyacinthus was in Greek myth the male love-object of the god Apollo; thus the name became generic, as here, for any physically attractive young man.

113–114 **Veiento . . . Eppia:** Veiento is probably the senator referred to in line 82 and husband of Eppia, a figure not as interesting to the infatuated Eppia as a gladiator, although the name was also that of a prominent informer under Domitian.

115 **Claudius:** This emperor (10 B.C.E.–54 C.E.) was said to have been both physically unattractive and mentally sluggish. Historical tradition attributes his death to poisoning by his second wife Agrippina. For a brutal parody of Claudius' apotheosis (deification after death), see the *Apocolocyntosis* of Seneca.

118–117: These lines seem to read more smoothly if their arrangement in the original Latin manuscripts is shifted.

117 **Palatine:** The Palatine hill was one of the seven hills of Rome and the site of an imperial mansion.

123 **Wolf-lady:** The Latin text reads *Lycisca*, which means "Wolf-lady"; the name is appropriate to the *lupanar* (compare *lupa*, "she-wolf"), a house of prostitution.

124 **Britannicus:** Britannicus was the emperor Claudius' son by his first wife Messalina. He was so-named from his successful military exploits in Britain.

126: This line appears only in fifteenth-century manuscripts. It could have been added by an interpolator who considered line 125 too abrupt, or it could have been deleted at some point by a prudish editor.

136 **Caesennia:** Although this Caesennia is unknown historically, her name suggests wealth, as the family of the Caesennii were socially prominent *circa* 60 C.E.

142 **Sertorius . . . Bibula:** The name Sertorius suggests a Sabine. The name Bibula is significant in that it suggests "(overly) fond of drinking," as does the English.

146 **"Collect your bags," a freedman will say, "and get out!:** The ex-slave was presumably still employed as housekeeper; thus here his job is to rid his employer's home of the unattractive woman. Under Roman law a man could divorce his wife by instructing her to leave his house.

150 **Canusian sheep . . . Falernian grapevines:** Sheep from the town of Canusium in Apulia were considered to produce wool of the highest quality. On Falernian and other varieties of wine, see the notes on Horace, *Satire* 2.8.14–15, 2.8.16, and Juvenal, *Satire* 1.70.

153–154 **the month of winter-cold . . . Jason . . . a white stall:** From 17 to 19 December ("the month of winter-cold") the Romans held a public festival called the Saturnalia, a period of revelry and even role reversal, with slaves being served by their masters. One of the notable aspects of this festival was the selling of figurines and other baubles from canvas booths lining the perimeter of the *Campus Martius*. These booths (for example, "a white stall") naturally obstructed from view the more permanent merchant-shops, some of which were located in the so-called Arcade of Agrippa, which contained a mural painted with the mythological scene of Jason and his crew in search of the Golden Fleece.

156–158 **well-known diamond . . . Berenice's finger . . . barbarian . . . Agrippa:** The diamond ring is said by the merchant (probably falsely) to have historical significance. Berenice was the granddaughter of "Herod" Agrippa, actually Marcus Julius Agrippa (10 B.C.E.–44 C.E.). Her brother was Agrippa II (the one mentioned here), who is called "barbarian" because, although a client-king of a Roman city-state, his origin was in Judaea. Tradition held that Berenice and Agrippa II co-habitated. There is some historical evidence that Jewish regals worshipped bare-footed and that the Jews generally abstained from pork for religious reasons.

164   **war-breaking Sabine with hair let loose:** The reference is to the quasi-historical "Rape of the Sabine Women," which caused the Sabines to attack the Romans, who, in order to populate their new city, had invited the Sabines to a festival and then abducted the women among them. The captured women were said to have interrupted the fighting.

167–168 **Venustina . . . Cornelia . . . the Gracchi:** Venustina is a generic name for "woman in the street" and perhaps even denotes "common streetwalker." Cornelia, on the other hand, was the noble mother of the famed Gaius and Tiberius Gracchus (known as "the Gracchi"), orators and populist social reformers of the second century B.C.E.

170–171 **Hannibal . . . Syphax . . . Carthage:** Cornelia is imagined to have set up in her house images of her illustrious father Scipio Africanus, who defeated first the Numidian Syphax and then the Carthaginian Hannibal at the Battle of Zama in 202.

172–173 **I pray you, Paean — transfix the mother herself:** Here Juvenal imagines the words of the mythical character Amphion. His wife Niobe had foolishly boasted that she had produced more children than Latona. Since Latona's children were Apollo ("Paean") and Diana (Greek Artemis), these two gods punished Niobe by killing all her seven sons and seven daughters.

174   **Amphion:** On this figure see the note on lines 172–173 above.

176   **Niobe . . . Latona's lineage:** On Niobe and Latona see the note on lines 172–173 above.

177   **more fertile than the white sow:** The white sow with its litter of thirty was a portent of the founding of Alba Longa, an ancient settlement near Rome traditionally founded *circa* 1152 by Ascanius, who was the son of Aeneas, Rome's traditional founder. Later Romans considered Romulus, one of Aeneas' descendants, to be the co-founder of Rome (along with his brother Remus), and Aeneas to be the founder of Lavinium, a preceding city.

186   **Tuscan:** A Tuscan was a native-born Italian from Etruria, the region just north of Rome.

187   **Sulmo . . . Cecrops:** Sulmo was an Italian town in the Sabine region. Cecrops was the quasi-historical first king of Athens.

188:   The relatively dull tone of this line has led most editors to view it as an interpolation.

195   **life and soul:** Juvenal's words in the original text, written in Greek script (transliterated *zoe kai psyche*), are translated "life and soul," a phrase the eroticism of which is to us elusive.

198–199 Haemus . . . Carpophorus: Both Haemus and Carpophorus were stage-actors known, evidently, for their ability to portray seductive characters. On Haemus compare Juvenal, *Satire* 3.99 and the note on Juvenal, *Satire* 3.98–99.

204–205 on well-endowed platter Dacian and German shine on inscribed gold coin: A platter filled with coins was evidently not common as a wedding gift but rather as a present to gladiators; thus Juvenal may be deliberately by careful choice of diction introducing martial imagery to what is ostensibly a peaceful union. At any rate, the gold coins referred to here probably were minted by the emperor Trajan (ruled 98–117 C.E.); they would have depicted his military victories over northern tribes.

236   **Archigenes:** This Archigenes was probably the famed Syrian physician working at Rome during the reign of Trajan. That such an illustrious doctor should be called to attend the woman who feigns illness to mask adultery is of course highly ironic.

243   **Manilia:** This figure is unknown.

245   **Celsus:** There were several legal experts by this name in Roman history. The point of the line is that women have become more versed in litigation than even renowned lawyers.

246   **Tyrian hue . . . feminine wrestling oil:** "Tyrian hue" was an ostentatious shade of purple, the dye for which was obtained from shellfish off the coast of Judaea/Palestine; "feminine wrestling oil" here is almost an oxymoron, as what follows is a description of women who practice the "manly" art of hand-to-hand combat.

247–248 the wounds of the post, which she makes hollow . . . and injures: Gladiators used a wooden stump ("post") as practice-dummy. The woman described attacks the stump with such persistence that she actually wears a depression in and damages it.

249–250 an utterly worthy lady of Flora's horn: Activities surrounding the public festival in honor of the flower-goddess Flora were announced by the sound of a trumpet. This festival was held from 28 April to 3

May and it is said to have had strong fertility aspects and the involvement of licentious women, even prostitutes. Thus, although the she-gladiator acts out a man's role, she is nevertheless pure female.

262–263 a great bandage . . . thick with tree-bark: The protective wrap ("bandage") worn by a gladiator was composed of layers of the dense inner bark of trees.

265–266 Lepidus . . . blind Metellus . . . Fabius Gurges: Lepidus, like the figures who follow, stand as representatives of the Roman noble aristocracy. Marcus Aemilius Lepidus was a founding member of the famous triumvirate created in 43 B.C.E. that included Marcus Antonius (Mark Antony) and Octavian. Tradition holds that Lucius Caecilius Metellus became blind when in 241 B.C.E. he heroically entered the burning Temple of Vesta and saved the Palladium, an ancient sacred image said to have protected Troy, until its removal allowed the city to fall, and later to have been brought to Rome by Aeneas. Quintus Fabius Maximus was consul in the early third century B.C.E.; he obtained the nickname *Gurges* ("Gullet") as a youth with an apparently insatiable appetite.

267 Asylus: A gladiator; the irony here is that even the consort of a gladiator does not imitate him.

280 Quintilian: See the note on line 75 above.

291 Hannibal . . . standing at the Colline tower: The historical reference is to the siege of Rome by Hannibal in 211 B.C.E. The Colline tower was an outpost on a protective wall standing on the Quirinal hill.

296–297 Sybaris . . . Rhodes . . . Miletus . . . Tarentum: Sybaris and Tarentum were early Greek city-states located in southern Italy. Rhodes was (even in antiquity) a prosperous Mediterranean island. Miletus was a city in Asia Minor with a reputation for sexual license.

300 a drunken Venus: Venus, goddess of sexual love, here denotes any woman who is both inebriated and sexually aroused.

303 undiluted Falernian: On Falernian wine see the notes on Horace, *Satire* 2.8.16 and Juvenal, *Satire* 1.70.

306 Maura: The name Maura is insignificant apart from the fact that it suggests "the girl from Africa."

308–307: On the reversal of lines, compare the note on lines 118–117 above.

308 altar of Chastity: There was a Temple of (the goddess) Chastity in the oldest of the Roman fora, the forum Boarium.

307   Tullia: This figure, if historical (which remains uncertain), is not literally the sister of Maura but perhaps the foster-sister. There were many members of the Tullian family, among them Marcus Tullius Cicero, the famous orator.

314   Good Goddess: It is not known exactly who the "Good Goddess" (Latin *Bona Dea*) was thought to be. She was celebrated by a fertility cult of women who were required to abstain from sex and who were supervised by the "Vestal virgins," who were themselves under a vow of celibacy. It was strongly forbidden for men to participate in or observe the ceremony.

316   Priapus' Maenads: There is irony combined with misrepresentation here. The Maenads were female revelers who celebrated the rites of Dionysus (Bacchus), yet here Juvenal places them in the setting of *Bona Dea* worship. Similarly, the women are depicted as celebrating sexuality and the watch-god Priapus, usually represented with a grotesquely enormous erect penis. Statues of Priapus, usually of wood, were commonly placed in gardens to ward off pests both animal as well as human. Threats of forced sodomy were likewise inscribed on these statues for those who might dare violate the god's territory.

320–323 Saufeia . . . swaying buttocks . . . gyrating Medullina . . . virtue equal to birth: Both Saufeia and Medullina are names that, while not specific to any known personages, imply an aristocratic background. Saufeia, with her "swaying buttocks," and Medullina, with her "gyrating," do not conduct themselves in the "noble" fashion expected of them; therefore "virtue equal to birth" is highly sarcastic.

326   son of Laomedon . . . Nestor: The "son of Laomedon" is Priam, the legendary king of Troy at the time when it was conquered and sacked by the Greeks in the Trojan war. Nestor, king of Pylos, was a Greek leader at Troy who was renowned for his very great age and wisdom. Both are typical examples of men who lived to be ancient.

337–338 which "cithara-girl" introduced a penis . . . two Anti-Catos of Caesar: The reference to a man disguised as a woman in order to witness the all-female celebration of the *Bona Dea* is in fact historically based. In 62 B.C.E. Publius Clodius Pulcher donned the garb of a woman cithara player and gained access to the rites that were being performed at the house of Julius Caesar. He was detected, however, and formally charged with violating the rites. Only by bribery did he avoid conviction and punishment. Caesar's works against his political opponent Marcus Porcius Cato (the "Anti-Catos") were notorious for their excessive length.

343   **Numa:** Numa Pompilius, as the quasi-historical second king of Rome, symbolizes the modest and inelegant lifestyle. Tradition attributes to Numa the primitive Roman religious doctrines; compare Juvenal, *Satire* 3.12 and keyed note.

344   **dishes ... the Vatican mountain:** The "dishes," including sacrificial bowls and the like, of very early Rome, suggests Juvenal, were made of modest black clay. Implied, however, is that contemporary Romans demand ornate vessels of precious metals. The Vatican mountain (not one of the "seven hills" of Rome) was slightly north-west of the city. The ground there was poor, as were any products of the region.

345   **Clodius:** This is the Publius Clodius Pulcher of line 337 above.

346–348: These lines are very similar to O 30–34, so they could be omitted.

351   **tall Syrians:** Syrian slaves, like Cappadocians and Liburnians, were most commonly employed as sedan-chair bearers.

352   **Ogulnia:** The name Ogulnia suggests a member of the plebs (the common class of poor people). Although poverty stricken, she must appear wealthy.

361   **the ant as their model:** For the moralistic motif "go to the ant" (and follow its example of industry and provision for the future), compare Lucilius, fragment 586–587 and Horace, *Satire* 1.1.31–35.

O 1–O 34: What follows line 365 is referred to either as the "O fragment" (after Oxford University, in whose Bodleian Library it was found) or the "Windstedt fragment" (after E. O. Windstedt, who discovered it in 1899). There remains critical debate both as to the authenticity of the fragment's thirty-six lines and as to their appropriate position within the larger satire; some editors place them after line 345. In the actual manuscript in which Windstedt found the lines, thirty-four are placed after line 365 and a further two (lines 373a and 373b) after line 373. The content of the fragment is obscene, which perhaps explains its exclusion from all manuscripts but one, and the meaning is somewhat obscure in places.

O 6   **Gourd-face . . . Bearded-swallow:** Both "Gourd-face" and "Bearded-swallow" are Greek names in the original text. They mean "Cunt-licker" and "Cock-sucker" respectively.

O 8–9   **Lisper . . . Big-tool:** The names of these two figures are problematic in meaning. Their original forms seem to be puns for two types of gladiators: "Lisper" = a light-armed fighter, its pun "Smoothie" (that is, pathic homosexual); "Big-tool" = a well-armed fighter, its pun "Well-equipped" (that is, one with a large penis).

O 15   **Alban . . . Surrentine wine:** These were better wines; compare the note on Juvenal, *Satire* 1.70.

O 25–26 **Thais . . . Triple-phallus:** Thais was a famous Athenian courtesan during the time of Alexander the Great; it is likely that many later prostitutes adopted her name for themselves. The actor (*Triphallus* in the Latin text) is a paradox: he plays a highly feminine role on stage but is actually a hypersexual male—hence "Triple-phallus."

367   **their hopelessness of a beard:** The castrated eunuch, due to hormonal deficiency, lacked facial hair.

373   **Heliodorus . . . the barber's loss:** Heliodorus is a Greek name, here of a surgeon who performs castrations. Eunuchs often wore long hair—to "the barber's loss."

373A–373B: From the O fragment (Winstedt's manuscript); compare the note on line O 1 above.

375   **garden's guard:** The reference here is to the god Priapus, on whom see the note on line 316 above.

377–378 **Postumus . . . Bromius:** Having abandoned the original addressee of the satire for some time, Juvenal now reintroduces him. Bromius was another name for Bacchus (Dionysus), the god of wine, nature, and ecstasy. It literally suggests the meaning "noisy one" and here it is evidently the pet-name of Postumus' (imaginary) young boy-friend. The enormous penis of the eunuch described would naturally injure such a boy physically but, implies Juvenal, could be accommodated by a woman.

380–381 **Instruments always are in her hands:** The sexual double-entendre of the woman handling "instruments" is deliberate.

383   **Hedymeles:** This Greek name may be Juvenal's own, as it means "sweet-singing."

385 **A certain woman of the number of Lamiae and Appius' name:** Aelius Lamiae was a famous patrician, while Appius was of *gens* Claudia ("the family of Claudia"). In both cases these names indicate descent from highly respectable and aristocratic families.

386 **Janus ... Vesta:** Janus, the two-faced god of beginnings and endings, was the first god to be invoked in a wide ranging prayer, Vesta, the hearth-goddess, the last; thus the woman actually prays to the entire Roman pantheon. Ground grain (meal) and wine were used commonly in sacrificial prayer whereby vows were made to the gods in return for their favors.

387 **Pollio ... Capitoline oak-crown:** This Pollio is mentioned elsewhere by Juvenal as well as by Martial and must have been a musician of some fame. The emperor Domitian instituted contests for music, horse-racing, and athletics in 86 C.E. These contests were in honor of Jupiter Capitolinus, whose temple stood on the Capitoline hill. The victors in these events were awarded crowns of oak-leaves.

397 **the seer will grow varicose:** The varicosity would supposedly result from constantly standing around watching for the divine portents hoped for by the praying women.

409 **Niphates:** Technically, the Niphates was not a river, as Juvenal implies, but rather a mountain range in Armenia. This confusion is probably deliberate, highlighting the ignorance of women who invent rumors.

430 **Falernian:** On this wine see the notes on Horace, *Satire* 2.8.16 and Juvenal, *Satire* 1.70.

435 **Vergil .. Elissa:** Vergil is Publius Vergilius Maro (70–19 B.C.E.), the famous Augustan literary figure, author of the *Georgics*, *Eclogues*, and *Aeneid*. Elissa is another name for Dido, the queen of Carthage who falls in love with Aeneas and kills herself when he leaves her; see book 4 of the *Aeneid*.

436–437 **Maro she suspends ... in the other part of the balance, Homer:** Maro is Vergil (see the note on line 435 above), who, by writing the *Aeneid* in obvious imitation of the *Iliad* and *Odyssey* ascribed to Homer (*circa* 750 B.C.E.), established himself as "the Roman Homer." Here Homer is literally "weighed" against Vergil by the would-be literary critic.

446–447 **ought to gird up as far as mid-knee her tunics, slaughter a pig for Silvanus, take a bath for a quarter:** The allusions all point to the idea that such a woman seems more male than female in her behavior. The tunic was normally the dress of males, the *stola* that of respectable women. Silvanus was a god of the woodlands and countryside, to whom only men were supposed to sacrifice. A coin of very little value, "a quarter" (Latin *quadrans*), was the usual fee for a man's bath, not a woman's.

452   **Palaemon's art . . . law of grammar:** As a historical figure, this Quintus Remmius Palaemon was known in the first century C.E. for his composition of a handbook on Latin grammatical usage.

460:   This line is deleted as an interpolation by some editors.

462–463 **with thick Poppaean mask:** Poppaea Sabina, originally the wife of Nero's friend Otho (emperor briefly in 69 C.E.), was first Nero's mistress and then (62 C.E.) became his second wife. Tradition held that it was Poppaea who persuaded Nero (reigned 54–68 C.E.) to murder his mother Agrippina and his first wife Octavia. She was certainly renowned for her beauty and she may indeed have devised a particular sort of facial treatment.

466   **face-oils . . . whatever you, slim Indians, send here:** Fragrant ointments were concocted from the spikenard plant, imported to Rome from India.

467–470 **face . . . caressed with that milk . . . she-ass companions . . . Hyperborean pole:** Again implied is a reference to Poppaea, who was said to have frequently washed herself in the milk of asses. As the Hyperboreans were a mythical race living beyond the bounds of the frozen north, the suggestion is that a woman such as this spares no expense in ensuring her beauty.

477   **Liburnian chair-carrier:** Compare the note on line 351 above.

486   **no softer than the Sicilian court:** Early Sicilian kingdoms were ruled by cruel tyrants. The most famous of these was Phalaris, who ruled as dictator in Agrigentum in the mid-sixth century B.C.E.; compare the note on Persius, *Satire* 3.39.

489   **Isis:** Isis was an Egyptian goddess brought to Rome as cult object in the second century B.C.E. Her later male counterpart was Serapis. The Temple of Isis, located in the *Campus Martius*, was a notorious locus for illicit sexual encounters.

490–492 Psecas loses her locks . . . naked breasts . . . bull-whip punishes: The Greek name Psecas is generic for any household servant who oils and combs her mistresses' hair. Here the irate mistress pulls out the hair of her servant and strips her for whipping.

503 **Andromache:** Andromache was the wife of the Trojan hero Hector. Like all quasi-mythological and heroic figures, she was imagined as having superhuman stature.

512 **mad Bellona:** The scenario involves worshipers not of two distinct goddesses, but of an amalgamation of decomposed forms. The original Asiatic fertility deity was Ma. She was confused and equated with Cybele (see the note on Juvenal, *Satire* 3.138–139) and identified with the primitive Roman war-goddess Bellona.

524–525 the "Proud King's" entire field: The "field" referred to is the *Campus Martius*, an area that before its dedication to Mars was thought to have been the property of the Etruscan kings of Rome. The last figure of the Etruscan monarchy, Tarquinius Superbus ("Tarquin the Proud"), was expelled from Rome in 510 B.C.E.

526 **gleaming Io:** The symbol of Isis was the cow. There is some syncretism of myth here, however. Io in Greek myth was a girl loved by Zeus. In order to protect Io from the jealous wrath of Zeus' wife, Hera, her father, the river god Inachus, turned her into a cow. Both Isis and Io are said to have had horns and to have wandered about in misery.

528 **Meroe:** An island in the Nile river in Egypt.

533–534 linen-clad flock and bald-headed herd . . . Anubis, mocker of the bewailing populace: The worshippers of Isis wore white linen and had shaved heads. One of these dons the persona of Anubis, the dog-headed companion of Isis, and mocks the people lamenting Osiris. The ritual is in part a re-enactment of the myth of Isis, who wandered grief-stricken after the murder and disarticulation of Osiris, both her brother and husband.

538 **silver serpent has been seen to have moved its head:** The symbol of divinity in Egypt was the asp. Here it is made to nod its head in disapproval of a superstitious woman's conduct.

543 **trembling Jewess begs in her ear in secret:** Compare Juvenal, *Satire* 3.13–16 and the note on Juvenal, *Satire* 3.15. Juvenal's representation of Jews is of course highly sarcastic, as they are said to loiter under trees and "sell" false prophesies. Emphasized above all, however, is the superstition and credulity of contemporary women.

544–545 interpreter of Jerusalem's laws and great priestess of the tree: The laws referred to comprise the Jewish Torah, the Mosaic code, also known as the *Books of Moses*. The Jews were permitted to meet among the trees outside the *Porta Capena*; compare Juvenal, *Satire* 3.11–16.

549–552 Armenian or Syrian seer — the guts of a puppy, sometimes too of a boy: Neither Armenians nor Syrians were especially famed for prophesy by the inspection of entrails. The early Etruscan practice of hepatoscopy was by Juvenal's time considered absurd and barbaric.

553   Chaldaeans: Babylonians in general were held to be expert astrologers, especially given the fact that some emperors consulted them for horoscopes.

555   Ammon: The north-African site of Ammonium (Siwah) was home of a spring assigned divine powers. It was believed that the amalgamated deity Zeus-Ammon issued forth oracles there. Delphi as prophetic center of the world had fallen into disuse due in part to the spread of Christianity.

557:   The two lines following this line (558–559) have been deleted by editors as non-sensical interpolations. They read:
>   cuius amicitia conducendaque tabella
>   magnus ciuis obit et formidatus Othoni.
>   (By whose friendship and purchased horoscope
>   the great citizen frightening to Otho died.)

566   Tanaquil: The reference to Tanaquil furthers the passage's irony. She was the wife of the first figure of the Etruscan monarchy at Rome, Tarquinius Priscus. Tradition held that she was skilled in the prophetic arts and played a role in the advancement to the kingship of her son-in-law, the second of the three Etruscan monarchs, Servius Tullius.

569–570 Saturn's grim star . . . fruitful Venus: The planet Saturn in the astrological scheme was a harbinger of disaster. Venus, on the other hand, was a positive sign.

576   Thrasyllus' numbers: The emperor Tiberius (ruled 14–37 C.E.) was evidently associated closely with astrologers and most notable among these was this Thrasyllus. His "numbers" are detailed horoscopic calculations.

581   **Petosiris:** Although there was a historical Egyptian astrologer-priest named Petosiris in the second century B.C.E., it is likely that by Juvenal's time this name had become generic for any self-professed expert on the zodiac.

582–584 **stadium-space . . . turning-posts . . . forehead and hand . . . lip-smacking:** The "stadium-space" referred to is the Circus Maximus, the elongated stadium used for chariot racing. The "turning-posts" were on either end of the circuit as markers for races. Various practitioners of occultism located themselves around the Circus. The woman's "forehead" as well as her "hand" (palm) would be inspected (read) by the seer, who would apparently require her to participate in the ritual by performing a prescribed series of "lip-smacking" noises.

585–586 **A Phrygian augur will give answers to the rich, thence hired:** The augur was hired directly from Phrygia and then imported to Rome. Editors question this reading, however, suggesting that a line following line 585 may at some stage been omitted from the text. The omitted line may have read "hired [at massive cost from the land where the crocus grows]"; if this line is accepted, the suggestion is then that a fortune-teller from Cilicia, famous for the crocus, is referred to here.

587   **some older character who disposes of the public's lightning-bolts:** Lightning striking the earth was a matter of public concern. A religious official such as a priest interpreted the significance of the accident and took ritual measures to ensure the common good. Whatever was burned by the lightning was gathered and buried as though to remove evidence of the occurrence.

588   **Plebeian fate is established in the Circus and on the rampart:** The "rampart" was a protective barrier of raised earth and stone, which tradition held was constructed during the Etruscan Monarchy—thus its name of the "Servian Wall." The common people (plebeians), suggests Juvenal, visited the fortune-tellers stationed near this wall and "in the Circus."

590   **before the wooden pillars and dolphins' columns:** The common woman, despite her show of wealth, here meets her fortune-teller in sight of two hallmarks of the Circus Maximus: the "wooden pillars," mobile towers employed in spectacles of mock warfare, and the "dolphins' columns," posts (seven in number) on the top of which a

hinged dolphin-statue was attached. As racers rounded the circuit, the dolphins "nodded" one at a time to mark the number of laps completed.

595–598 So great are the arts of *this* one — offer her to drink whatever it will be: Juvenal here makes reference to a professional abortionist. There seems to have been among ancient Romans little or even no practical distinction between sterilization and abortion. The killing of unborn children was neither illegal in ancient Rome nor for most a moral issue. The advent of popular Christianity, especially its embracement by Constantine the Great, eventually caused many Romans to question the traditional idea that an unborn child was a mere animal without a soul.

603–605 dirty cess-pools . . . priests, "Leapers" . . . the names of Scauri with false body: The "dirty cess-pools" are either public toilets or the civic reservoirs. Unwanted infants were evidently often abandoned in such places by their real parents. In some cases an abandoned child might be fortunate enough to be rescued and raised by foster-parents. "Leapers" (Latin *Salii*) were a class of "priests" who took their name from the Latin verb *salire* ("to leap, dance"). The religious function of the Salii remains somewhat enigmatic, but certain prerequisites for admission to the college are known: one had to be of high birth, that is, from the patrician class, and had to have both parents surviving. The Scauri were a wealthy and socially prominent family of patricians. There is great irony in Juvenal's assertion that such children eventually become priests, since only members of the aristocracy were normally eligible to do so—hence his reference to "carry the names of Scauri with false body."

610–611 Thessalian love-potions: Thessaly and its environs were infamous in antiquity as a source of black magic and witchcraft.

612   beat his rump with shoe-sole: The wife beating her husband involves two ideas: first, the man becomes so demented by the drugs he is given that he seems a mere child; secondly, recalled is the mythic image of sex-role reversal—the dominant (by Roman standards) husband is made subservient to his wife. One of the most famous myths involving sex-role reversal is that of Hercules and Omphale; see, for example, Terence, *The Eunuch* 1027.

**614:   ** The three lines following this line (614A–614C), which describe a man who is maddened by a love potion and cannot satiate his lust, have been deleted by most editors as non-sensical interpolations. They do not appear in the most authoritative manuscripts; nor do they seem to fit here (not even if they replace line 615) or after line 601, where one manuscript actually places them. The lines read:

> semper aquam portes rimosa ad dolia, semper
> istud onus subeas ipsis manantibus urnis,
> quo rabidus nostro Phalarim de rege dedisti.
> ([If you do not] constantly carry water to a cracked vat,
> bearing a load with the jars themselves leaking,
> by which you become mad and turn into a Phalaris from a king.)

615–616 uncle of Nero . . . Caesonia poured an entire forehead-philter of trembling foal: The "uncle of Nero" was the emperor Caligula (reigned 37–41 C.E.). Ancient writers attributed one of the causes of Caligula's alleged insanity to an aphrodisiac potion prepared for him by his wife Caesonia. A well-known aphrodisiac was a concoction made either from the forehead-scrapings of a newly born horse or from the mucosa of a mare in heat. It was usually called by its Greek name *hippomanes*, which means something like "horse-madness."

619   her husband: Jupiter/Jove.

620–622 Agrippina's mushroom . . . checked the heart-throbs of one old man: Agrippina, second wife of the emperor Claudius and mother of Nero, was thought to have murdered her husband by means of a dish containing a toxic mushroom, probably the "death cap," or *amanita phalloides*.

628   it's right to kill off a stepson: The murder of one's (step)son was of course illegal. There is heavy irony here. The idea of mother killing son and wife killing husband naturally leads to Juvenal's recollection of similar mythical themes in the lines that follow.

634–635 high stage-boot of tragedy . . . limit and law of precedent: Performances of Athenian tragedy involved actors who wore platform-boots to make them more visible to the audience—hence "high stage-boot of tragedy." The "limit and law of precedent" to which Juvenal self-consciously refers is the generic convention of Roman satire, which did not favor excessively lengthy composition. Compare the note on lines 636–637 below.

636–637 Sophoclean gape . . . unknown to Rutulian hills and Latin sky: Sophocles was a fifth century B.C.E. Athenian tragedian; "Sophoclean gape" works on two levels: first, *Satire* 6, like Sophoclean (and other) tragedies, which usually comprised roughly 1,400 lines, is expansive; secondly, the masks worn by tragic actors frequently displayed a sort of gaping grimace. Since *Satire* 6 has gone on for nearly 700 lines, Juvenal acknowledges here the fact that he has composed an extraordinary poem, one "unknown to Rutulian hills and Latin sky," referring, of course, to his native Italy. Compare the note on lines 634–635 above.

638 **Pontia:** A Pontia, likely the same one as here, is mentioned by Martial, *Epigrams* 2.34.6, 4.43.5, and 6.75 as an infamous and accomplished poisoner.

639 **aconite:** A toxic potion made with the root of a particular flower of the monkshood family.

643–644 fierce Colchian ... Procne: The "fierce Colchian" is the mythological fratricide and child-killer Medea. She is a major figure in the myths of Jason and the Golden Fleece. Procne, likewise the subject of Greek myth, had a sister called Philomela. When Procne's husband, Tereus, king of Thrace, raped Philomela and cut out her tongue, Procne fed to Tereus a dish made of the dissected body of their son.

652 **Alcestis undergoing the fate of her husband:** Euripides, in his play *Alcestis*, relates the tragic story of Admetus, king of Thessaly, and his wife Alcestis. Admetus could avoid death only if he could find someone willing to die in his place. His father and mother refused and his wife heroically died for him before being rescued from the underworld by Heracles. As Admetus and Alcestis were emerging into the light of the upper world, he looked back too soon upon his wife and she was lost to him again as the underworld claimed her back. For her willing sacrifice to save her husband, Alcestis is thus the mythological paragon of spousal loyalty.

655–658 Belides ... Eriphyles ... Clytemnestra ... daughter of Tyndareus ... axe: The mythical Belides were otherwise known as the Danaids, since they were the fifty daughters of Danaus, who was the son of Belus—hence Belides. These daughters, apart from one (Hypermnestra), murdered their fifty husbands on their wedding night. Their divine punishment for this crime was one of frustration—to spend eternity in a futile attempt to pour water into leaky vessels. Eriphyle was the wife of one of the famed "Seven Against Thebes," Amphiaraus; the others were Adrastus, Polyneices, Tydeus, Capaneus, Hippomedon, and Parthenopaeus. She persuaded her husband to join a doomed expedition in return for a pearl necklace given to her by Polyneices. Clytemnestra, "daughter of Tyndareus," her name here used generically, was the wife of Agamemnon, the Greek leader of the expedition against Troy. She lived in adultery with Aegisthus and on the return of her husband from the Trojan war the two axed him to death in the bath.

659   **slim lung of a toad:** Certain toads were believed (erroneously) to have lethally toxic body parts.

660   **Atrides:** The name Atrides means "son of Atreus," that is, Agamemnon or Menelaus. Here the name is used generically (and humorously) for the husband of any potentially murderous woman.

661   **thrice-conquered Pontic king:** Mithridates IV (120–63 B.C.E.) was king of Pontus and nemesis to Rome. His vision of an eastern empire conflicted with Roman imperialism. He was defeated three times by the Romans: first by Lucius Sulla, then by Lucullus, and finally by Pompeius. Tradition held that he had immunized himself against poison by ingesting certain prophylactic potions.

INDEX OF NAMES

This index lists *biographical, mythical, geographical,* and other names that appear in the Introduction, English translations, and Notes; names of modern scholars are excluded, as are most titles of ancient and modern literary works. When names in the English translations are discussed in the keyed notes, they are listed in most instances as appearing only in the translations in order to avoid unnecessary duplication of the citations. Citations with authorial abbreviations refer to satire and line numbers. Numbers without preceding authorial abbreviations refer to page (and sometimes footnote) numbers; when a name appears in the text and notes of the same page, only the page number is given.

The following abbreviations are used: Lucil. = Lucilius, fragments; Hor. = Horace, *Satires*; Pers. = Persius; prol. = prologue; Juv. = Juvenal.

Accius: Pers. 1.76; Juv. 6.70
Achaeans: Juv. 3.61; *see* Greeks
Achilles: Juv. 1.4–5n.; Juv. 1.60n.; Juv. 1.163; Juv. 3.205n.; Juv. 3.280n.
Admetus: Juv. 6.652n.
Adrastus: Juv. 6.655–658n.
Adriatic: Juv. 3.239–240n.
Aeacus: Juv. 1.9
Aegean: Juv. 1.73n.; Juv. 3.69–70n.
Aegisthus: Juv. 1.4–5n.; Juv. 6.655–658n.
Aelia: Juv. 6.72
Aemilius: Juv. 6.32
Aeneas: Pers. 1.72–73n.; Pers. 4.8n.; Juv. 1.100n.; Juv. 1.162; Juv. 3.60n.; Juv. 6.177n.; Juv. 6.265–266n.; Juv. 6.435n.
Aeolus: Juv. 1.8
Aeschylus: Juv. 1.128n.
Africa: Pers. 3.44–45n.; Juv. 1.49–50n.; Juv. 3.89n.; Juv. 6.306n.; Juv. 6.555n.
Africans: Juv. 3.79n.

Agamemnon: Lucil. 570n.; Juv. 1.4–5n.; Juv. 6.655–658n.; Juv. 6.660n.
Agrigentum: Pers. 3.39n.; Juv. 6.486n.; *see* Agrigento
Agrigento: Pers. 3.39n.; *see* Agrigentum
Agrippa (Marcus): Juv. 6.153–154n.; Juv. 6.158
Agrippa II: Juv. 6.156–158n.
Agrippina: Juv. 6.115n.; Juv. 6.620; Juv. 6.462–463n.
Alabanda: Juv. 3.70
Alba Longa: Juv. 1.70n.; Juv. 6.177n.
Alban (wine): Hor. 2.8.16; Juv. 1.70n.; Juv. 6. O 15
Albina: Juv. 3.130
Albinus: Lucil. 1196; *see* Postumius (Aulus) *and* Postumius (Spurius)
Albucius: Lucil. 87; Lucil. 93; Hor. 2.1.48; *see* Titus
Alcestis: Juv. 6.652
Alcibiades: 11; Pers. 4.3n.; Pers. 4.8n.; Pers. 4.20n.

207

Nereus: Pers. 1.94

Nero: 9; Juv. 1.71n.; Juv. 1.155n.; Juv. 3.116n.; Juv. 3.251n.; Juv. 6.462–463n.; Juv. 6.615; Juv. 6.620–622n.

Nestor: Juv. 6.326

New Comedy: Hor. 2.8.19n.; Juv. 3.93–94n.

Nike: Juv. 3.68

Nile (river): Juv. 1.26; Juv. 6.83; Juv. 6.528n.

Niobe: Juv. 6.172–173n.; Juv. 6.176

Niphates: Juv. 6.409

Noah: Juv. 1.81–84n.

Nomentanus: Hor. 2.1.22; Hor. 2.8.23; Hor. 2.8.25; Hor. 2.8.60

Numa: Juv. 3.12; Juv. 3.138; Juv. 6.343

Numantines: Lucil. 714n.

Octavia: Juv. 6.462–463n.

Octavian: 6; Hor. 2.1.14–15n.; Juv. 6.265–266n.; see Augustus, Caesar (Augustus)

Ogulnia: Juv. 6.352

Old Comedy: 1; Pers. 1.123–124n.; Pers. 1.126n.

Omphale: Juv. 6.612n.

Oppian hill: Hor. 1.9.1n.

Orestes: Pers. 3.118; Juv. 1.5

Orontes: Juv. 3.62

Osiris: Juv. 6.540; Juv. 6.533–534n.

Otho (Caesar): Juv. 6.462–463n.; Juv. 6.557n.

Otho (Luscius Roscius): Juv. 3.154n.; Juv. 3.159

Ovid: Pers. 4.21n.; Juv. 6.1n.

Pacuvius: 4; Pers. 1.77

Paean: Juv. 6.172; Juv. 6.174; see Apollo

Palaemon: Juv. 6.452

Palatine hill: Hor. 1.9.1n.; Juv. 3.71n.; Juv. 6.117

Pales: Pers. 1.72–73n.

Palestine: Juv. 6.246n.; see Judaea

Palestrina: Juv. 3.190–192n.; see Praeneste

Palilia: Pers. 1.72

Palladium: Juv. 6.265–266n.

Pallas: Juv. 1.109

Pantolabus: Hor. 2.1.22

Parcae: Juv. 3.27n.; see Atropos, Clotho, Fates, Lachesis, Moirae

Paris: Lucil. 570n.; Juv. 6.87

Paris (Trojan): Juv. 1.162–163n.

Parnassus: Pers. prol. 2; Juv. 1.81–84n.

Parthenopaeus: Juv. 6.655–658n.

Parthians: Hor. 2.1.15

Pasiphäe: Juv. 3.25n.

Patroclus: Juv. 3.280n.

Peace: Juv. 1.115

Pedius: Pers. 1.85

Pegasus: Pers. prol. 1n.; Pers. prol. 14; Juv. 3.117–118n.

Peleus: Juv. 3.280

Peloponnese: Pers. 3.9n.; Juv. 3.69–70n.; see Greece

People's Games: Juv. 6.69

Perseus: Juv. 3.117–118n.

Persians: Pers. 3.53n.

Persicus: Juv. 3.221

Persius: 3; 8–12; 15; Lucil. 2n.; Lucil. 3–4n.; Lucil. 70n.; Lucil. 713–714n.; Hor. 2.1.11n.; Pers. prol. 1–14n.; Pers. prol. 2n.; Pers. 1.4n.; Pers. 1.16n.; Pers. 1.29n.; Pers. 1.109–110n.; Pers. 1.134n.; Pers. 3.13n.; Pers. 3.28n.; Pers. 3.40n.; Pers. 3.79n.; Pers. 3.105–106n.; Pers. 3.107–108; Pers. 4.8n.; Juv. 1.154n.; Juv. 6.486n.

Petosiris: Juv. 6.581

Petronius: 3; 7; Juv. 1.109n.

Phalaris: Pers. 3.39n.; Juv. 6.486n.

Pharos: Juv. 6.83

Philemon: Pers. 4.21n.

ABOUT THE AUTHORS

William J. Dominik, PhD (Monash University, 1989), has taught at a number of academic institutions, including Texas Tech University (USA), Monash University (Australia), and the University of Leeds (UK). He is the author or editor of the following books: *Speech and Rhetoric in Statius' Thebaid* (1994); *The Mythic Voice of Statius: Power and Politics in the Thebaid* (1994); *Roman Eloquence: Rhetoric in Society and Literature* (1997); and *Concordantia in Sidonii Apollinaris Epistulas* (1997). Forthcoming books are: *Flavian Rome: Culture, Image, Text; Literature, Art, History: Studies on Classical Antiquity and Tradition; Concordantia in Anthologiam Latinam;* and *Words and Ideas.* He is currently Associate Professor (Reader) of Classics at the University of Natal, Durban (South Africa) and has been Editor of the international classics journal *Scholia* since its founding in 1991.

William T. Wehrle, PhD (University of Southern California, 1991), has taught at the University of Santa Barbara, the University of Southern California, and the College of William and Mary (USA). His publications on Roman literature include *The Satiric Voice: Program, Form, and Meaning in Persius and Juvenal* (1992). He is currently Visiting Assistant Professor of Classics at the University of the Pacific and teaches Latin at Lincoln High School in Stockton, California (USA), where the late Robert Hanlon, to whom this anthology is co-dedicated, was William J. Dominik's Latin teacher.